START A RIOT!

START A RIOT!

Civil Unrest in Black Arts Movement Drama,
Fiction, and Poetry

Casarae Lavada Abdul-Ghani

University Press of Mississippi / Jackson

Margaret Walker Alexander Series in African American Studies

The University Press of Mississippi is the scholarly publishing agency of
the Mississippi Institutions of Higher Learning: Alcorn State University,
Delta State University, Jackson State University, Mississippi State University,
Mississippi University for Women, Mississippi Valley State University,
University of Mississippi, and University of Southern Mississippi.

www.upress.state.ms.us

The University Press of Mississippi is a member
of the Association of University Presses.

Portions of "Our King is Dead" by Henry Dumas are used by permission
of the Henry L. Dumas Literary Estate. Copyright @ 1968–2021
by Loretta Dumas and [Estate Executor] Eugene B. Redmond.

Works by Gwendolyn Brooks reprinted by consent of Brooks Permissions.

Any discriminatory or derogatory language or hate speech regarding race,
ethnicity, religion, sex, gender, class, national origin, age, or disability that
have been retained or appear in elided form is in no way an endorsement
of the use of such language outside a scholarly context.

First printing 2022

∞

Library of Congress Cataloging-in-Publication Data

Names: Abdul-Ghani, Casarae Lavada, author.
Title: Start a riot! : civil unrest in Black Arts Movement drama, fiction, and poetry /
Casarae Lavada Abdul-Ghani.
Other titles: Margaret Walker Alexander series in African American studies.
Description: Jackson : University Press of Mississippi, 2022. | Series: Margaret Walker Alexander
series in African American studies | Includes bibliographical references and index.
Identifiers: LCCN 2022002589 (print) | LCCN 2022002590 (ebook) |
ISBN 9781496840455 (hardback) | ISBN 9781496840448 (trade paperback) |
ISBN 9781496840431 (epub) | ISBN 9781496840400 (epub) | ISBN 9781496840417 (pdf) |
ISBN 9781496840424 (pdf)
Subjects: LCSH: Black Arts movement. | African American arts—Political aspects—History—
20th century. | Arts—Political aspects—United States—History—20th century. |
Black nationalism—United States—History—20th century. |
United States—Race relations—History—20th century.
Classification: LCC NX512.3.A35 A23 2022 (print) | LCC NX512.3.A35 (ebook) |
DDC 700.89/96073—dc23/eng/20220605
LC record available at https://lccn.loc.gov/2022002589
LC ebook record available at https://lccn.loc.gov/2022002590

British Library Cataloging-in-Publication Data available

Dedication:
To my parents Linnie and James Gibson.
To my husband Husan I and son Husan II
I love you dearly.
In memory of Mamie Ruth George, Lottie Mae Sanders, and Mary Evans

CONTENTS

ACKNOWLEDGMENTS

I am blessed to see this book finally making it to print. I wrote this book to shine a light on the Black American protest tradition that is often a controversial topic, but a necessary conversation as we continue to seek justice and equality in the Western hemisphere. I want to thank Dr. Venetria K. Patton for believing in my talent and being a great sister and friend. Dr. Patton's comments in the initial stages of this manuscript set the tone for how I approached writing the chapters. I want to sincerely thank my dear friend Dr. Janis Mayes for meeting with me on numerous occasions to discuss drafts and help me think through ideas that were central to formulating my argument. Dr. Bill Mullen, Dr. Marlo D. David, Dr. Shanna Greene Benjamin, and Dr. Sonja Watson are great friends and I want to thank them for supporting this book project and going above and beyond to help me in other areas of my career.

To the University Press of Mississippi acquisitions editor Katie Keene and many members of the staff who graciously put time and effort into this book project, thank you from the bottom of my heart.

To Dr. Gwendolyn D. Pough, Dr. Joan Bryant, and the Lender Center for Social Justice co-founders Marvin and Helaine Lender, I want to thank each of you for supporting my book project. To the Lenders for granting me the inaugural Lender faculty fellowship award that supported my research trips to the Bancroft Library at UC Berkeley. In addition, to the Special Collections Research Center at Syracuse University's Bird Library.

To Eugene B. Redmond and Mrs. Loretta Dumas for granting permission to use Henry Dumas's poetry in the manuscript; I sincerely appreciate the best wishes.

To Khari "Discopoet" Bowden, thank you for inspiring the title of *Start a Riot!* This manuscript has the spark it needed because of your inspirational poem. Thanks for always staying true to the spoken word poetry tradition.

To Boyd Smith, thank you for designing the book cover. Your vision and creativity speaks to the essence of the book and I am forever grateful.

To Eric Goddard-Scovel, I'm indebted to your attention to this book in its infant stages—my sincere thank you!

To my friends in academia Philathia Bolton, Cassander Smith, Jolivette Anderson-Douoning, Juanita Crider, Daphne Penn, Keturah Nix, Lisa Young, Shana Hardy, Kyla Carter, Heather Moore Roberson, Dana A. Williams, LaVonda N. Reed, Thabiti Lewis, Joanne V. Gabbin, Tyriana Evans, Nardia Lipman, Antonio D. Tillis, Jennifer Freeman Marshall, Cornelius L. Bynum, Tithi Bhattacharya, Renee Thomas, and Bill Caise thanks for your unwavering support throughout the years.

To my sorority sisters of the Alpha Kappa Alpha Sorority, Incorporated, thank you for your ongoing support and love—Kiosha Ford, Akiba Griffin, Holly Smith, Yolanda Brooks, Arethea Brown, Tanya Hicks, Tamar Smithers, Vivian Gunn, Tamara Hamilton—Gamma Delta, Chi Phi Omega, Iota Nu Omega, and Theta Phi Omega chapters.

Lastly, to my husband Husan-Iddin Abdul-Ghani I, you are my rock, my lover, and best friend. Thanks for supporting me through the years as I worked on this project. You've always encouraged me to believe in the creative process that takes place when writing a manuscript and I am forever indebted to your loyalty. Thanks to my son Husan-Iddin Abdul-Ghani II, my parents Linnie and James Gibson, my brothers Gabriel and Nick, my extended family the Hunters, Gibson-Powell's, Hines/Floyds, Scotts, and in dedication to Mamie Ruth George, Lottie Mae Sanders, and Lavada Barnes— thank you to the Olivet Missionary Baptist Church family in San Francisco, California, for your prayers and everlasting love.

START A RIOT!

ABBREVIATIONS

BAM	Black Arts Movement
CRM	civil rights movement
BPM	Black Power Movement
#BLM	Black Lives Matter
DBWYCW	Don't Buy Where You Can't Work
NYCHA	New York City Housing Authority
OAAU	Organization for Afro-American Unity
SNCC	Student Nonviolent Coordinating Committee

INTRODUCTION

"I'm Gonna Start a Riot!"

We need to recognize that this is not just an issue for Ferguson,
this is an issue for America. We have made enormous progress
in race relations over the course of the past several decades.
I've witnessed that in my own life. And to deny that progress
I think is to deny America's capacity for change.
—BARACK OBAMA, "STATEMENT ON THE FERGUSON
GRAND JURY DECISION," 2014

In 2014, Barack Obama, then president of the United States, issued a state-ment about the Ferguson grand jury decision. The St. Louis grand jury decided not to indict the policeman who killed eighteen-year-old Michael Brown Jr. In a White House briefing room, Obama tells the public that what took place in Ferguson is an American issue, and insists that the country has made great progress in race relations. Obama makes his point by stating that he has seen racial progress in his own life. He solidifies his comment by telling the public that America's advancement in race relations cannot be overlooked because of incidents such as Ferguson that exemplify regression. Rather, Obama persists that Americans must see the country's evolvement so as to believe America's capacity to change. Six years later, one-term president Donald J. Trump responds to the rioting after the death of George Floyd in Minneapolis-St. Paul with a tweet that reads "we will assume control but, when the looting starts, the shooting starts," exacerbating race relations and reverting back to law-and-order tactics exhibited by past US presidents, most notably Richard Nixon.[1] Both former presidents respond to civil unrest strikingly different. Obama's communicative style is through a hybrid modal-ity—a mix between a television screen and a press room. Obama recites an impassioned speech to draw emphasis on unity and nationhood. Whereas

5

Trump's communicative style is through text, using Twitter as his preferred modality, eschewing the White House briefing room altogether. His tweet is simplistic but emotive, ratcheting up language that trigger historical wounds of "looting" and "shooting" that are a familiar flashpoint paralleling civil unrest of the 1960s and the present moment.

During the latter part of twentieth century history, riots in American cities gleaned as disruptive outbursts in predominantly Black low-income neighborhoods alienated from the more significant demographics of US society. According to Janet Abu-Lughod, initially, *race riot* referred to "interracial violence . . . initiated by collectivities of whites against blacks" (Abu-Lughod 11).[2] However, the term evolved into interracial violence of Blacks against whites' property in response to their racial insubordination. These volatile acts, enacted by Black Americans as an alternative strategy to be heard, were a tactic to raise awareness about their dissent with the status quo. I agree with many scholars of today who state that Black-initiated riots are actually uprisings against state violence and oppression. For the purposes of this book, I am not making a case for such language. Instead, I am arguing to read riot iconography in Black literature that makes a case for Black rage as a legitimate form of grievance. The United States government trivialized Black America's rage and reframed it as a pathological problem within Black communities rather than exploring the structural and institutional factors that contribute to the expressions of Black America's rage. The National Advisory Commission on Civil Disorders (known as the Kerner Report), headed by Governor of Illinois Otto Kerner, released a report in 1968 that investigated riot-affected areas in American cities where large Black populations resided. Kerner and other committee members, including then president of the NAACP Roy Wilkins, concluded that America was "moving toward two societies, one black, one white—separate and unequal" (*Report of the National Advisory* 1). The civil unrest that the report documents between 1963–67 in cities such as Tampa, Cincinnati, Atlanta, and Newark was the "accumulation of unresolved grievances by ghetto residents against local authorities (often but not always, the police)" (147). While the summaries of each riot are detailed in the Kerner report, the authors contend that the real reason that many Black Americans live in impoverished neighborhoods is because of "segregation and poverty" that is "unknown to most white Americans" (20). However, as Keisha Bentley-Edwards et al. note in an essay based on the report, "whites are relegated to the roles of saviors of black people, and bystanders to addressing systemic racism's repercussions" (Bentley-Edwards et al. 546). The report locates blame solely within Black communities, rather than interrogating the extent to which Black discontent unfolds.

The Kerner Report intentionally frames the language of Black riots in a manner that shows concern and empathy for Black Americans, while also assigning them blame. The report calls on the state to initiate racial reform even as it pushes for more state control to quell racial dissent, which could result in over-policing and further exacerbate tensions in Black communities. Grace Hong explains the neoliberal aim in the Kerner Report as an "invitation to respectability" that "becomes a way of regulating and punishing those populations it purports to help; thus in the neoliberal moment, 'care' becomes the conduit for violence" (Hong 20).[3] In other words, as the report attempts to push for an active, progressive agenda to satisfy the real demands behind Black dissent, in actuality, it exacerbates racial relations. The document leaves police officers off the hook, positioning them as victims instead of disciplining their overt use of state-sanctioned authority to harass and murder Black citizens.

Since the turbulent 1960s, rioting has remained a contradiction in contemporary American politics when race is the primary signifier. Toward the end of Obama's presidency, civil unrest mounted, and the call for police reform was paramount. When Robert McCulloch, the prosecuting attorney, relayed the devastating news that a grand jury would not indict the former Ferguson police officer, a second riot ensued. Before the rebellion, peaceful protest demonstrations were conducted around Ferguson and throughout St. Louis County while surrounded by militant police. Following the non-indictment, the National Guard was ordered in by then-Governor Jay Nixon after looting and arson took place in the city. In particular, the news media focused on two specific businesses where looting and vandalism took place in the initial civil unrest that occurred following Brown's death. The first was the Ferguson Market & Liquor convenience store, where Brown had allegedly stolen cigars before his confrontation with the policeman. The second was a Quik Trip convenience store; at first a site where residents came to memorialize Brown, it had now become a site of vandalism.

In December 2014, then-President Obama signed Executive Order 13684 to create a task force on twenty-first-century policing. Co-chaired by then commissioner of the Philadelphia Police Department Charles H. Ramsey and George Mason University Professor Laurie O. Robinson, the committee was ordered to create a report based on building trust and legitimacy between police and the communities that they serve; strengthening policy and oversight by having more collaboration between community leaders and police; incorporating social media and technology (body cameras) as a basis for examining police-civilian relations and reporting police misconduct where necessary; and finally, promoting community policing in marginalized communities to reduce crime, promote educational workshops for police to refine their skills, and provide wellness and safety.[4]

However, the following year in Baltimore, Maryland, amid protests in response to the death of Freddy Gray, a fire was set to a local CVS pharmacy in West Baltimore, burning it to the ground. The media centralized the CVS as a main talking point about the upheaval among Black residents in Baltimore. This focus often overshadowed the actual grievance of Gray's death that protesters and residents of the city were making in the first place. The razed CVS became a metaphor for how the lasting impression of destruction of property conveyed by the media overshadowed complaints made by Black citizens and their allies about police brutality. In other words, the media's focus on the expendability of Black lives when they do not specifically provide capital—or as Jared Ball connotes, participate in the "myth of Black buying power" (Ball 29)—resulted in focusing on property as more important than Freddy Gray's life.[5]

Now as the Trump presidency settles into history, its cementing of ethnonationalist and fascist ideologies in American discourse sustains racial wounds as anti-Black racism abounds.

In 2017, the University of Virginia campus experienced a racial nightmare when white nationalists of far-right extremism marched in unison chanting, "You will not replace us!" and "Jews will not replace us!" This incident shook the Charlottesville community, but also shocked the nation as discussions about explicit racial bias resurfaced on the national stage. The white nationalist revolt was an orchestrated response to the city's decision to remove the Robert E. Lee Confederate statue. Lee, a general and a proslavery advocate, wanted to maintain American slavery. Lee did so by fighting for it as a commander of the Confederate states in the Civil War. When Trump was asked to respond to the Charlottesville incident, which led to the death of opposing protester Heather Heyer, he stated that "many sides" were to blame (qtd. in Chan and Cumming-Bruce).[6] Trump's refusal to call out examples of racism caused by acts of white supremacy illustrated his reliance on racism, particularly the vestiges of it that solidified his agenda of law and order as well as suppression of multiracial groups that do not define the white majority. Because, as Michelle Alexander asserts "[i]n the 1968 election, race eclipsed class as the organizing principle of American politics," Trump's words harkened back to Richard Nixon's campaign of law and order and later Ronald Reagan's War on Drugs policies; his rhetoric shoehorned racial anxiety and fear from his followers (Alexander 46). For example, Trump's administration issued a travel ban against Muslim majority countries in the same year as the Charlottesville debacle, specifically barring Syrian refugees.

Barbara Ransby asserts, "the anti-immigrant rhetoric of the Trump administration threatens more deportations and harassment of the undocumented residents. The threat of repression remained constant as Trump praise[d] and cavort[ed] with dictators around the world and malign[ed] the media at home" (Ransby 163). While the travel ban was contested continuously throughout the US court system, those of various racial identities in solidarity with Black Americans continued to challenge and resist the Trump administration. Angela Davis notes, "within the sphere of Black politics . . . [the challenge is] to include gender struggles, struggles against homophobia and struggles against repressive immigration policies" and how "anti-Muslim racism has really thrived on the foundation of anti-Black racism" (39). In other words, and particularly during the Trump era, multiple forms of racial discrimination are indicative of previous iterations, most notably displayed from anti-Black racism.

Similarly, in 2020, riots erupted in the twin cities Minneapolis-St. Paul in response to the police killing of George Floyd after he allegedly paid for an item with a counterfeit twenty-dollar bill at a convenience store. People across the world watched a rogue cop kneel on Floyd's neck for eight minutes and forty-six seconds, killing him slowly on the hard street pavement. Several days after the video aired on social media, Black Americans and their allies of multiracial backgrounds protested peacefully. Others, including those of varied racial backgrounds, also rioted throughout the Minneapolis-St. Paul metro area as well as in cities like Atlanta, Oakland, and Richmond, Virginia.[7] Rioting in twenty-first-century America, particularly when examining the multiracial resistance that took off in Minneapolis-St. Paul following the death of Floyd and its implications, link back to circulatory ways Black people have historically used rioting as an act of consciousness raising to address longstanding grievances associated with polity, police brutality, and economic inequality. These tragic incidents and the ongoing racial polarization exhibited in the United States inspired me to write a book about how Black politics during the Black Arts Movement (BAM) era critically shaped the way artist-writers sought to address citizenship rights, housing (in)security, and economic inequality.

Start a Riot! Civil Unrest in Black Arts Movement Drama, Fiction, and Poetry examines representations of riots in BAM literature. The book argues that rioting as emphasized in the works of Amiri Baraka (LeRoi Jones), Gwendolyn Brooks, Ben Caldwell, Sonia Sanchez, and Henry Dumas exemplifies a shift in the political mindset for Black Americans. During the late 1960s, Black people increasingly embraced more violent methods for calling attention to the United States' refusal to address anti-Black state-sanctioned violence in their communities. This study aims to broaden the discussion of riots in BAM texts to understand how Black artist-writers during the civil rights era responded to the urban uprisings in Black American cities from 1964–68 through the utilization of Black protest politics. The book makes three critical interventions regarding the reasons why we research and teach the BAM. First, studies about the BAM have neglected to include a clear understanding of rioting and its place within BAM discourse. *Start a Riot!* offers a much more nuanced discussion of how and why rioting mattered in BAM literature. Second, the book illuminates how BAM artist-writers' works served as a proactive way to address Black urban America's discontent, which became more pronounced after the assassinations of pivotal leaders such as Malcolm X and Martin Luther King Jr. Finally, the book challenges misconceptions regarding Black American protest that its historical significance within the American lexicon ended after the dismantling of Jim Crow.[8] As this book illustrates, the depictions of late-1960s rioting in literature published during the BAM era reinvigorated Black America's discussions about revolt as the answer to anti-Black racism, police brutality, and economic inequality. BAM's protest literature becomes the through line to contemporary aesthetic responses to state violence, offering a lens to explore how artists in the twenty-first century deal with endemic themes of racism.

For instance, in 2016 spoken word poet and community-based artist Khari "Discopoet" B. performed his poem "Start a Riot" at Hamilton Park in Chicago for a commission project funded by the Jazz Institute of Chicago.[9] According to Ytasha L. Womack, Discopoet "uses live soul bands reminiscent of funk as the backdrop for his fireball political poetry" (Y. Womack 119).[10] Discopoet's presentation honored renowned poet Gil Scott-Heron. The poem was also dedicated to #BlackLivesMatter (#BLM) in the aftermath of civil unrest in Ferguson, Missouri, and Baltimore, Maryland, following the deaths of young Black men and women at the hands of police within the last several years. Bowden belts out during his poetic incantation, "I'm Gonna Start a Riot," with great enthusiasm, and the crowd responds, "riot."[11] He builds up the momentum in his performance, calling for the disorder—a liberatory technique to gain the audience's commitment to the rebellion intensifying in the park. As the voices, now syncopated, build on the foundation of Discopoet's chant. This music guiding the performance calls to mind 1960s and 1970s era–style funk, soul, and jazz, the same kind of music that accompanied the dramatic performances of BAM artists, for whom rioting also was central to their expressions.

Sonically, the spoken word poem sounds like a chaotic crescendo. There is an integral link between the literary, cultural, and performative responses to racial injustice that mobilizes the masses in a public declaration of Black political, artistic expression. The performative and interactive nature of Discopoet's poem illustrates precisely how Black Americans collectively formed a liberating and politicized identity to counteract centuries of gruesome proletariat conditions and police violence. Discopoet's performance pays tribute to protest slogans "I Can't Breathe," "Hands Up, Don't Shoot," and "Say Her Name," espoused during the current #BLM movement. Also, his performance makes a case for why understanding the sociocultural responses to civil unrest adopted in twenty-first-century Black life also must attend to its cultural predecessors in the BAM as more than a mere point of comparison. Instead, the comparison illustrates how rioting exemplifies a decades-long political strategy that has defined Black artistic expression.

For example, Ben Caldwell anticipates Discopoet's riotous evocation some forty years earlier in his 1968 drama, *Riot Sale or Dollar Psyche Fake Out*. In the play, he depicts a cast of Black characters banding together to protest the killing by a white police officer of a fifteen-year-old Black teenager in Harlem, New York. The community demands the policeman be held accountable for his brutal actions. The protestors are loud, armed, and ready to fight to end police brutality even if it means death. Policemen attempt to quell the unrest, "but the blacks do not retreat. Most of them stand, fearlessly, out in the open" (Caldwell, *Riot Sale* 42). As one of the characters notes, "It looks as though the black man has finally, really, become himself" (42).

Noticeably, the protesters are not all men. Black women and children join the uprising, all appearing militant. The Black community, however, does not loot property; instead, they stand up to law enforcement. The police in bulletproof "fiberglass-shingle" outfits that protect them from the armed community repeatedly tell Black people to go home and "let [their] appointed leaders handle [their] grievances and negotiate [their] demands" (41). Black protesters stand their ground and do not leave their staged protest until they accept money. Caldwell's play serves as a caution to Black America not to become sidetracked with America's bribes for their freedom, but to stand up to the US power structure and demand that their humanity is recognized and that the revolutionary consciousness emerging from the civil unrest continues to strengthen organically. In the play, Caldwell ultimately illustrates that the US state government and its actors (the police) are incapable of relinquishing their dictatorial power and forceful suppression to protect Black citizens from racial violence or acknowledge the payment due for their long suffering. What connects Discopoet's real-life call-and-response chant and Caldwell's fictive rally call is that both illustrate how BAM literature evokes a kind of collective Black consciousness that embraced rioting in the aesthetical sense as a political strategy. It was a call to action, which, as Larry Neal has argued, "speak[s] directly to Black people" (Neal, "Black Arts" 56).

In his representation of rioting, Caldwell evokes what I call "conscious revolt." The term is distinguished from mere rioting because it pushes against simplistic and often racist readings of Black activism as spontaneous, violent outbursts that are destructive. Instead, conscious revolt draws attention to how rioting, as an aesthetical framework, is a political act written in BAM writers' works as a method intended to address how Black Americans fought for their liberation during the turbulent 1960s. Therefore, the core argument of *Start a Riot!* is that BAM literature represents rioting as a viable form of Black political speech and protestation. In "In Search of the Revolutionary Theatre," written in 1964, Amiri Baraka (then LeRoi Jones) demanded that Black artists harness their stories to expose the sentient forms of rebellion expressed in urban uprisings in Black communities. The process of revolt Baraka argues, "must isolate the ritual" and thus create "historical cycles of reality" (22). Rioting, then, is a historical event, and BAM literature, like Caldwell's play, represents a rewriting of Black resistance. As Cheryl Finley notes, Baraka's revolutionary theatre "subvert[s] and over[turns] the traditional boundaries between audience and performer" (135).[12] The literature humanizes Black protestors and casts such civil unrest not as a disorderly or disobedient act seen as unpatriotic and un-American, but as inherently American responses in line with a long history of revolt in the United States from slavery to the present.[13]

Start a Riot! provides a literary analysis mainly of noncanonical works of several prominent writers during the BAM era. In particular, the book examines *The Slave* by Amiri Baraka (LeRoi Jones), *Riot Sale, or Dollar Psyche Fake Out* by Ben Caldwell, *Riot* by Gwendolyn Brooks, *The Bronx Is Next* by Sonia Sanchez, and "Riot or Revolt?" by Henry Dumas. The literature these artist-writers explore suggests that civil unrest can serve as educational contexts to help us understand complex problems associated with hard truths about America's racial present. For these artist-writers, discussing riots in their works showcased rebellion in northern US cities as Black Power inspired new directions and organizational forms in the pursuit of social justice.

In 1966 Kwame Ture, then Stokely Carmichael, became the lead organizer of the Student Nonviolent Coordinating Committee (SNCC). Ture/Carmichael defined a concept of Black Power that he would proclaim in public during a SNCC rally in Greenwood, Mississippi, to address the non-fatal shooting of James Meredith, during the March Against Fear protest in Jackson. In "What We Want," Carmichael speaks to Black youth's militant attitudes in northern ghettos.[14] He argues that the southern civil rights movement's cause "was adapted to an audience of liberal whites" that neglected the anger and frustration Blacks felt when seeing on television "Martin Luther King get slapped" and "four little black girls bombed to death" (Carmichael 419). Ture/Carmichael called for a Black politics that would realize "human rights" rather than succumbing to "disenfranchisement, maintained by racist terror" (420). The ideologies, strategies, and tactics to achieve civil rights among leaders and groups kept referring back to white liberalism as antagonizing or the only option for achieving equality. In "The Spirit of Neoliberalism: From Racial Liberalism to Neoliberal Multiculturalism," author Jodi Melamed describes racial liberalism as "the new flexibility in racial procedures after World War II" (Melamed, "Spirit" 3). The meaning, Melamed contends, is "that racism constantly appears as disappearing according to conventional race categories, even as it takes on new forms that can signify as nonracial or even antiracist" (3). Melamed maintains that racial liberalism is an "ideology" and "race regime" that proliferates certain racial structures or hegemonies that "[contribute] vitally to U.S. global hegemony after World War II" (4). I will speak more candidly in chapter 4 about neoliberalism and its attempts to decentralize Black Power politics in Dumas's "Riot or Revolt?" However, it is essential to highlight how white liberalism within Black civil rights discourse functions as a dominating force that relegates the direction in which Blacks should fight for their equality. While Rustin and King believed that a coalition between Black Americans and white liberals would guarantee Blacks equality, Carmichael and SNCC thought that an all-Black movement with "the people" at the forefront was necessary to extol self-determination among Black people. SNCC rejected Bayard Rustin and the philosophy of King's southern civil rights strategy, suggesting that white people cannot "relate to the black experience . . . because these things are not a part of their experience" (Student Nonviolent Coordinating Committee 425). Instead, they called for self-determination to be achieved through a Black politics administered entirely without white interference (429).[15]

The battle over the attainability of civil rights has remained a conflict within the Black freedom struggle. Bayard Rustin, the civil rights strategist for Martin Luther King Jr.'s Southern Christian Leadership Conference (SCLC) and a stalwart activist who practiced nonviolent protest and socialism, confirmed that America was racially divided. He understood the tension over Black civil rights mounting into "two Americas." Rustin believed that Black Power activists could not achieve civil rights based on "one-tenth of the population" accomplishing such a massive undertaking (431). Rustin argued that Black Power "not only lacks any real value for the civil-rights movement but that its propagation is positively harmful. It diverts the movement from a meaningful debate over strategy and tactics, it isolates the Negro community and it encourages the growth of anti-Negro forces" (430). Rustin pushes against a Black-centered movement because he believed that the only feasible way of achieving civil rights for Blacks was to join with "a liberal-labor-civil-rights coalition which would work to make the Democratic party truly responsive to the aspirations of the poor" (431).

Duly noted, Huey P. Newton addressed reactionary politics among some leaders in the Black Power Movement. He asserts that such responses resulted in "the oppression of the people" that rejects "a people's revolution with the people in power" (Newton, "To the Black" 90). Through a socialist framework, Newton's instruction for the people to "stage a revolution" means that Black people must not replace their white oppressors and become oppressors themselves. Instead, Black Americans must form a cooperative politics among each other and allies that "[strengthens] their resistance struggle" (Newton, "Correct Handling" 19). In chapter 3, for example, the arsonist act committed by the revolutionaries in Sanchez's play *The Bronx Is Next* is a form of reactionary nationalism that stifles a growing Black population to resist the dominant society. The men take on the leadership of their Western oppressors by dividing and conquering Black communities living in ghettos that do not question their motives. The revolutionaries' politics does not allow for every Black person living in the tenement to learn, study, and observe a Black Power that promotes a Black agenda that would liberate them from systemic racism. The revolutionaries' plan to migrate South pacifies racism and, according to Huey Newton, does not "awaken the people and teach them the strategic method of resisting a power structure which is prepared not only to combat with massive brutality the people's resistance but to annihilate totally the Black population" (Newton, "Correct Handling" 15). In chapter 3, Sonia Sanchez emphasizes that the revolutionaries' action clarifies why civil rights leaders such as Bayard Rustin believed Black Power was a reactionary political ideology, understanding it not through Huey Newton's analysis, as a Black movement demanding the abolishment of institutionalized racism. These intraracial disputes on activism illustrate the polarizing viewpoints taken by Black activists during the Black freedom struggle.

Kwame Ture and Charles V. Hamilton refined the Black Power argument to combat racism they contended "is both overt and covert. It takes two, closely related forms: individual whites acting against individual blacks, and acts by the total white community against the black community" (Ture and Hamilton 4).[16] These various forms of discrimination are systemic and have, for centuries, remained institutional practices in the United States, where Black people overtly and covertly have experienced death, injury, and property damage that have been allowed without careful redress from the United States government. Ture and Hamilton believe that "continued subjection [from] a white society that has no intention of 'giving up' their 'power willingly or easily its position of priority and authority'" squanders Black Americans' demands for justice (4). For Ture and Hamilton, Black Power meant more specifically "that black people see themselves as part of a new force, sometimes called the 'Third World'; that [they] see our struggle as closely related to liberation struggles around the world" (xix). Ture and Hamilton comparatively framed the Black American efforts within a Third World global struggle context. A Third World framing contesting Western imperialism exemplifies a theoretical strategy that the two men believed would act as a practical strategy toward liberation for all Africans and non-whites. The artist-writers treated in this book attended to political rioting as a Black Arts method to intervene in philosophical debates about activism.

To have these discussions about activism, the Black revolutionary artist adopted Black music, specifically the genres blues and jazz, as the methodology to explain Black Power as a concept and driving force toward liberation. The utilization of music was an experimental form of knowledge that, at times, eclipsed more standard or conceptual theoretical practice of understanding art through a social and political context.[17] Blues and jazz as a methodology gave the BAM its uniqueness and cemented a praxis for today's understanding of the BAM aesthetic. For instance, James T. Stewart asserts, "it is jazz and it is firmly rooted in the experiences of black individuals in this country" (Stewart 8). Notably, jazz "is a social activity, participated by the artists collectively" that "affords the participants a collective form for individual group development in a way white musical forms never did" (9). In other words, from its various cultural derivatives (the Black Baptist church, Haitian voodoo, or Afro-Brazilian samba among others), is a social activity that can break Black communities from "existing white paradigms or models [that] do not correspond to the realities of black existence" (3).[18] As Baraka connotes, "The blues is formed out of the same social and musical fabric that the spiritual issued from, but with blues the social emphasis becomes more personal" (Baraka, *Blues People* 63). The personal manifests itself in the Black revolutionary artist, what Tony Bolden argues is the Black resistance poet. The "African American resistance poets . . . blues poets, engage in expressive acts of cultural resistance" and "use these forms to counter (mis)representation, describing and responding to black experiences in styles that challenge conventional definitions of poetry, resisting ideological domination" (Bolden 37).[19] While Bolden situates the resistance poet within the Black blues poetic form, I would extend his point to say it happens within the BAM literary tradition. I discuss this more explicitly in chapters 1 and 2. In addition to understanding Black Power and Black music as the fuel that BAM writers use to illustrate resistance, the riot iconography and its treatment in Black American literature also are historically significant.

Even as BAM literature emerged in the 1960s, there already was a long history in the twentieth century of Black American literary treatments of rioting and revolts. In 1944, for example, Ann Petry depicted civil unrest in her novella *In Darkness and Confusion*, which reveals residents' riot as in response to a Black soldier being harassed by police after coming to a Black woman's aid.[20] Riot imagery is also displayed at the end of Ralph Ellison's *Invisible Man* when the unnamed narrator and main character becomes part of a riot. At the end of the novel, he observes that communities of Black individuals participating in the riot, like his friend Scofield, "had a plan. Already [he] could see the women and children coming down the steps" (Ellison 537). These families succumb to living in dilapidated housing. Because of the civil unrest that ensued, Scofield was able to transition these women and children to a more stable environment, one without the dark windows and unstable roofs that had been their previous condition. Therefore, riot iconography is worth revisiting, as featured through artistic mediums such as fiction and dramatic works and again in nonfiction spanning the twentieth century up to the BAM period. Such a presentation makes seamlessly a connection with fiction and reality that suggests Black writers were conduits for enlivening a dialogue about rioting unfolding because of the racial animus toward Black people that manifests within United States society and culture. *Start a Riot!* situates BAM literature within that tradition while also mapping out key departures.

James Baldwin perhaps anticipated the role rioting would assume in BAM literature when he penned his 1963 *The Fire Next Time*, an implicit warning about the violence to come as a result of American racism. To avoid the violence, Baldwin called on conscious Black and white Americans to actively engage in loving discussions about race and issues of equality and fairness (aligning well with US governing democratic principles) to end the racial discontent across the country. Baldwin insists that love is the greatest weapon to conquer the hate that diminishes America's potential to be a great country. Such a proposition depends on Black and white America's understanding of their racial existence in the United States and the binaries of hierarchy (white vs. Black) and hegemony (superiority vs. inferiority) it creates. He explained the "racial nightmare" in *The Fire Next Time* in the form of a letter written to his fifteen-year-old nephew, also named James, on the 100th anniversary of the emancipation of African slavery in the United States. Utilizing the symbolism of the moment, Baldwin made plain that celebrating the Emancipation Proclamation is "celebrating one hundred years of freedom one hundred years too soon" (Baldwin, *Fire* 10). The reality is that Black America "cannot be free until [white Americans] are free" (10). Also, Baldwin explains to his nephew the reason for Black America's inability to truly be free: that white Americans "in effect, [are] still trapped in a history which they do not understand; and until they understand it, they cannot be released from it" (8). Baldwin also explains to his nephew that he accuses his country and countrymen of such acts that "have destroyed and are destroying hundreds of thousands of lives and do not know it and do not want to know it" (5). For the dominant society to indeed relinquish itself from the psychological effects of power inherited through the period of United States slavery, they must learn how to "accept and love themselves and each other," and by extension, Black people. Then "the Negro problem will no longer exist, for it will no longer be needed" (22). Baldwin advocates a self-corrective course that would avoid the imminent violence and doom suggest by the text's title.

As for Black America, Baldwin insists that they cannot retaliate against white America with the same hate targeted at them because fighting hate with hate only creates a divided nation. He explains to his nephew James that he "must accept [white America] and accept them with love" (8). According to Baldwin, Black America will assume the moral high ground and become the model for racial tolerance if they chose the pathway of love. But Baldwin admits that this path is risky and difficult to ascertain because "the danger in the minds of most white Americans, is the loss of their identity" due partly to their inherited belief that "black men are inferior to white men" despite knowing better (9). Baldwin illuminates Black America's anger and frustration that stems from generations of racial hegemony extending through the periods of slavery, Jim Crow, and systemic racism, particularly relating to acts of police brutality in predominantly Black American neighborhoods. Baldwin points to this reality when he speaks of his subjugation to police harassment in *Fire*: "It was absolutely clear that the police would whip you and take you in as long as they could get away with it" (21).[21] During a pivotal moment in US history, Baldwin's message in *Fire* reverberates as Black people are once again faced with an anti-Black sentiment as they fought to gain civil equality and full citizenship. These times reinvigorate a conversation among Black Americans about how to move forward in a turbulent moment then and now. Like Baldwin, Ta-Nehisi Coates in *Between the World and Me* (2015) writes to his fifteen-year-old son in a similar way, recalling that "[i]n 1863 [equality] did not mean your mother or your grandmother, and it did not mean you and me" (Coates 6). His words confirm that Black

Americans remain in a longstanding fight for civil equality despite all of the constitutional underpinnings that have been enacted by the US government that guarantee a Black person's freedom. Because white America, or as Coates says those who "believe that they are white" (7), believe in America's exceptionalism, racial injustice persists because of white America's moral ineptitude. Thus, Coates insists to his son that America is his country and that he has to find a way to live in it.

Again like Baldwin, famed Harlem Renaissance poet and writer Langston Hughes understood rioting as central to Black protest in the 1960s. Unlike Baldwin, however, he did not write about rioting with a sense of foreboding. Instead, Hughes seemed to embrace its political efficacy. He advocated for swift action and a strategy that would improve the lived conditions of Black people. In his essay "The Harlem Riot—1964," he exclaims that "words are rather useless at the moment" and "what is needed now is quick, effective, and immediate practical action" (Hughes 214).[22] For Hughes, the fire has come and continues to burn as more Black people are subjected to anti-Black violence and killed by police or racist vigilantes. His attendance at the funeral of fifteen-year-old James "Jimmy" Powell in 1964, who was shot by off-duty policeman Thomas Gilligan, raised his consciousness about the reality of Black life in the mid-twentieth century.[23] While Hughes's primary demand is justice for Powell, his piercing statement simultaneously interrogates America's unending racial inadequacies. In particular, America's general public remains silent about increased racial violence and unrest that are known most visibly through acts of police misconduct and vigilante violence that have become a recurrent narrative, in Black life and death in the United States.

In his remarks following Powell's funeral, Hughes tries to make sense of his death and his shock and disbelief about what happened. Hughes writes:

> the placing of blame for the current riots goes far beyond the simple shooting in front of a public school of little Jimmy Powell by Police Lt. Gilligan. Knife or no knife, Jimmy was a little boy. I saw him lying in his coffin looking very small and dead. And I heard people wondering in front of the funeral parlor why a very big man with a pistol—who had received medals for disarming grown criminals without shooting them—felt the need to shoot and kill this kid who looked, in his coffin, small even for the age of 15. (214)

Hughes's observations are a futile effort to make sense of what Gail Williams O'Brien notes as "an arbitrary criminal justice system and a social order that controlled black Americans in their relations with whites but that offered blacks little protection from whites or from one another" (O'Brien 143). The vulnerability of Powell's Black body is a reminder of a horrific past examined alongside twentieth- and twenty-first-century practices of systemic racism against Black Americans. Such trauma reveals the continued invalidation of human life that Black people experience in the United States. Hughes's and Baldwin's unwavering call for action as they incite conscious revolt is no different from what they were familiar with during the early twentieth century. Baldwin's "The Harlem Ghetto," written in 1948, is a commentary that cements riot as inevitable. He writes, "if an outbreak of more than usual violence occurs, as in 1935 or in 1943, it is met with sorrow and surprise and rage; the social hostility of the rest of the city feeds on this as proof that they were right all along, and the hostility increases; speeches are made, committees are set up, investigations ensue. Steps are taken to right the wrong, without, however, expanding or demolishing the ghetto" (Baldwin, *Notes* 58).[24] As Hughes's and Baldwin's texts point out, rioting was not a sociopolitical phenomenon unique to the 1960s and the BAM. Violent insurrections and plots to revolt were a frequent recourse for enslaved Black Americans, and riots rocked American cities like Chicago and New York in 1919, 1935, and 1943. *Start a Riot!* points out that rioting assumed a new significance in the 1960s with BAM writers wrestling with questions about implicit and explicit racism occurring in the aftermath of the passage of civil rights laws supposed to guarantee equal protection for Black Americans. BAM writers endeavored to capture in their works the images of Black people rioting as a humane act to seek racial justice. In this way, rioting is a language—a cultural code that Martin Luther King Jr. stated in his "The Other America" speech. This language is articulated by the unheard; more precisely, it is a ritual within Black politics that is vital in understanding the evolution of protest strategy conveyed in Black literature.[25]

As the above examples illustrate, images of rioting and its usefulness as a political strategy of protestation have factored into Black American literature throughout contemporary American history. However, BAM scholars have been slow to acknowledge the centrality of rioting as part of a BAM literary aesthetic. The Black Arts Movement of 1965–75 is well known for its radicalization of Black American artistic production. The movement was a critical moment in American history, where Black writers and artists departed from writing about Black themes rooted in Anglo-American aesthetics and culture. Instead, founders of the movement centered Black culture and aesthetics in their works, intentionally calling it "revolutionary" to direct other Black Americans to rethink and reshape how literary texts were read among Black communities across the United States and abroad. Beyond discussing the influence of the BAM, scholars pay little attention to how and why riot scenes appear in the works of BAM artists. Current scholarship about the BAM approaches the movement as a leftist, Marxist phenomenon, or examines the literary movement's gender and sexual politics and general literary aesthetics.[26]

The scholarship emphasizes the movement's insistence on Black self-determination. When we turn our attention toward rioting as a significant thematic of the BAM, we see how BAM artist-writers were concerned not just about aesthetics or leftist politics; they also protested the state-sanctioned violence and lack of economic independence that made their Black bodies vulnerable to death and made it virtually impossible to achieve civil autonomy.

Lisa Gail Collins and Margo Natalie Crawford's edited anthology *New Thoughts on the Black Arts Movement* (2006) is one of the few studies to address rioting extensively in the BAM. They argue that BAM's artistic production mirrors the politics of the Black Power Movement (BPM), but they also point out that a wave of riots in the mid-1960s influenced the strategic thrust in BAM creative works—specifically, toward a message of liberation as a move away from Westernized constructions of Black literature and politics to pan-African ideals and philosophy. Also, Soyica Diggs Colbert's essay "A Pedagogical Approach to Understanding Rioting as Revolutionary Action in Alice Childress's Wine in the Wilderness" (2009) recognizes rioting. She notes that BAM texts often paid close attention to fiction and nonfiction works by male writers. Women writers' works, particularly poetry and drama that examined riots and civil unrest, were overlooked. *Start a Riot!* builds on Collins, Crawford, and Colbert works by providing a nuanced exploration of the movement's contribution to Black aesthetics and culture. This book seeks to build on their work to reconstruct the multidimensional nature of Black Art's expressive culture and show how it contributed to the development of political ideologies. Also, *Start a Riot!* is part of a broader ongoing discussion about Black radical politics that reappraises the significance and relevance of the BAM.

BAM art was massively produced and created in US cities and across the world among Black artists who, after Malcolm X's death, became agents in their literary cadres.[27] After the assassination of Martin Luther King Jr. in 1968, BAM artists and writers had an established Black consciousness framework expressed through a Black literary aesthetic that allowed them to produce mass media content and shape the minds of its Black readers. A vital component of that aesthetic was rioting. Take, for example, *Black Fire:*

An Anthology of Afro-American Writing, published in 1968 by Black Classic Press. The book theorizes Black art's meaning through the articulation of essays that focused on economic and political topics and the artistic literature that today we canonize in works that celebrate the BAM. Notably, the anthology discusses civil unrest extensively. Peter LaBrie's essay "The New Breed" addresses rioting as a political activity among young Black Americans in retaliation against state violence. He contends:

> It is this threat of violence among the young breed which makes them a highly political group. They are political not because they may like to go on demonstrations or engage in organized political activities, but because certain of their actions have far-reaching political consequences. Their willingness to use force and violence to get what they want upsets the traditional socio-economic organization of American cities. The white businesses and political leaders of the cities cannot stand for widespread looting and rioting because it means destruction of their properties and disturbing their political and social positions. This they fear much more than they do peaceful demonstrations and thus become willing to make token concessions to the black community. (LaBrie 75)

Embedded within LaBrie's discussion of riot as a political act, his essay also examines the economic circumstances within Black society. Amiri Baraka and Larry Neal's editorial decision to include LaBrie's essay intertwined the kinds of social and cultural politics that made up the BAM, but that clarify our contemporary understanding of the economic landscape in the 1960s that shaped Black America's discontent. For instance, Kenneth B. Clark asserts that in New York City, "only one in twenty-five Negro families [had] an income above $10,000, while more than four in twenty-five of the white families [did]" (K. Clark 35).[28] Clark's data meant that many Black families and individuals were more than likely experiencing minuscule wages within their households.

The destruction of property (white property owned in Black communities) was a symbol of the dominant society's socioeconomic power. Mehrsa Baradaran asserts that "Black rioters destroyed white business establishments, but even more specifically, according to press accounts and government research, the pent-up anger was directed at the ghetto lenders" (Baradaran 143). The overwhelming irritation was due to predatory credit lenders that sold them worn or low-quality furniture and other household items. Many families stopped making payments on these things once they were no longer useful. These rioters responded to their economic depression by destroying those same faulty credit lenders' businesses. BAM drama, fiction, and poetry become the lens through which are seen the stories about rioting and its social, economic, and political connections.

BAM literature picks up on narratives of anti-Black and anti–civil rights violence as well as Black America's insistence on utilizing Black nationalism and human rights sentiment as a political ideology. Such doctrines draw attention to the structural inequalities that circumscribe Black life and revolutionize those social structures. Furthermore, they suggested annihilating racism–white supremacy and recreating a system through self-determination that would fit within the confines of a highly capitalistic society, where exploitation is necessary for the US system to work. How BAM drama, fiction, and poetry address anti-Black and anti–civil rights backlash in US society is deliberate. The texts' language is unapologetic and does not shy away from representing violence as a protest to express Black America's discontent with America's racist, white supremacist structures.

However, the majority of non-canonical works treated in the book (except for *The Bronx Is Next* and *Sister Son/ji* by Sanchez) shy away from multigendered narrations of civil unrest. Farah Jasmine Griffin eloquently describes that the early conceptions of contemporary Black women's literature surfaced out of a need and "were a direct response to the masculinist bias of the civil rights and especially the black power and black arts movements" (Griffin, "That the Mothers May Soar" 337). For example, Larry Neal's pioneering essay "The Black Arts Movement," published in the *Drama Review* in 1968, heavily uses male-centered pronouns to solidify that Black cultural production is centered in Black men's ideas, feelings, and expressions. For instance, Neal defines Black artistry in its relation to politics as "the black artist takes this to mean that his primary duty is to speak to the spiritual and cultural needs of Black people" and "the main thrust of this new breed of contemporary writers is to confront the contradictions arising out of the Black man's experience in the racist West" (Neal, "Black Arts" 55). Black men's experiences become the singular form of oppression that Black communities must combat when addressing racism. The "community" is not described as women and children collectively with Black men as being part of the freedom struggle.

Scholars have engaged with the gender politics of exclusion within Black freedom movements. Robert J. Patterson notes that "these writers have called into question the cultural and historiographical tendencies to champion male leadership, to promote models of leadership that diminish the significance of mass mobilization, to conceptualize racial rights as disconnect from gender and sexual rights, and to restrict the modern civil rights movement to the years between 1953–1965" (R. Patterson 2). Patterson contends that past glo-rifications of male civil rights leadership have undermined and to a degree erased the inclusion of gendered and "sexual rights" that illustrate past and current calamity within Black leadership and attaining civil rights. Patter-son's further contextualization of this crisis is what he calls "the paradoxes of exodus politics" (2). In fact, the singular leadership of Black men taking on the responsibility for the entire race, without women's input, becomes an act of what Patterson labels "masculinizing black leadership" (4). In the BAM literature examined in this book, particularly *The Slave* by Baraka, *Riot Sale, or Dollar Psyche Fake Out* by Caldwell, and "Riot or Revolt?" by Dumas, Black women subjects are absent, seldom visible, or overtly silent. In Sonia Sanchez's *The Bronx Is Next* and *Sister Son/ji*, Black women subjects have a voice, are visible, and the reader is offered exploratory ways of understand-ing their humanity and how it maneuvers within a Black cultural politics. Simultaneously, Sanchez's works of fiction, which we will focus on more in depth in chapter 3, reveal the abusive actions of Black male revolutionaries that, as Patterson suggests, "disallows the possibility of female leadership . . . but also produces a gender hierarchy that prioritizes black men, black men's leadership, and black men's political interests" (3). These insular interests among Black male radicals are motives that disempower the communities they seek to represent or "save" from racial oppression. Furthermore, San-chez's characters such as Old Woman and Black Bitch in *The Bronx Is Next* who reject the Black male revolutionaries' leadership either die or experience physical abuse. Black women become the consequence of Black male leader-ship gone rogue. Sanchez narrows in on the fact that Black women do fight for their lives and to dismantle consequential male-centered leadership, but it comes with a high price.

In similar fashion, but through another perspective, Erica R. Edwards's analysis of singular Black male leadership points to mythological narrations of Malcolm X's and Dr. King's influence that shaped civil rights histories. Edwards argues that "African American Narrative helps us to understand the myth of messianic black political fulfillment" (Edwards xxi). In other words, the projections of Malcolm X's and Dr. King's images become the fictions that forward a cultural consensus from the general public, but Black people specifically, that singular Black male leadership is what progressed the civil rights movement (CRM) and BPM. However, as Edwards suggests, these "fictions" make "black manhood the privileged site of political subjectiv-ity and activism" (7). The works treated in this book illuminate Edwards's point as the overemphasis on regarding Black male leadership consumes many of the works to a point that they often echo the sentiments of Neal's

deciphering about male-centered crises explored in BAM literature. One of
the components that my book addresses, particularly in chapter 4 examining "Riot or Revolt?" by Henry Dumas, is the idea of a singular charismatic
leader. Micheval LeMoor, the protagonist in the short story, is recognized as
a chosen leader of his community to combat and interrogate police brutality.
As a charismatic leader, Micheval engages with government and city officials
about police brutality, but he also challenges the position as singular leader
to an ongoing CRM. Revealingly, the concerns of charismatic Black male
leadership undergird the argument that Edwards and Patterson bring to the
fore regarding the overemphasis and embellishing of Black male-centered
leadership as the catalyst for civil rights and Black power.

Thus, what is left to ponder, when thinking of BAM's literary attention to
rioting, is recognizing the concurrent economic failures as a result of King's
assassination that maintained Black America's inaccessibility to material
wealth and how this further strained race relations. That is to say, when
we rely on singular Black male leadership as the basis for actualizing civil
rights promises of equality, what then happens to the collective? The crux
of male-centered leadership as the only source of revelation in the literature
presented in this book illustrates the looming polarities that emerge as crises
of radical Black activism.

Gene Andrew Jarrett asserts that works of Black American literature that
seek to "transform society on multiple ideological, cultural, and political
levels have not yet been treated carefully enough" (Jarrett 5). How do we recognize and acknowledge more Black American literature's influence within
Black people's call for civil rights and citizenship? One of those routes, I
argue, is to examine BAM literature's treatment of the attention to riots in
the 1960s as a marker of intraracial crises within Black politics. Jarrett notes,
rightfully so, that political histories read within Black Literature tend to focus
greatly on modern periods. Insightfully, he indicates that his "elimination on
a book chapter on the decades of the 1960s and 1970s captures my belief that
this famous period has dictated too much of the recent political approaches
to African American literary history" (13). What is evident in my exploration of civil unrest read in BAM literature is that the political approaches
are not explored enough. If Black literature contributes to our understanding of social transformation when exploring (or, as Jarrett indicates, when
"addressing or redressing the attitudes of readers and stimulating social
action" [6]), then BAM literature is an entry point to further understanding
the conundrums that arise out of civil unrest—in other words, how riots, or
what I call "conscious revolt," emerge out of the need to dismantle emblems
of white capitalism that exploit Black people and communities.

For instance, Lisa M. Corrigan assesses the outcomes from the 1960s riots and explores their place in BPM politics as a "mood" that "exposes the paradoxes of liberalism that promoted and foreclosed freedom and equality as black activists" grappled with "capitalism and disciplinarity" (Corrigan xvii). The feelings read within Black politics that placed a "psychological strain of movement disappointment, particularly with liberals (black and white)," ignited what Corrigan calls a "public grief" that "influenced new rhetorical and emotional paradigms in the black freedom struggle as it operated with and against liberal hope" (xvii, xx). The analysis of structural emotions attached to despair and pain that Corrigan poses is a direct correlation to King's examination in *Where Do We Go from Here?* that the call for Black Power among male revolutionaries "is a reaction to the failure of White Power" (King, *Where* 33). In other words, the Black Power slogan is seen not as a reference of self-determination but as "a cry of disappointment" relative to the legal guarantees that were supposedly an outcome of civil rights acts (King, *Where* 33). The inclusion of Black literature, particularly from a BAM standpoint, is vital because it brings clarity to the real tactics of working-class and poor Black people living in cities. Similarly, rioting of the early to mid-1960s read as a product of Black urbanity can be perceived as what King points out as a feeling of despondency or what Corrigan calls "black nothingness of the absence of black being" (Corrigan 76). The post–civil rights focus, echoing Cornel West's examination in *Race Matters*, which I explore briefly in chapter 1, is the attention to Black nihilism that evokes lovelessness and hopelessness in Black communities. In recalling the self-determination aspect in BAM literature, I have to point out that I interpret Black rioting analyzed in Corrigan's analysis, which focuses on the nihilistic attenuation to inhumanity, which subdues the self-determination and empowerment rhetoric that also ricochets through readings of Black rioting. The vitality of reading civil unrest within BAM literature opens the door to understanding the complexity of moods, feelings, and expressions associated with revolt. After the end of a riot in Gwendolyn Brooks's long-form poem *Riot*, there is jubilee. Black people have the autonomy to recalibrate their lives in the way they see fit. Likewise, in Dumas's "Riot or Revolt?" when the rioting subsides, it leads to true activist building for Black youth, the next generation; pride and self-determination are restored. BAM cultural production provides us with the opportunity to understand and see rioting beyond its despair, pessimism, and slow death. We see the possibilities of the rising of a new Black politics in the way we see in contemporary collective protests after the brutal police murder of George Floyd. Black rioting through its ugliness gives us possibility to learn and get right our politics. And, to echo

Gene Andrew Jarrett, Black political history represented in Black American literature promotes the imagined possibilities of social change the mainstream media denies to show about rioting: liberation, instead of recurring narratives that attribute the rioting to Black self-destructive behaviors that are normalized in historical representations of revolt.

Herein, chapter 1 examines Amiri Baraka's and Ben Caldwell's underexamined plays *The Slave* (1964) and *Riot Sale, or Dollar Psyche Fake Out* (1968). Both plays are during a riot. Walker Vessels, the protagonist in Baraka's play, and Caldwell's unified crowd both demand material and compensatory restitution from the US government for centuries of oppression. They seek reforms that will end rampant, systemic racism. Through protest, Black characters in both plays use rage to actualize self-determination and fight to achieve reparations from the status quo, even if it means death or long suffering. Black rage represents a form of protest that emerges from the Black proletariat. They intentionally demand that America devote critical and sustained attention to transformative justice, to endeavor to truly understand the cultural and economic devastation of Black America resulting from centuries of slavery, Jim Crow, and mass incarceration. Baraka's and Caldwell's dramatic theatre reveals that transformative justice materializes only when Black rage takes center stage. In this chapter, I argue that BAM artist-writers like Baraka and Caldwell employ Black rage as a central component of revolts designed to protest and dismantle the systemic racism that white America does not acknowledge. Ironically, through the seemingly chaotic and disparate expression of rage and rebellion, Black Americans derive a sense of racial unity as they work toward the common goal of social and economic equality. Through its representations of revolt (and the rage that energizes it), the "revolutionary theatre" of Baraka and Caldwell ultimately delineates and affirms a Black political subjectivity.

In *The Slave* and *Riot Sale*, Black rage occurs in moments of perpetuated pessimism that often reinforces a destructive impulse. However, in Gwendolyn Brooks's *Riot*, Black rage is exemplified through more respectable outlets seen as optimistic and constructive. In chapter 2, *Riot* uncovers Black America's rage and discomfort with a white northern backlash to Black progress gained in the earlier years of the CRM. It is a tale about Black America's revolt to avenge King's death and addresses the unresolved racial tensions between Blacks and whites. The poem includes leitmotifs such as sermons, the blues, and love as a challenge to Black America to emerge from the dark and destructive nature employed by the riot. Whereas most literary scholars label Brooks a writer of the Chicago Black Renaissance, in this chapter, I argue that her poem *Riot* employs a Black blues aesthetic. She does so by contemplating the place of rage and rebellion in Black racial progress to accentuate her vision for a new collective Black consciousness, which situates her within a BAM literary tradition. Baraka and Caldwell utilize Black revolutionary theatre as a method to advocate for rebellion. They do so by emphasizing Black communities' divisiveness, most readily exemplified through the tensions between nonviolent movements and those that accept violence as a bold response to racism. Caldwell's and Baraka's plays do not offer antidotes for that Black dissension. Their plays leave central conflicts unresolved; Black rage abates. Brooks explores those same divisions in *Riot* to model a dialogue that moves toward reconciliation and empowerment. However, I argue that her representation of rioting presents a more optimistic way forward by emphasizing rioting as a necessary catharsis with the potential to regenerate Black communities and produce opportunities for intraracial reconciliation.

Unlike Baraka, Caldwell, and Brooks, Sanchez does not strive to create a collective Black consciousness or advocate self-determination. She does not see rioting as a necessary evil to burn down the master's house in an apocalyptic display of rage or as a cathartic release that will lead to Black love and unity. Instead, she critiques rioting as divisive and self-mutilating—not to mention misogynistic. The so-called revolutionary act of rioting leaves the poor behind and burns down public housing, which does not alleviate Black suffering. In chapter 3, the actions of protest that revolutionaries enact in Sanchez's *The Bronx Is Next* do not disrupt the white social order; instead, they turn rage on themselves, blaming each other, not the oppressive institutions.

Moreover, acts of rioting oppress Black women in specific ways, Sanchez argues in *Bronx*. She challenges chauvinistic impulses of Black male revolutionaries who incite violence throughout the play. In this chapter, I argue that, unlike the works of Caldwell, Baraka, and Brooks, which center revolt through a male-focused lens, Sanchez's play forwards Black women's voices to question the efficacy of Black rage as a productive means of safeguarding Black humanity. Through my exploration of variegated feminisms such as womanism and Africana womanism exemplified in Sanchez's second play *Sister Son/ji*, I contend that she draws attention to the BPM, exposing the fractures of gender, race, and class that signal contradictory and polarizing views that emerged out of Black citizens' quest to achieve liberation.

In the first two chapters rioting is examined as a necessary move toward Black unity. In the third chapter, Sanchez exposes the collapse of Black politics. In the final chapter, I analyze further the crumbling of a Black revolution. Henry Dumas's short story "Riot or Revolt?" departs from *Bronx* through anchoring the discussion as it explores police brutality, integration, and political education. Specifically, I examine neoliberalism's free-market capitalism and how it manifests itself in recent Black politics. Through an exploration of state and vigilante violence committed against Black people, the chapter traces back to the Black radicalism of the 1960s through close readings of Dumas's short story "Riot or Revolt?" to understand racial violence and Black people's counter-responses through riotous protest. As a result, I argue in this chapter that Dumas draws attention to how the rise of neoliberalism within US social policy threatened to decentralize Black politics and render Black people vulnerable to structural inequalities such as state-sanctioned violence.

In the twenty-first century, it becomes abundantly clear that Black art depicting riots and revolts during the BAM is still polemical in today's society but also needed for the unapologetically original and raw language that captures the stories of the unheard. In real time, we reflect on an Obama presidency that experienced heightened civil unrest because of increased anti-Black violence that is state-sanctioned. In a post-Trump presidency, now settling into a Biden presidency, domestic terrorism is at the center of US politics and culture. American citizens continue to debate law and order rhetoric that continues to hinder #BLM justice claims of police reform, immigration, and LGBTQ rights.

Such examples underscore the need to locate Black stories written during the BAM. These stories situate this literary movement as a cohesive subfield within Black American literature because of its response to the neoliberal moment of its time. Also, BAM literature helps readers locate the progression of a neoliberal agenda that is interested in doing away with a discussion about racism altogether. Toni Morrison once said that "race has become metaphorical—a way of referring to and disguising forces, events, classes, and expressions of social decay and economic division far more threatening to the body politic than biological 'race' ever was . . . it is perhaps more necessary and more on display than ever before" (Morrison, *Playing* 63).[29]

These words stand as a reflection of past and present history with the racial debate. Jodi Melamed suggested that antiracism became the post–World War II rhetoric that ushered in new racial capitalism. According to Melamed, racial capitalism refers to the "official U.S. antiracisms since World War II" ("Represent and Destroy" 2). These antiracisms "have disconnected racism from material conditions, even as they have detrimentally limited the horizon for overcoming racism to U.S. global capitalism" (2). Herein, race is a controlling metaphor confined to an abstract narrative within US political and economic discourse. For example, the uprisings in Ferguson, Missouri, and Baltimore, Maryland, where civil unrest occurred in response to the grievances made about the police deaths of Michael Brown Jr. and Freddy Gray, illustrate race as a structural marker the disguising force did not acknowledge by the state. BAM drama, fiction, and poetry are conduits for conveying subject matter that addresses the oppression faced by Black communities as a result of systemic racism.

In conclusion, this book provides a literary framework to understand civil unrest as a critical form of study in Black literature to give relevant meaning to riots and revolts that continue to permeate US society. The fictional stories told are committed to educating our world about the ongoing consequences of racial inequality and how racism as a social construct continues to diminish the route to progressive race relations. Conceptually, this book returns to the critical conversation about Black politics initially outlined in Larry Neal's essay "The Black Arts Movement." I am interested in situating Black artist-writers' drama, fiction, and poetry that examines their political motives for transformative justice, thus paying attention to how it is revealing through artistic mediums.

Chapter 1

THE INABILITY TO COMPROMISE

Examining Black Rage and Revolt in the Revolutionary Theatre of Amiri Baraka and Ben Caldwell

In 1964 Amiri Baraka, then LeRoi Jones, wrote an essay for the *New York Times* titled "The Revolutionary Theatre." In that essay, Baraka argues for a theatre that exposes Western imperialism and its suppression of Black culture and creativity. His essay seeks to give voice to Blacks often marginalized and discouraged from participating in the American theatre—a space that he contends is nonpolitical, but fantastical, and centers Anglo-American life as the model for all lived experience.[1] Baraka encourages Black artists to disrupt a privileged white space with stories that are political and culturally progressive. The *Times* refused to publish the essay.

Baraka then attempted to publish it with the *Village Voice*. When that magazine also refused, he published it a year later in the Black magazine *Black Dialogue*. It appeared again in 1966 in *Negro Digest*. His inability to publish his essay in white publications perhaps reflects the unwillingness of mainstream American culture to confront the oppression of Black Americans and the silencing of their voices through, in this particular context, creative arts like theatre. Baraka's struggles to get the essay published are well known and repeated in historical accounts of the development of the BAM.[2]

In "The Revolutionary Theatre," Baraka understands art as the "expressed attempt to document the feelings of the community" (Baraka, "Revolutionary Theatre" 21). In other words, art has the potential to correct the image of Blackness in Western art. He calls on Black people to use art as a revolutionary practice to achieve liberation (21). What is necessary, he argues, is a theatre of reality, one that expresses their experiences through a dramatic lens onstage; Black drama, he anticipated, would ignite a reckoning that would change the fundamental approaches to racism within the existing power structure. This chapter uses Baraka's concept of "black revolutionary theatre" to illuminate the significance of rioting as a motif in his play *The*

Slave and Ben Caldwell's play *Riot Sale, or Dollar Psyche Fake Out*. Baraka's and Caldwell's works focus on the themes of slavery, reparations, and Black nationalism—which are all residual effects of systemic racism embedded within US culture. Both plays explore the consequences that result when white America refuses to acknowledge or relinquish race and class privilege for the sake of social equality and justice for all. The plays, emphasizing Black rage, become the cornerstone of conscious revolt, serving as mechanisms to expose the treachery of Western theatre, which renders Black people as victims complicit in their victimization.

Baraka's and Caldwell's plays make clear that demonstrations of revolt among Black America are a response to the unwillingness of white Americans to dismantle racial hierarchies and challenge white supremacy. Importantly, the Black rage represented in each play should be understood not as uncontrollable anger but instead as a manifestation of what Cornel West calls the "nihilistic threat" that pervades Black society. For West, Black nihilism is a byproduct of liberal and conservative strategists' failure to understand decrepit economic and political collapse in Black communities. The standard self-made man narrative implies that poverty and other forms of suffering that exist in Black communities occur because Blacks do not work hard and apply themselves. The notion of pulling oneself up by the bootstraps insists that "Black people . . . see themselves as agents, [and] not victims" of racism, of white supremacy (West 39). However, West contends that "inspiration slogans cannot substitute for substantive historical and social analysis" (39). The only viable antidote for the rage that emerges from a Black proletariat, West argues, is for mainstream America to devote critical and sustained attention to transformative justice. Such a tactic articulates an understanding of the cultural and economic devastation of Black America resulting from centuries of slavery and Jim Crow. Now mass incarceration circumvents the rage that ultimately emerges from a Black proletariat. The revolutionary theatre of Baraka and Caldwell reveals that transformative justice only materializes when Black rage takes center stage. In this chapter, I argue, then, that BAM artist-writers like Baraka and Caldwell employ Black rage as a central component of revolts, designed to protest and dismantle the systemic racism that white America does not acknowledge. Ironically, it is through the seemingly chaotic and disparate expression of rage and revolt that Black Americans derive a sense of racial unity as they work toward the common goal of achieving social and economic equality. Through its representations of rebellion (and the rage that energizes it), I argue, the "black revolutionary theatre" of Baraka and Caldwell ultimately delineates and affirms a unified Black subjectivity.

To illustrate this point, in the first half of the chapter I provide an overview of the two plays. Then I discuss the theme of Black rage that was central to the emergence of the BPM, in the wake of Malcolm X's assassination, to provide context for the political exigencies that characterize Baraka and Caldwell's plays. I also discuss their personal experiences that were central to how and why they chose to represent riots and revolts in their works. In the second half of the chapter I provide close readings of the two plays to map out how they represent rage and revolt as central to Black unification and progress. This reading of their works helps reorient predominant discussions of the BAM that almost exclusively emphasize the aesthetics of the movement while disregarding the literature's more overt politics. The artist-writers' artistic choices implicate the political agendas centered on rioting and revolts. That is to say, Baraka and Caldwell do not content themselves with writing plays that simply represent political protest. The dramas, themselves, are acts of protest. It is out of this call for riotous and revolutionary action that Baraka and Caldwell imagine Black unity or the Black nationalism advocated by foundational figures like Malcolm X.

BARAKA'S *THE SLAVE* AND CALDWELL'S *RIOT SALE, OR DOLLAR PSYCHE FAKE OUT*

The Slave is a two-act play that Amiri Baraka first performed in 1964. Set in both the antebellum South and a more modern-day time, the play features a Black man named Walker Vessels, who is a poet and revolutionary. In the play's prelude, he is an enslaved field hand on a nineteenth-century plantation. In the regular acts, he is the leader of a twentieth-century Black liberation movement that demands the US government provide Black Americans restitution for centuries of enslavement and other forms of oppression. A riot erupts when the government ignores the movement's demands.

The riot provides a backdrop to the story of Vessels, his white ex-wife, Grace, and their two biracial daughters. As the riot rages, Vessels breaks into the home that Grace and his daughters share with Grace's new husband, a white man named Bradford Easley. Vessels intends to remove his daughters from the home to raise them himself to ensure that they will inherit a Black consciousness. During his confrontation with Grace and Easley, Vessels espouses the virtues of Black culture, as represented by an emphasis on the blues. He insists that his daughters grow up with a strong sense of their Black lineage and the cultural experiences of Black Americans. Essentially, with his ex-wife and her new husband as an audience, Vessels insists on a

Black subjectivity for himself, for his daughters, for Black Americans. He insists that Black subjectivity means a "meta-language" that describes the Black experience—the blues—and its emphasis on detailing the suppression of Black Americans (Baraka, *The Slave* 45). He argues that the blues provides a soundtrack of sorts for the pain and suffering of Black Americans, which makes it a central art form in the tradition of American poetry.[3] Grace and Easley reject Vessels's artistic stance and, consequently, Black America's claim to restitution. Vessels, who initially saw his marriage to Grace as an act of interracial solidarity, now considers the marriage to be a mistake; it delayed the inevitable rebellion necessary for Black progress. In Baraka's play, a riot becomes the center of a justice claim against Vessels's ex-wife and the US government in general.

Baraka's play focuses on the struggles of one individual, Vessels. He positions this character to petition white America to atone for the atrocities brought upon Black Americans; in Ben Caldwell's *Riot Sale, or Dollar Psyche Fake Out*, Black Americans collectively band together to hold the United States government accountable. First published in 1968, the play begins with a crowd of armed Black protestors marching down Lenox Avenue in Harlem, New York.[4] They are confronting the local police, one of whom has just killed a fifteen-year-old Black boy in the neighborhood. They demand answers. Instead of providing information, the police instruct the protestors to go home and offer vague promises that they will get more information from their community leaders and allies. The crowd ignores the police's instructions; instead, they charge at the police officers. To quell the rage of the angry protestors, police use cannons to shoot money into the air, right in the middle of the crowd. The protesters throw down their weapons to scoop up the money. With the protestors distracted, the police confiscate their weapons and laugh at the protestors and their new interest in collecting money rather than fighting systemic oppression. Seemingly, the play calls into question the ability of Black protest movements to simultaneously advocate for justice and also seek financial restitution. It is a cautionary tale that Black rage can be bought, which would consequently delay Black Americans' efforts to gain faithful, legible American citizenship.

Both Baraka and Caldwell's plays have received scant critical attention. Scholars tend to dismiss *The Slave*, first performed at St. Mark's Playhouse in New York City, deeming it a piece of political dogma that presents no solution to systemic racism. The play, as some critics argue, advocates for forms of ritualistic violence that perpetuate the degradation of Blackness rather than presenting solutions. They determine that the play's Afro-pessimism does not allow for solutions or racial progress.[5] Scholar Samy Azouz, who analyzes

Baraka's *Dutchman* and *The Slave*, contends that the "characters are victims of their own failures because they use rituals to kill instead of using them to interact positively with each other" (Azouz 20).[6] Azouz's examination of Baraka's characters assumes that Black Americans, like Vessels, are responsible for seeking out common ground with their oppressors, represented by Grace and Easley in the play. This perspective misses the point that white America, as represented by Grace and Easley, rejects Vessels's demands for cultural appreciation and refuses to relinquish race privilege for the sake of Black Americans and racial equity. The demise of Grace and Easley at the end of the play—Vessels murders Easley and Grace dies after an explosion during the revolt—is partially self-inflicted. In contrast, scholars more open to *The Slave* pay attention to the theme of slavery and how its afterlife manifests in contemporary iterations of Black life.[7] In many ways, *The Slave*, published and performed a year before the BAM begins in earnest, is the movement's precursor.

The BAM formalized in 1965 with a definitive statement written by Larry Neal, in which he describes the movement as a reevaluation of "western aesthetics, the traditional role of the writer, and the social function of art" that places at the center a "black aesthetic" (Neal, "The Black Arts Movement" 55). *The Slave* rejects white dominance and embraces a radical Black identity, anticipating BAM texts. Furthermore, it foregrounds the mechanisms of revolt that were responses by Black Americans in response to Western imperialism and capitalist oppression. This early play of Baraka's also sets the foundation regarding riots as central to the grounding of the African story in America that crystallizes in his more mature work, 1969's *Slave Ship*, published at the height of the BAM.[8]

Ben Caldwell, in his own words, aligned his short play with Baraka's "black revolutionary theatre" concept. He goes on to say in an interview with Kenneth Bowman that he considered himself "a Black Revolutionary playwright, by definition given by Amiri Baraka in a *New York Times* article, and by Larry Neal" (Bowman 814).[9] He defines his plays as a move toward action rather than a representation of activity. Caldwell affirms that his plays must "influence change" (813). BAM scholars have often described *Riot Sale* as a Black nationalist satire that exposes the contradictions embedded within revolutionaries' ideas of enacting social change.[10] Scholars reading *Riot Sale* often miss Caldwell's intention of "revolution" as a method to redirect Black America's "attitudes and the behaviors that are the result of the slave condition and the post-slavery condition" (815). Caldwell is referring to attitudes and behaviors of Black Americans that embody negativity, or that are detrimental to social change (815). In other words, Caldwell's vision of social change happening within his play to effect action in real life can only emerge when the playwright is intentional and conscious about rallying the people to action. Thus, Caldwell's plays intend to be understood not as satire but instead are meant to engage the audience's reaction to illustrate the consciousness of Black Americans through art successfully. Therefore, in this chapter, Baraka and Caldwell's plays are analyzed to uncover methods through which they use theatre as sufficient space for Black nationalists' political engagement.

THE MAKINGS OF BLACK RAGE IN BARAKA'S AND CALDWELL'S REVOLUTIONARY THEATRE

The BAM directly resulted from the politics surging within the BPM following the assassination of Malcolm X. His death in 1965 was an act of anti-Black violence because what he stood for until the end of his life was redressing the humanistic wrongs brought upon Black lives. BAM artists participating in Black nationalism because of Malcolm X's influence strategized ways to engage Black America in Black radical politics through art. Black art served as a medium for Black artists to reignite Malcolm X's call for a Black revolution as a formidable continuation of the Black freedom struggle. Notably, this aspect is revealing during a crucial time when the division between Black Americans centered nonviolent and more militant approaches to civil rights protests.[11] Inspired by the legacy of Malcolm X, Black artists such as Baraka and Caldwell built their united fronts to provide a platform for cultural nationalism. Through drama, this intention restores the place of Black radical politics in Black Americans' consciousness as a necessary means to achieve their liberation.[12] Malcolm X's image and what he stood for, Black nationalism, became what Howard Rambsy II asserts is "a unifying force for a diverse range of poets" (Rambsy 104). I would add to Rambsy's analysis the poets treated in this book, such as Baraka, who was a playwright along with Caldwell. Baraka's and Caldwell's dramatic works were interested not only in paying homage to the fallen leader but also in reimagining his image as a staple of Black leadership in ways that placed him in a favorable light rather than in a controversial one.

A year after Malcolm X's assassination, Baraka argued that "the concept of Black Power is natural after Malcolm" (Baraka, "November 1966" 29). He further explained that "the thrust of Black Art was to free our images to disentangle them from the image(s) of the oppressor, so Black Power is the thrust of our total" (30).[13] Such comments speak to Baraka's discontent with the Civil Rights Act of 1966, which he labeled a "symbol more than a reality" (29).[14] The 1966 Civil Rights Act aimed to ensure nondiscrimination in jury selection at the federal and state levels. Since the passing of civil rights acts in 1964 and 1965, increased white rage became a national conversation, as many believed that Black Americans were aggressive in the pursuit of racial integration. The bill, which would build on civil rights activists' interests in eliminating discrimination in education and housing, and protect Black people's lives from acts of domestic terrorism, particularly when asserting the right to vote, was killed by a Senate filibuster. Baraka believed that the civil rights bill was an empty promise made by the Lyndon B. Johnson administration, exclaiming, "the bill never meant anything except one kind of promise. Nothing was to be done . . . [t]hey hated Black people anyway" (29). Baraka saw the 1966 civil rights bill as a smokescreen that leaders such as Roy Wilkins, A. Phillip Randolph, Bayard Rustin, Whitney Young, and Martin Luther King Jr. acquiesced to without considering "the genuine workers for Black independence" (32). In other words, he saw Black Power as the answer to Black people claiming full autonomy over their lives. The disjuncts between civil rights and Black Power, according to Baraka, stemmed from the failed promises of a white majority to make racial equality a reality. Baraka's disenchantment with a civil rights plan, as well as that of other BAM artist-writers, is partly framed from the ideological perspective of Malcolm X. He believed that the goal of human rights, instead of civil rights, should be the primary focus for Black people as the answer to a deeply racist United States government.[15] Agreeing with Malcolm X's take on international relations, Black artists and writers such as Larry Neal placed Black Power politics within the purview of Third World unification.[16] In his essay "Black Power in the International Context," Neal argues that "the African American struggle is inextricably linked to the worldwide struggles of oppressed people against decadent political and economic systems" (Neal, "Black Power" 133). Neal examines the history of Black radical freedom fighters since Malcolm X, and the internationalization of the US Black civil rights struggle. Neal, similar to Malcolm X, criticizes civil rights leaders such as Roy Wilkins and Whitney Young for approaching racial equality through a non-nationalist's lens that "is dangerous" (135). Neal states that civil rights leaders do "not see the struggle in nationalist terms" because they have "no independent international position" (135). Malcolm X's solution was taking Black Americans' justice claim to the United Nations while in the meantime building institutions for Black "people who originated in Africa and now reside in America" (Malcolm X, "Program"). Therefore, to plan "courses of action that will conquer oppression, relieve suffering, and convert meaningless struggle into meaningful action" (Malcolm X, "Program"). Malcolm X's powerful words became deeply rooted in the mind of Baraka, who has helped to cement art as a pivotal force to transmit ideological messages that would gain people's attention. As noted by Lisa Gail Collins and Margo Natalie Crawford, Malcolm X's influence exemplified a "Black nationalism, namely racial consciousness and black solidarity and pride," that remained central within the civil unrest happening in American cities (Collins and Crawford 6).

While Baraka's and Caldwell's plays emphasized political struggles within the public sphere of Black protest, the plays also underscored deeply rooted and internal conversations—seemingly, topics taking place in Black households about self-hatred and inferiority that have resulted from Westernized depictions and caricatures of American Blackness. For Baraka, the creation of the Black Arts Repertory Theatre and School (BARTS) in 1965 and the art that came out of it were intended to fulfill the social responsibility felt by Baraka and others. BARTS became the engine to eradicate Western ideals of Blackness and to use African diasporic identity as the methodology through which Black people could realize a cultural nationalism predicated on what Komozi Woodard has called "self-transformation of black consciousness" (Woodard 50).[17]

Black solidarity and pride became a more personal reality for Baraka when he returned to his hometown of Newark, New Jersey, with his wife, Amina Baraka. In 1967 the couple founded Spirit House, a cultural center similar to BARTS in Harlem that advanced Baraka's mission of Black nationalism and political coalition building.[18] According to James Smethurst, what differentiated Baraka's Spirit House from BARTS was his ability "to make an impact on the city that would have been impossible in New York" (Smethurst 101).[19] In addition to Smethurst's assertion, Baraka chose not to align Spirit House as close to the artistic work he had done at BARTS.

As an illustration of Baraka's investment in themes of riot and Black rage, at Spirit House he produced a play titled *Arm Yourself, or Harm Yourself: A Message of Self-Defense to Black Men!* The play is a direct response to the police brutality he experienced as a result of the 1967 Newark Uprising. The Newark Uprising was a five-day revolt that occurred July 12–17, 1967. Black residents of Newark's Central Ward came to the defense of a Black cab driver who had been brutally beaten by police. Black residents ignored the call for peaceful protest in response to the inhumane treatment of the cab driver. The police responded by brutally beating and violently harassing Black residents who were in opposition to their authority. The uprising claimed the lives of twenty-six Black residents, a white firefighter, and a white police detective. Similarly, 700 people were wounded, and the city of Newark paid some ten million dollars in damages.[20]

Baraka was among the protesters participating in the rebellion. He suffered a head injury during the uprising and was taken to the hospital. Once released from the hospital, he was later arrested by Newark police for allegedly possessing illegal firearms.[21] The conditions for the Newark Uprising began to arise eight years earlier, when the city initiated an urban development plan. Redevelopers under Mayor Leo Carlin's administration wanted to return the city to its wealthy and white middle-class roots. Carlin confirmed that "the surgery of redevelopment, [is] the most valuable tool in the entire kit of Urban Renewal" (qtd. in Rabig 69).[22] The growing Black community that had migrated to Newark during the Great Migration in the first half of the twentieth century were in confrontation with a city that wanted them gone. Newark city officials attempted to displace Black residents through methods such as suppressing political power and enacting employment discrimination.

Furthermore, many Black residents were renters living in buildings that were poorly maintained by the city. The city failed to address issues related to the quality of living, and by extension, poorly funded schools. The clash between Black residents and police that started the uprising in 1967 was inevitable. When journalist Saul Gottlieb asked Baraka for *Evergreen Review* about his interactions with Newark police during the uprising, he responded, "they just chopped us off at an intersection and jumped on us. They pulled us off the car [beating us] with guns and clubs and handcuffs" (qtd. in Gottlieb's "They Think" 27).[23] These interactions with the police are retold fictionally in *Arm Yourself, or Harm Yourself*, directly addressing Black men's subjugation to police violence at extreme levels. The play, published in 1967, introduces several Black men, known as First Brother and Second Brother, who witness and experience daily police harassment in their neighborhoods. The Second Brother believes that armed defense is a means of preventing harassment or death caused by contact with the police. First Brother hesitates to arm himself, as he believes that handling police interactions with morality and levelheadedness will result in no lives lost. However, the two meet their unfortunate demise when a group of cops kills them anyway for what they believe to be a fight between the two men. The overarching lesson revealed in *Arm Yourself, or Harm Yourself* is the emphasis on ending Black genocide as a result of police brutality and internal fights between Black people. The Black men in the play and, by extension, the community that witnesses the killings, are vulnerable to the police and easily targeted. They are harassed daily, for unknown reasons in some cases, and in other examples, scuffles between the men come across as a threat to the police that causes them to kill the men. The essential point that Baraka connotes in the fatal tale is that without Black unity, there is no self-defense.[24] Malcolm X once called self-defense an act of intelligence, remarking that "I am not against using violence in self-defense. I don't even call it violence when it's self-defense" (Malcolm X, "Communication" 313). Baraka asserts that self-defense among Black men and women is warranted.

Baraka determined that his art would act as a method of revolution, thus rebirthing radical political activism that called for action. He stressed in "The Revolutionary Theatre" that American art must "begin to be peopled with new kinds of heroes" (24). These heroes, the new breeds that Malcolm X alluded to in his "Black Revolution" speech, would now see their stories reflected on stage and were, as he called them, "better able to understand that they are the brothers of victims and that they themselves are victims if they are blood brothers" (22).[25] The call for unification within Baraka's dramatic works exemplified the manifestations of a Black nationalism, written for Black communities specifically as an avenue to convey their sentiments about anti-Black violence brewing in US society.[26]

Similarly, Caldwell also emphasizes Black nationalism in his work and is compelled to do so as a result of his personal experiences. In *Riot Sale*, there is a defining moment where Black Americans unify in protest to challenge the police to address the death of an unnamed fifteen-year-old teenager. The police dismiss their complaint and respond, "We don't want anyone hurt or killed. You people surrender your weapons and go home—it's all over—everything will be alright" (Caldwell, *Riot Sale* 41). Unsatisfied with the policeman's response, the individual members in the crowd shout, "Liar . . . Ain't nobody 'fraid of dying! . . . We tired you fuckin' over black men and women and ruinin' our children! [*sic*]" (41). The police repeat their previous response.

When the crowd refuses to surrender, the white male police brigade, coupled with their white male civilian allies and government officials, disperse tear gas into the air to disorient the crowd. The Black protesters do not retreat; instead, they continue to fight. When the police fire cannons of money into the air and watch the Black crowd scramble for the bills, they observe that, "[t]he black crowd's purpose and direction is lost" and "look at [the] black bastards go after that money" (42). Caldwell's play underscores what Soyica Diggs Colbert describes as "a [Black] political collectivity that remains invisible in normative formulations of citizenship. . . The scattering of revolutionaries at the sight of the money . . . highlights the desire to achieve bourgeois subjectivity" (Colbert, "Black Rage" 338; "Pedagogical" 80).

Colbert is correct in assessing the limitations of citizenship among the Black crowds that are only concerned with financial restitution that results in a bourgeois status. However, the moment is also indicative of making legible their right to citizenship and compensation long denied to them and their ancestors.

Riot Sale denotes Black America's attempts to actualize their political autonomy. The Black protesters' self-determination is undercut by the policemen's aversion to redress their brutality and, by extension America's prolonged, systemic oppression. In *Riot Sale*, the status quo weaponizes Black people's restitution. This activity is done by subduing Black American political collectivity and relegating them to the invisible confines of American society (Caldwell, *Riot Sale* 21). As a result, protesters enact rage as a method to ascertain why the killing of Black youth matters and to seek redress. Shermaine Jones declares that what she terms a "radical ethic of rage" hinges on Black America's call for immediate action in response to the violent deaths caused by anti-Black racism (Jones 180).[27] Jones further explains, "the need to not only mourn the dead but also protect the living is black rage" (180). It is a convergence of Caldwell's Black crowd mourning the death of the slain teenager and forming an aggressive response to that death, which challenges the status quo to reconcile the murder, but which reveals the perpetual insignificance of Black life.

Consequently, Black America remains exploited by US imperialism, and their rage is programmatically silenced. The setting of a riot, Colbert notes, serves as a "useful theatrical device for the BAM by showing the dichotomy inherent in rioting, chaos, and confusion on the one hand, and a mass of people unified in destroying white supremacy on the other" ("Rioting" 80). In other words, as Shermaine Jones contends, "rage becomes a kind of cultural capital. It is manufactured, commoditized, and performed by those committed to Black Power" in exchange for having immediate demands met (181). Rage is a kind of cultural capital that is effective in Black protest depicted in *The Slave* and *Riot Sale*.[28] The making of revolutionary action is indicative of the resistance to persistent marginality that Black people are tired of, and hence why they form communities of rebellion. Walker Vessels builds his community of rioters in *The Slave*, and the Black crowd in *Riot Sale* band together and socially transform the narrative.

Moreover, rage becomes a utility for which ending white supremacy and moving toward American democracy is tantamount.[29] Together, Black rage with Black nationalism bring to bear broader illustrations of how Black protesters respond to violence, whether state-sanctioned or vigilante. In response, Black characters enact their mission through self-determination to overturn racial antagonism and, by extension, proclaim their rights to true American citizenship.[30] As we shall see in the next section, slavery iconography and the Black Power ethos are utilized by Baraka to fortify racial justice and commemorate a lasting impression of radical politics and pride that provoke a movement for liberation and civil rights that would characterize the remainder of the 1960s.

THE INABILITY TO COMPROMISE, PART I: THE RISE OF CONSCIOUS REVOLT IN *THE SLAVE*

Baraka's characterization of Vessels's revolt reflects the civil unrest occurring during the emerging BPM era. Also, the characterization harkens back to slave resistance that occurred throughout the colonial and early nationalist days of America. In Act I, Vessels resembles an old plantation slave, but by the time he confronts Easley and ex-wife Grace, he appears as a contemporary radical, emblematic of the era of Black Power. Baraka's conflation of Vessels's appearances that are representative of the old and new revolutionary enlivens a conversation about the mechanisms of Black rage—specifically, intraracial communication among Anglo-Americans, and the consequences that it has on Black Americans whose heritage of African slavery in the Americas directly traces back to the Middle Passage.

The transatlantic slave trade is integral to understanding slavery iconography presented throughout *The Slave*. Gerald Horne investigates and challenges the longstanding history of America's founding by contemplating those factors that led to African resistance in colonial America.[31] He calls for a more nuanced understanding of the transatlantic slave trade that provides "a more accurate descriptor of [Africans'] plight [as] a collective political (and economic) persecution" (Horne 262). Black resistance, he argues, was a reaction to this kind of persecution; they refused "to accept passively the proclamation of a slave holder's regime, then a Jim Crow regime, then massive inequalities stemming from the two" (262). Put another way, Walker Vessels's revolt is the recognition of what Horne terms the "continuing invidious discrimination that undermines the descendants of enslaved Africans on the mainland," the massive importation and enslavement of whom "laid the foundation for the concomitant growth of capitalism" (22, 7). Slavery as a thematic focus in *The Slave* does not address the precariousness of the transatlantic slave trade as it relates to "the denied wealth from African labor that built a first world economy" (21). Still, it does interrogate the racial and historical consequences that have led to lingering traces of Black rage. Today, we understand race as a caste hierarchy in which the descendants of white Europeans who migrated to America are recipients of wealth and racial privilege in the United States. Those descendants of enslaved Africans reside at the bottom of a national caste system in terms of economic and social status.[32]

Baraka's *The Slave* helps readers understand the detrimental barriers caused by African chattel slavery that have resulted in centuries of civil unrest and Black uprisings. Importantly, he points out how the unrest is exacerbated by white America's refusal to acknowledge systemic inequality and to strive for interracial coalitions. In *The Slave*, there is a polemical moment between protagonist Walker Vessels and his ex-wife's husband, Easley. The two find themselves in a contentious debate about the US government dismantling its common practice of white supremacist politics that has perpetually disenfranchised Black Americans. Vessels explains to Easley, "We [Black Americans] called for a strike to show the government we had all the white intellectuals backing us . . . the only people who went out were those tired political hacks. No one wanted to be intellectually compromised" (Baraka, *The Slave* 76). Easley responds, "And it was an intellectual compromise. No one in their right mind could have backed your program completely" (76). Easley's response to Vessels reveals his complicity in the racial order, thus what Charles Mills contends in *The Racial Contract* as "securing the privileges and advantages of the full white citizens and maintaining the subordination of nonwhites" (Mills, *Racial Contract* 14). In a nation-state that is built on racism, Easley knows that backing Vessels's strike means the end of deeply rooted white supremacy and the move toward a truly racial egalitarian society, a move he conscientiously chooses to reject. Thereafter, Vessels's unsuccessful organizing of an interracial coalition against racial injustice turns into a revolt.

Vessels fails to find support among whites like Easley. Grace's husband perceives Vessels as being racially unpalatable, that is, too radical, too Black, too deviant within the context of mainstream (white) America. While Easley sides with Vessels's point that American society must be racially inclusive, he refuses to relinquish any measure of comfort or privilege to dismantle the white hegemonic rule. Instead, when Vessels mentions that "No one but Negroes" would participate in the strike, Easley responds, "Well, then they weren't in their right minds. You'd twisted them" (Baraka, *The Slave* 77). The conversation diverges as Easley places the blame on Vessels for starting a revolt and manipulating the minds of Black Americans who participate in the riot. He further calls the rebellion a "politics of self-pity" (77). Black rioters again are blamed for their victimization. What is more apparent, for acceptance to happen within the dominant social order, Vessels (and by extension Black people) has to conform to Western ideology, aesthetics, and customs, a move that is impossible even if Vessels wants to, which he emphatically does not. Baraka makes clear that Black American plays are essentially Western. However, some of its heroes, such as Vessels, have to represent "Anti-Western[ism]" because their sensibilities build the dismantling of racial hierarchy in America that goes against the making of a uniquely Western persona (Baraka, "The Revolutionary Theatre" 22).

Gerald Horne makes clear that the "necessity of slavery . . . at least for the Africans meant a counter-revolution" (Horne 7). Walker Vessels is the embodiment of counter-revolution-conscious-revolt and is enacting it through the language of physical violence but also the literary diatribe of Western poetry. When Grace asks Vessels if he is still writing, he remarks, "Oh, God, yes. Want to hear the first lines of my newest work?" (Baraka, *The Slave* 50). Vessels does not perform his original poetry in front of Grace and Easley; instead, he mockingly recites W. B. Yeats's "News for the Delphic Oracle." Grace, unfamiliar with Yeats, does not recognize Vessels's mocking of Western poetry. Vessels admits the poem is Yeats and facetiously remarks to Grace, "didn't you recognize those words as being Yeats's? Goddamn, I mean if you didn't recognize them . . . who the hell would?" (51). On Grace's behalf, Easley remarks, "I knew they were Yeats's . . . the second part of 'News for the Delphic Oracle'" (51). Vessels's reciting of a Yeats poem at that moment has twofold significance. On the one hand, he attempts to impress both Grace and Easley with his knowledge of the foremost poet in Irish and American history. On the other hand, the particular lines from Yeats that he chooses insinuate disorder and tragedy.[33] The revolt happening outside of Grace and Easley's house foreshadows their demise. Grace emphasizes this point when she indulges a drink with Easley during the riot, lamenting, "one of the few real pleasures left in the Western world" (47). The other pleasure is listening to and reading Western poetry. However, there is a moment in *The Slave* where Easley transitions the discussion with Vessels and begins to argue with him about Black poetry. In the play's "Prologue," Vessels, an aging man in his old field slave attire, ends his speech with a lyrical poem:

As the sky when the moon is broken
Or, old, old blues people moaning in their sleep
Singing, man, oh, n----r, n----r, you still here
As hard as nails, and takin no shit from nobody
He say, yeah . . . Goin' down slow, man. Goin' down slow. (45)

Easley claims Vessels's aesthetic is an example of "a bad poet always a bad poet . . . even in the disguise of a racist murderer" (Baraka, *The Slave* 50). Easley declares Vessels's poetry is lousy because it does not conform to traditional Western aesthetics rooted in classical and European Renaissance traditions or through praised white American poets such as Carl Sandburg or W. B. Yeats. Easley's critique also invokes the racial liberalism that absolves him from interjecting his prejudice. As discussed earlier regarding Easley and Grace's intraracial screening of Vessels's behavior, specifically, their critique is what Charles Mills argues is an "intra-white agreement" (Mills, "Black Rights/White Wrongs" 39). Mills goes on to say, "European expansionism, colonialism, white settlement, slavery, apartheid, and Jim Crow—shapes the modern world. Whites contract to regard one another as moral equals who are superior to non-whites and who create, accordingly, governments, legal systems, and economic structures that privilege them at the expense of people of color" (39).[34] Vessels resists the notion that his poetry is second-rate. Instead, he understands his poetry as a direct correlation to Black liberation, which is political. Easley and Grace reject this kind of poetry because it claims a Black autonomy; it is too Black. Easley critiques Vessels's poetry, further calling it "the poetry of ritual drama" (Baraka, *The Slave* 56). A trait of ancient Greek and Roman drama, the ritual took precedence, particularly when a disruptive scene such as a fight between a king and a god took place.[35] In modern times the ritual, as Samy Azouz notes, "is constituted by collective practices and activities that have significant potential for oppositional power" so that "Baraka's theatre stresses the relatedness between ritual and theatre by blending the real and symbolic, the ceremonial and the spiritual" (Azouz 18). Baraka's theatre is what Harry Elam terms social protest theatre that manifests into a space of racial liberation and truth-telling.[36] Therefore, as Terrance Tucker asserts through his exploration of comedic rage, Vessels's poetry (and by extension ritual drama) exhibits a rage that makes it impossible for Easley "to be [a] passive" uncritical spectator (3). Instead, Easley and Grace are "forced to confront the continued legacy of racial oppression," as exhibited through Walker's bold delivery (Tucker 3).

Vessels's and Easley's riffs about adequate methods for writing Western poetry get at what Tony Bolden defines as "resistance poetry" that includes a "blues network . . . [a]central position in African American vernacular culture" (Bolden 43).[37] Vessels's poetry involves a blues aesthetic Baraka once termed "primitive blues" (Baraka, *Blues People* 60). Such blues birthed "a kind of singing that utilized a language that was almost strictly American. It was not until the ex-slaves had mastered this language in whatever appropriation of it they made that blues began to be more evident than shouts and hollers"

(63). Easley degrades Vessels's poetic remastering of Black vernacular and diminishes the form by addressing it as "inept formless poetry" (Baraka, *The Slave* 55). Easley's lack of appreciation for Vessels's poetic efforts reflects what Bolden asserts is the critic's inability to "envision an alternative to a script-centered poetics" (Bolden 61). Such critics "often mistakenly assume that a blues method can only be reflected in stanza patterns on a page" (61). The poetic mastery of Vessels—and by extension, Baraka—is not reflected in the conventional forms of seasoned white male poets who set the standard for how poetry should be read and written. Baraka's attention to Black American expression is precisely why BAM artists sought to define and differentiate Black poetry, which, as Larry Neal explains, has "a concrete function, an action"; it ". . . affirms the integral relationship between Black Art and Black people" (Neal, "The Black Arts Movement" 58). Vessels's poetic delivery, then, speaks to a collective consciousness that incorporates conventional and unconventional modes of Black vernacular to convey a radical expression that embeds resistance.

Importantly, Western art, as Baraka notes, does not have the same politi-cal obligation as Black art. In "The Revolutionary Theatre" he maintains that "white Western artists do not need to be 'political' since usually, whether they know it or not, they are in complete sympathy with the most repres-sive social forces in the world" (Baraka, "The Revolutionary Theatre" 23). Thus, because of this proclamation, they "will hate the Revolutionary Theatre because it will be out to destroy them and whatever they believe is real" (23). White America's refusal to address racial politics is the very reason that the interracial coalition Vessels imagines never materializes. Easley and Grace do not compromise with Vessels or acknowledge gross injustices. Because of this rejection to acknowledge racism exhibited by the couple, the irony is that they experience the same violence and death that initiated Vessels's rage, what Grace calls "twisted logic" (Baraka, *The Slave* 49). When Walker explains that before his revolution, when he "was crying out against three hundred years of oppression; not against individuals" (72), Grace refuses to see his plight; instead she calls it the "destruction of white people" and the "politics of self-pity" (72). The flippant remark made by Grace disavows Vessels's rage, and she remains unaccountable more broadly for perpetuat-ing white hegemonic rule. Grace and her new husband's inability to give up racial power is why Vessels resorts to violence; in his mind, that is the only solution to ending Black suffering. Not only do Easley and Grace reject racial compromise, when the riot begins their real bias also comes to the fore. In a heated conversation, Grace calls Vessels a "second-rate Bigger Thomas" (57). Vessels responds with a bit of wry humor when he quips, "but remember when I used to play a second-rate Othello?" (57). As the exchange continues, the scene becomes crasser and viler.

To exert his opinion about Easley's and Grace's inadvertent denial of racial compromise, Vessels employs comic rage. Speaking directly to the couple, Vessels says, "Oh . . . I was Othello . . . Grace there was Desdemona . . . and you were Iago . . . Ah ah, that's the basis of an incredibly profound social axiom . . . I mean if they ever rebuild the university. What was I saying to you, enemy?" (Baraka, *The Slave* 57). Baraka's references to Shakespeare's *Othello* are particularly appealing in these passages because they evoke the kinds of cultural and comedic expressions that zero in on the covert racism exemplified by Easley and Grace's speech. Terrance Tucker defines *comic rage* "as an African American cultural expression that utilizes oral tradition to simultaneously convey humor and militancy" (Tucker 2).[38] He merges both comedy and rage to explain the reasoning behind Black people making justifications for their racial suffering, but also to explain how they are determined to overcome the anxiety of their oppression through comedic storytelling that permeates their daily lives. I argue that Vessels's humor becomes a way to, as Tucker connotes, "construct responses to racist attack by exposing white folly, highlighting American hypocrisy, and celebrating African American difference" (Tucker 2). In *The Slave*, Baraka purposely uses humor as a trait for his characters to expose white American fragility when confronted with conversations about institutional racism within society.[39] However, before the humor emerges, he illustrates white liberal America's inability to compromise their privileges in a way that will actualize a civil and equitable society for all racial and ethnic groups. As stated earlier in reference to Charles Mills's racial liberalism, Vessels's humor and Grace and Easley's flippancy is an example of "an artifact of racial privilege . . . of injustices that do not negatively affect whites" (Mills, "Black Rights/White Wrongs" 35). Therefore, the tension leads to Vessels's conscious revolt.

Easley and Grace's rejection of Vessels's efforts toward interracial cooperation illustrates for Baraka the unwillingness of white liberals to compromise their livelihood and privilege. Fundamentally, Vessels fails to find support among (liberal) white Americans because his ideas are too radical, too Black. Thus, what Mills characterizes as the "white citizenry increasingly [insisting] that the surest way of bringing about a raceless society is to ignore race" (35). Moreover, Vessels's struggles against what sociologist Ted Thornhill notes is an intra-white code of screening that happens among white Americans whereby they reject or accept Black Americans based on the racial salience of the person (Thornhill 695).[40] In modern society, white administrators can select the Black American prospective student or job applicant that appears

race-neutral or apolitical. To this end, if an applicant seems to be the opposite, more aware of racial lineage, conscious of one's identity, and prideful,
they face the risk of being passed over for opportunities that could enhance
their material and social circumstances (695). Thornhill's research reveals the
longstanding struggle that Black Americans who are descendants of African
chattel slavery in the Americas experience. For example, Black Americans
have been denied admission at predominantly white institutions because of
whites' perceptions of their race consciousness and politics.[41] As a result, in
The Slave, because Vessels is unable to pass Easley and Grace's intra-white
code of screening, he retaliates by killing all of them. This violent act is supposed to symbolize the death of Western imperialism and white supremacy,
or more precisely what Baraka explained in "The Revolutionary Theatre" as
the "strike back against any agency that attempts to prevent this widening"
of Black consciousness (21). Before Easley's and Grace's demises, instead of
understanding the crux of racial liberalism, they instead perceive Vessels as
the real racist, hence why they call him a "racists murder" and "n----r murder"
(*The Slave* 50, 54). Again, the couple takes no responsibility in acknowledg-
ing that their liberalism has contributed to unsatisfactory racial progress.

   Ultimately, *The Slave* interrogates white supremacy and those, such as
Easley and Grace, who appear to be liberal allies to Black America but who
are opposed to giving up their privilege for real racial equity in America.
In the end, Walker Vessels struggles and confronts this racism through an
armed revolt to seek true citizenship and wholeness in American society,
a country that is his home and where his lineage resides. Seemingly, Vessels's racial awakening is the rallying cry for the early foundation of Baraka's
insistence that art acts as a method to urge what John H. Bracey Jr., Sonia
Sanchez, and James Smethurst define as the ability of "African Americans
to determine their own political and cultural destiny," and that is exhibited
in Baraka's revolutionary theatre (Bracey Jr., Sanchez, and Smethurst, "Black
Arts Movement" 1).

THE INABILITY TO COMPROMISE, PART II:
BLACK POLITICS, REPARATIONS, AND RACIAL (IN)JUSTICE

Ben Caldwell's one-act play is a direct enactment of rage that incites social
change and promotes self-determination—primary tenants attributed in
"The Revolutionary Theatre." In *Riot Sale*, white men assume positions of
authority (police officers and government officials) and set the tone for
racial justice by compensating the Black crowd with US dollars in return

for ending their protest of a Black teenager who was killed by law enforcement. White men mock newly rich Black folks for immediately spending their money in stores or taking it home. The police officers call the Black protesters "N----RS" (Caldwell 42), an incendiary term that negates their willful claim to collectively reap the financial gains for which their ancestors fought and died. The general use of the n-word here reduces the protestors to inhumane commodities, much the way the word reduced their ancestors. As R. A. T. Judy notes, n----r was the primary marker "to designate African American slaves as commodity . . . labored commodities" (Judy 222).[42] The white police officers denigrate the Black protesters. Such an action from public servants undermines the protesters and intentionally mischaracterizes what reparations would mean to Black people by linking their humanity to the exploitation of capitalism. Melvin L. Oliver and Thomas M. Shapiro have argued that over the years, US economic policies produced the Black inequality that undergirds white wealth accumulation. For example, the authors exclaim: "slaves were by law not able to own property or accumulate assets. In contrast, no matter how poor whites were, they had the right . . . to buy land, enter into contracts, own businesses, and develop wealth assets that could build equity and economic self-sufficiency for themselves and their families" (Oliver and Shapiro 95). Even after the emancipation of enslaved Africans following the Civil War, Blacks were prohibited from accumulating advantages in sectors such as social security, federal housing, and the Internal Revenue Service. Oliver and Shapiro further make known that today "the seemingly race-neutral tax code thus generates a racial effect that deepens rather than equalizes the economic gulf between black and white" (100). In other words, the state policies enacted by federal and state governments ensured the financial security of white America while at the same time disadvantaging Black America. The call for reparations made by individual and collective groups of Blacks are about redress, rather than what is understood today as a governmental handout.

Discussions surrounding reparations for African descendants have centered on the impossibility of such an act truly compensating Black Americans. Given that impossibility, Stephen Best and Saidiya Hartman concede, "if what has been done cannot be undone, then the forms of legal and social compensation available are less a matter of wiping the slate clean than of embracing the limited scope of the possible in the face of the irreparable, and call attention to the incommensurability between pain and compensation" (Best and Hartman 1–2). Put another way, Black people's newfound wealth (in a fictional context) does not solve racial injustice or end white supremacy because politics are traded in for monetary gain. Best and Hartman go on to say that their 2005 Redress Project "is not a volume on reparations; . . . this volume represented, is the attempt to interrogate rigorously the finds of political claims that can be mobilized on behalf of the slave (the stateless, the socially dead, and the disposable) in the political present" (5).[43] The scholar-writers are not concerned with repayment but rather "the contemporary predicament of freedom, with the melancholy recognition of foreseeable futures still tethered to this past" (5). Such a stance in the twenty-first century, particularly in the same year when the US federal government made a public apology to the families of lynched victims during the Jim Crow era without also providing restitution, points precisely to how the United States has refused to acknowledge in its totality the trauma and centuries-long consequences of dehumanizing the enslaved and making them into human capital.[44]

A close reading of *Riot Sale*, then, focuses on the significance of the reparations debate. Through an economic-historical lens, I will illustrate how Caldwell's play probes the problematic notions of restitution as compensation for America's original sin (slavery) that still haunts its present as well as its past. Utilizing the reemergence of reparations discussions within US politics, particularly surrounding the racial wealth gap, this section will explore what scholars Harry and Michelle Elam call "staging reparations" (Elam and Elam 102). The Elams suggest that the story of American slavery must be told and retold, "daily enacted by people" confirming that "racial justice will be had whether or not whites are willing participants" (103).[45] The intervention here is that Caldwell's play broadly recognizes a critical dialogue about redress.

In *Riot Sale*, the Black protesters receive restitution from the policemen only after collectively rousing their political activism and putting pressure on law enforcement and their federal superiors. Before that, a police officer tells the impatient protesters to turn to their civil rights leaders: "Let your appointed leaders handle your grievances and negotiate your demands," he insists (Caldwell 41). The dissenters disregard the statement and press forth in their rebellion, invoking interpolations from H. Rap Brown's rallying cry "If America don't come around, America need to be burnt to the ground" (qtd. in Baraka, "Black Liberation" 216). The crowd responds, "We gon' tear this motherfucker down to pieces!"—emphasizing Caldwell's intentional melding of rage and obstructive language that connotes the crowds' association with civil disobedience. Thus, the reimagining of repair through proper restoration becomes the method by which Black dramatists such as Baraka and Caldwell attempt to provoke questions about restitution for

Black Americans.[46] Drama stands as a conduit for reinserting reparations into an American imaginary that becomes reconfigured in both fictional and nonfictional spaces.

It is vital to understand how reparations figure in *Riot Sale*. Reading about restitution in Caldwell's play, it is essential to examine redress in nonfictional spaces. On June 19, 2019, members of the US House of Representatives met at a congressional hearing to commemorate the quadricentennial of the first enslaved Africans to arrive at Point Comfort, Jamestown, Virginia. The hearing was led by Congresswoman Shelia Jackson Lee, who serves as chairman over H.R. 40, the Commission to Study and Develop Reparations Proposals for African Americans Act, formally introduced by the late Congressman John Conyers, representative from Georgia 1989–2017.[47] The hearing included testimonies from former NFL athletes, clergy, entertainers, and politicians, notably Senator Cory Booker and journalist Ta-Nehisi Coates. The moment was historic because the discussion about a potential study for reparations was not taken seriously since 2007, the last time there was a congressional hearing about restitution for the African descendants of American slavery.

The telling of the historic moment was raised not in the hearing but in testimony written by scholar William Darity Jr., who was unable to attend the hearing, in remarks on behalf of the commission. In "The Case for Reparations: Is the Nation Ready to Give African Americans Reparations," Darity contends that Black Americans are the heirs of restitution in the form of cash payments. These payments will eliminate the centuries-long racial wealth gap that has kept the racially marginalized group an economic underclass. To defend his claims, Darity argues that "Black Americans constitute approximately 13 to 14 percent of the nation's population, yet possess less than 3 percent of the nation's wealth" (16). Wealth, as he argues, is "insurance against economic anxiety and economic disruption for individuals and families" (16). Due to a historical lineage tied to enslavement, Black citizens remain at the bottom of the economic ladder. They are vulnerably susceptible to "inferior housing and educational products, predatory finance, and ongoing housing and labor market discrimination" (Darity and Hamilton 62). Darity and Darrick Hamilton go on to say in "The Political Economy of Education, Financial Literacy, and the Racial Wealth Gap," that "Black students are 25 percent more likely to accumulate student debt and are, on average, borrowing over 10 percent more than their White student counterparts" (62). The case for reparations made by Darity concludes that by lawfully restituting the descendants of America's formerly enslaved with compensatory payments that equal to 13 to 14 percent of their actual population will sufficiently change the collective economic position of Black Americans.

The stance on reparations emerges in *Riot Sale* when the protesters do not back down from the police because they are demanding redress. To build off of the observation made in this book's introduction, we have to understand how we read the history of redress as it relates to the extreme measures Black Americans endured being first human commodities through slavery and then disposable humans during Jim Crow. In *Riot Sale*, before the Black protesters receive their money, they stand in unison for a substantial amount of time. The police repeatedly state: "[t]his is to warn you—we are prepared to handle whatever situation arises. We don't want anyone hurt or killed. You people surrender your weapons and go home—it's all over—everything will be alright" (Caldwell 41). The protesters, not deterred by the policemen's supposedly empathetic stance, confront them about the many injustices they have committed against Black people. Responding to the police, angry protesters shout: "'Liar' . . . One of you motherfuckas [*sic*] killed a innicent [*sic*] fifteen year old boy! . . . We are tired of you fuckin' [*sic*] over black men and women and ruinin' [*sic*] our children! . . . You can't stop my people now, goddamn! . . . We ready to go all the way!" (41). The consistent demand from Black protesters to be heard by the police (their oppressor) exhibits how police officers and their unwillingness to recognize their brutal actions contests what Black citizenship is and what it means. Keeanga-Yamahtta Taylor argues: "police brutality has been a consistent badge of inferiority and second-class citizenship . . . when the police enforce the law inconsistently and become the agents of lawlessness and disorder, it serves as a tangible reminder of the incompleteness of formal equality" (K. Taylor, *From #BlackLivesMatter* 108).[48] The protesters in *Riot Sale* are poor and working-class Black citizens. The police do not protect them; rather, they remain silent about how they killed a Black teenager. The policemen's actions, of suppressing Black protesters' voices, illustrate what Taylor contends is "the police function to enforce the rule of the politically powerful and the economic elite: this is why poor and working-class communities are so heavily policed" (108). The Black protesters' inability to receive an adequate response from the police also illustrates that, because they do not possess economic elitism or political dominance within US society, Black Americans' call for respect is ignored. The protesters' willingness to stand their ground by not walking away from the police makes a case for what Soyica Diggs Colbert contends is a "rite of repair" (*The African American* 2).[49] Fundamentally, Black America's political voice about reparations is isolated and relegated to the margins. To be sure, *Riot Sale* melds the possibility of reimagining the US getting reparations right. Still, it also critiques the propaganda propagated by the white elite in addition to its examination of police brutality. Caldwell showcases a police officer stating to the protesters in a sarcastic tone, "You n----rs sure all you want is freedom?" (Caldwell 42). The protester's response is, "You hear that?! Come on let's get these m.f.'s now!" (42). The police forcefully try to jettison Black protesters' demand for transformative justice and, in the end, try to recharacterize what it means to give reparations as a way to direct the narrative that mocks the protesters. Once the protesters begin to charge, the police throw money in their direction and mockingly state, "Look at the black bastards go after that money" (42). In this example, the implication, on the one hand, is that money will not solve racism and, on the other hand, that Blacks do not deserve their newfound wealth. Once the protesters begin collecting their money, "those few still bent on revolution are now easily subdued by the police" (42). Also, "the (anti-poverty) cannon roars again!" (42). Like Baraka, Caldwell uses light humor to forge a conversation about reparations with the inclusion of Lyndon B. Johnson's War on Poverty programs. The police shoot money in the air and laugh about it as Black protesters collect it. The police officers' actions reveal how the War on Poverty platform, as the US Congress admitted, "are not programs to bring about major structural change in the economy or to generate large numbers of additional jobs" (qtd. in Baradaran 151).[50] In other words, Johnson's program did not include elements like financial literacy or economic programs that would build wealth. The play can potentially be read as the money that Black people collect is a charity, instead of a means to build generational wealth. But this type of reading becomes apparent because, for so long, the American narrative about reparations reduces to negative connotations.

Black Americans have repeatedly been denied reparations, presumably due to the legal and logistical difficulties of figuring out what the atonement should be and precisely who should qualify for restitution. While there have been individual examples of reparations cases won by Henrietta Wood in 1878 and for the Rosewood Massacre of 1923, these are rare exceptions that reflect a general idea "that ex-slaves were owed nothing more than emancipation" (McDaniel 7). For example, stories about unsuccessful reparations cases, such as that of Callie House, survived over successful ones such as Wood's.[51] Henrietta Wood was born into slavery in Northern Kentucky and freed by her mistress Jane Cirode in 1848. However, in 1853, Cirode's daughter Josephine and her husband Robert White conspired with deputy sheriff Zebulon Ward to kidnap Wood and sell her back into slavery. The plan was successful, and Wood remained enslaved in Natchez, Mississippi, until she was freed in 1869. In 1870, after settling as a freedwoman in Cincinnati, Wood's lawyer Harvey Myers sued Zebulon Ward for $20,000 to seek restitution for the illegal kidnapping and re-enslavement. In 1878 Wood was granted a $2,500 reparations settlement against her former slave owner Zebulon Ward.[52] As W. Caleb McDaniel cogently remarks, "Wood's pursuit of damages argued for a less popular view that the past might make continuing claims on the present" (6).[53] The lasting stories that are part of America's historical memory do away with Henrietta Wood because her case "was about what former slaves were owed for their enslavement, as well as about the real differences that restitution could make" (6). Such a divergence from reparations as a realized possibility of restitution for Black Americans instead places the memorialization of a debt owed and its impact on the socially dead and disposable. Caldwell delves into the contestation of Black politics and cash reparations. He fictionally refashions the story into a history that settles the score and makes apparent the need to revisit the question on restitution and transformative justice for the descendants of the formerly enslaved—thus illustrating how rioting as a theme undergirds the restitution and transformative justice narrative rooted within the play and bringing together full circle how oppressive systems and practices have shaped the Black experience and, moreover, how Black characters within *Riot Sale* challenge and work to hold the US government accountable for those systems and practices of oppression.

CONCLUSION

Amiri Baraka's *The Slave* and Ben Caldwell's *Riot Sale, or Dollar Psyche Fake Out* focus on the demonstrations of rage among its Black characters that bring to bear the status quo's inability to compromise and make real an equitable society that benefits all citizens. Such a revelation within this chapter presents challenging iterations about racial compromise through the examination of Black rage. The revolutionary theatre reveals that revolt among the characters is a direct result of Black rage that becomes the cornerstone of lasting political changes that promote Black subjectivity and address their legislative concerns such as nationalism, slavery, racial violence, and reparations. The artist-writers also get at how revolution leads to defining change if and only when the compromise institutes otherwise, as we see in Brooks's poem *Riot*, Black rage escalates. Civil unrest prolongs as the status quo continues to challenge racial compromise.

Chapter 2

"BLACKBLUES"

The BAM Aesthetic and Black Rage in
Gwendolyn Brooks's *Riot*

Most literary scholars understand the Pulitzer Prize–winning poet Gwendo-lyn Brooks as a vital figure of the Chicago Black Renaissance Movement of the 1930s–50s. This chapter examines her literary evolution in the 1960s and the BAM. Brooks's writing was precipitated by the larger political events and forces surrounding her in the latter part of that decade.[1] In her autobiography, *Report from Part One*, Brooks writes that "until 1967 [her] own blackness did not confront [her] with a shrill spelling of itself" (Brooks, *Report* 83). She always knew "that to be black was good," but the social realities of 1960s America made her think broadly about the deaths of and violence against Black people, particularly its leaders. Brooks "lived through the rebellion in Chicago after King's death while listening with disbelief to Mayor Daley's 'Shoot to Kill' orders" (22).[2] Daley's draconian directive was in response to rioters, who were labeled as arsonists and looters. Anyone caught doing such acts during the riot were ordered to be killed.[3] The combination of the riot and murders of Black leaders, like Malcolm X and Martin Luther King Jr., led Brooks to think more about how her poetry could respond to the state-sanctioned and vigilante violence committed against Black Americans.

In 1969 Broadside Press published Brooks's poem *Riot*.[4] Like Baraka and Caldwell, discussed in the previous chapter, Brooks's preoccupation with the rage outpouring from Black communities proposes a different response. The difference in this scenario, however, is that the rage erupting is in reaction to the death of Martin Luther King Jr. Set in Chicago, rage takes center stage as Black citizens rebel in response to persistent racial inequality. They also react to what they perceive as white America's backlash to Black progress made in the earlier years of the CRM. The assassination of King halted that progress. The poem is a tale about Black America's effort to avenge the death of King and address unresolved racial tensions between Blacks and whites.

For Brooks, rage (and the violence it engenders) is a necessary evil in the fight for racial justice. Rage is a preliminary tactic that Chicago's Black residents utilize in response to white America's insensitivity toward racial oppression and the grief of Black America caused by King's death.

In *The Slave* and *Riot Sale*, Baraka and Caldwell employ Black rage to articulate an overall pessimism about racial reconciliation and progress. Riots, then, come to represent communal hopelessness and resignation. It is a destructive impulse in Black communities. Brooks, however, sees rioting as a regenerative response. Black rage illuminates through more respectable outlets seen as optimistic and constructive. For example, she presents a sequence motivating affirmations such as King's quote, "a riot is the language of the unheard," the rising phoenix mythology, and love as a challenge to Black America to emerge out of the dark and destructive nature employed by the riot.

Most scholars who examine Brooks's *Riot* read her as a Chicago Black Renaissance poet, concerned with the poverty and oppression of urban Black America.[5] Such approaches overlook the poem's aesthetic roots in the BAM. That is to say, *Riot* not only reflects Brooks's Chicago Black Renaissance identity but also illustrates the extent to which she embraced the political imperatives of the BAM. In *Riot*, Brooks makes use of a Black blues aesthetic, which undergirds much of the creative output of BAM artists, to protest racial oppression and provide a constructive avenue through which Black America could vent its rage.[6] Although understudied, *Riot* is a quintessential representation of BAM politics, and Brooks adds her creative voice to that of other BAM artists who imagine their art as forms of protest. As I stated previously in the book's introduction, a Black blues aesthetic refers to how writers included blues and jazz within their writings.

Moreover, the music is the fuel to illustrate acts of resistance against "existing white paradigms or models [that] do not correspond to the realities of black existence" (Stewart 3). Therefore, it is vital to read Brooks in this way, because her voice is in sequence with a Black revolutionary view, similar to Baraka and Caldwell's, that corresponds to the dissent employed by a Black Power generation. In response to writing in the BAM era, Brooks stated, "My newish voice will not be an imitation of the contemporary young black voice, which I do so admire, but an extending adaptation of today's G.B. voice" (183).[7] That adaptation manifests itself in how Brooks uses certain artistic elements from the BAM, like blues imagery. In this chapter, I argue that Brooks's poem *Riot* employs a Black blues aesthetic to contemplate the place of rage and rebellion in Black racial progress and to elucidate her vision for a new collective Black consciousness. Baraka and Caldwell utilized the

Black Revolutionary Theatre as a method to advocate for liberation. They did so by emphasizing the divisiveness within Black communities, most readily exemplified through the tensions between nonviolent movements and those movements that accept violence as an authentic response to racism; Caldwell and Baraka's plays do not offer antidotes for that Black dissension. Their dramas leave central conflicts unresolved and Black rage abates. Brooks explores those same divisions in *Riot* to understand how "political organizations were increasingly divided between the late Martin Luther King's non-violent program and Black Power groups' call for self-defense" to model a dialogue that moves toward reconciliation and empowerment (Malewitz 541–42).[8] I further argue that Brooks's representation of rioting presents a constructive way forward by emphasizing rioting as a necessary catharsis with the potential to regenerate Black communities. This chapter begins with a synopsis of Brooks's *Riot*, then discusses several other poems she wrote in the 1960s, all of which illustrate an evolution in Brooks's racial awareness over the decade, leading her to embrace the politics of the BPM and the BAM. The chapter ends with a close reading of *Riot*, one that emphasizes its use of the blues to articulate Brooks's vision.

GWENDOLYN BROOKS'S *RIOT*

Riot, published in 1969, is a long-form poem that depicts a rebellion led by Black Chicagoans in the aftermath of Martin Luther King Jr.'s death. In the first poem, titled "Riot," Black Americans protest, loot, and burn property in a wealthy and upscale part of the city. The rioters encounter a white man named John Cabot, a symbol of wealth and power. Rioters ambush Cabot after he has enjoyed a relatively normal day, driving his Jaguar, visiting the museum, and dining at a nice restaurant. As the rioters charge at him, all Cabot sees is a Black underclass. He says, "Que tu es grossier!" (You are rude) (Brooks, *Riot* 9). He cannot see the Black Chicagoans as human and does not recognize his racist critiques of Black people, failing to understand that his dismissal of their suffering ironically is the cause of his demise. The poem transitions to its second part, titled "The Third Sermon on the Warpland." At this moment, Black American life is in a period of uncertainty. As the riot escalates, Black people continue to permeate the streets with their blues and their sorrows as they try to find vital resources such as food and clothing. Two narrators remark on the riot in this second section, a Black philosopher and a white philosopher; they illustrate different perspectives affecting the rioters within the same moment. The Black philosopher tells the reader that the formerly enslaved Black Americans are still in bondage as they invoke their experiences through blues song. The white philosopher tells the reader that Blackness is a curse of darkness. Specifically, he says, "It is better to light one candle than curse the darkness . . . These candles curse—inverting the deeps of the darkness" (15). Furthermore, the darkness will remain if Black people choose to invert their rage rather than seeking optimism amid their plight. The Black philosopher counters by insisting that even when Black people practice moral uprightness through respectability, they still are killed.[9]

In the final part, "An Aspect of Love Alive in the Ice and Fire," the riot has ended. Black people gather together pridefully by physically expressing love toward one another. Love is a method that connects the rioters in one direction, while their scattered divisions caused by racial conflict are no longer relevant. This final section of the poem emphasizes the main themes of Black nationalism and pride. The community comes together for the sake of racial cohesion and forward progress. Importantly, this reunification can happen only out of the chaos of the riots in the first two parts of the poem. *Riot* is a disjointed poem, consisting of pieces that stand alone as separate poems. The first poem was written on April 8, 1968, four days after King's assassination.[10] The other two poems were an addition to what would become *Riot*, the chapbook published by Broadside Press. When reading the parts as individual poems, it is challenging to ascertain Brooks's more extensive political maneuvers or trace the blues aesthetics shaping the poem. *Riot*, when read as a whole, brings to bear Brooks's Black Arts intervention and her preoccupation with rioting as a political strategy for racial progress.

BLACK NATIONALISM AND THE BLUES AESTHETIC
TROPE IN BROOKS'S SIXTIES POETRY

Brooks's understanding of Blackness as a political identity emerged through her experience at the second annual Fisk University Black Writers' Conference in Nashville, Tennessee. The inaugural conference in 1966, was a historic gathering where writers, activists, and artists came together to discuss the Black American's image in literature.[11] Brooks participated alongside Amiri Baraka and other Black writers. They spent their time reading poetry and listening to the pride messages of Black Power from speakers such as Baraka, Hoyt Fuller, and John Henrik Clarke, among others. The Fisk meeting and subsequent experimentation with Black Power themes led Brooks to pen many poems that would interrogate the Black nationalism concept. In the appendix of her autobiography, *Report from Part One*, she writes:

My aim, in my next future, is to write poems that will somehow successfully "call" (see Baraka's *SOS*) all black people: black people in tav-
erns, black people in alleys, black people in gutters, schools, offices,
factories, prisons, the consulate; I wish to reach black people in
pulpits, black people in mines, on farms, on thrones; not always to
"teach"—I shall wish often to entertain, to illumine. (183)[12]

With this moving passage, Brooks acknowledges the need for a new approach
in her poetry, an approach that would speak to Black Nationalism and
support a collective Black consciousness. She endeavored to join with the
younger generation's "call" to urgently reach Black people, to teach but also to
entertain and enlighten. After returning from the Fisk Black Writers' Conference, Brooks realized that her language was outdated. A new Black generation
that represented the BAM was employing the term "Black" while she was still
saying "Negro" (*Report* 167). Brooks's shift to a new Black consciousness at
this conference and her experience giving writing workshops to Black youth
made her "aware of a new general energy, an electricity, in look, walk, speech,
gesture of the young blackness" that she encountered (84). After her various
visitations with the rising youth, figures that included Baraka, she concluded
that "there is indeed a new black today. He is different from any the world
has known. He's a tall-walker" (84). Recognizing her growing awareness of
this shift, she referred to herself as "the new black sun" that is "qualified to enter
at least the kindergarten of new consciousness now. New consciousness and
trudge—toward—progress" (85–86).

With a growing sense of the shift that was happening in Black America,
Brooks published *In the Mecca* (1968).[13] The poetry book is a symbolic
appraisal of the rise and decline of the rich cultural, political, and social
foundations of early twentieth-century Black Chicago. Particularly in the
second part, titled "After the Mecca," there are a series of poems dedicated
to civil rights leaders such as Medgar Evers and Malcolm X, artifacts of
Black Chicago such as the Wall of Respect, and the youth street gang the
Blackstone Rangers. Brooks writes the poems in a singular format dedicated
to leaders of the CRM and BAM, such as Charles Evers and Dudley Randall, that Brooks either had personal relationships with or admired. "After
the Mecca," as Cheryl Clarke asserts, "comes to represent the struggle of
black people, during the late twentieth century, to envision a world in which
African American culture occupied the center" (2). For instance, the two
poems concluding "After the Mecca," "The Sermon on the Warpland" and
"The Second Sermon on the Warpland," are metaphorical representations
of the harsh lived experiences of Black people during the turbulent sixties.

Furthermore, in "After the Mecca" Brooks addresses the downfall of a strong Black community, the demise of which was precipitated by white resentment regarding the progress Black Americans made through constant civil rights protests and persistent demands for equality. The poem "Medgar Evers" is dedicated to Evers's older brother Charles, also a civil rights activist who fought for voting rights. In the poem, Brooks eulogizes Evers, who was assassinated in 1963 in the driveway of his home in Jackson, Mississippi, by a white supremacist. Her free verse, which employs a slant rhyme, constructs the image of Evers as a man who was committed to civil rights, not only for Black Americans but for all citizens. Evers's final breath is depicted in the poem's last stanza, which begins, "Roaring no rapt arise-ye to the dead, he / leaned across tomorrow" (Brooks, "Medgar Evers" 38). Here, Brooks signals Evers's effort to survive another harsh reality in the segregated South by envisioning a call for justice that, though he may not see it in his day, would eventually come to fruition in the future. She ends the poem with the image "People said that / he was holding clean globes in his hands," contending that Evers's call for justice was a global fight that all humane society had to undertake (38). The death of Evers and other significant events of the 1960s compelled Brooks to refocus her poetry and target it solely toward a Black audience, again, part of her aim to "call all black people."

The poem that follows, "Malcolm X," focuses on the authenticity of the slain civil rights leader as a coming-of-age model of leadership and Black masculinity. His heroic stature became the symbol and motivation for a younger generation interested in his conception of Black Power to continue the mission of political organizing—not only for Blacks in America but for the African diaspora at large. Malcolm X's "Original / ragged-round / rich-robust" frame represented for Brooks the "maleness" she and her peers identified as "he opened [them]" (Brooks, "Malcolm X" 39) to a world where "black boy-men" shout on rooftops "Black Power" while "women in wool hair chant their poetry" (Brooks, "The Wall" 42). Here is how Clarke characterizes the influence of the BAM on Brooks's work: "Wherever [Black women] stood in relation to the Black Arts Movement, most black women writers of that time wrote because of it—and still do" (2). In other words, whereas Baraka and Caldwell utilized the rhetoric of Malcolm X in their plays to invoke the Black revolution, Brooks evokes his image and stature to acknowledge his unifying effect on men and women part of the BPM.

Brooks ends "After the Mecca" with two poems: "The Sermon on the War-pland" and "The Second Sermon on the Warpland." Lesley Wheeler notes that Brooks's metaphorical use of "Warpland" conveys the "war planned" by "black nationalists against white America and even a 'warpland,' a carrier for this militant message" (Wheeler 231).[14] In the first sermon, Brooks arrives at the moment where she has to discuss the lived realities of Black people in 1960s America. This poetry was for the street, from the people from the housing projects to the Wall of Respect in Chicago (Brooks, *Report* 152). When questioned by George Stavros for *Contemporary Literature* on why she chose to focus on Black subjects for a Black audience, Brooks writes: "I am in the Black community; I see what's going on there. I talk with these people. I know how many of them feel" (Brooks, *Report* 160). Brooks stands by her commitment to treat Blackness with great care and relate her poetic voice to a people who are confident in their identities and steadfast in their journey toward liberation. In so doing, she incorporates radical sixties Black nationalism in her first sermon, beginning with an epigraph that states, "the fact that we are black is our ultimate reality," highlighting the harsh actuality of Blackness (160). Martin Luther King Jr. frames this actuality in "The Other America," noting that Black people "find themselves forced to live in inadequate, substandard, and often dilapidated housing conditions. In these conditions, they don't have wall-to-wall carpets, but all too often, they find themselves living with wall-to-wall rats and roaches" (156). The lived reality of poverty in Black America is a reality that America has "failed to hear that the promises of justice and freedom have not been met" (159). It appears that Brooks is engaging with the same strife that King is grappling with as he learns to understand Black America's plight. Her way of addressing Black people is through a prophetic lyrical tone that alerts them to turn their despair into a political action of love that is "luminously indiscreet; complete; continuous" (Brooks, *Mecca* 50). The prophetic voice tells the congregation to:

> Build now your Church, my brothers, sisters.
> Build never with brick nor Corten nor with granite.
> Build with lithe love.
> With love like lion-eyes. (49–50)

According to Lesley Wheeler, Brooks calls for communal engagement among Black people through an organization "around the imperative and inspiring rhetoric of the pulpit" (Wheeler 231). The language of the Black church becomes a central leitmotif in Brooks's poetic sermons. Brooks's preachments last well into "The Second Sermon on the Warpland" as she inserts King's call for the fierce urgency of now, demanding that the urgency for Black America is to "live" through "your blooming in the noise of the whirlwind" (Brooks, *Mecca* 51). The whirlwind, a repetitive metaphorical device Brooks employs

to explain the Black freedom struggle, is undoubtedly a tumultuous process
for Black America that is experiencing the social and political turmoil that
defined the CRM. Joanne V. Gabbin underscores these moments, calling out
some of Black America's "major victories" such as "The Montgomery Bus
Boycott, which brought Rosa Parks and Martin Luther King Jr. to national
prominence . . . [and] the Freedom Riders" that led to "the Civil Rights Act
of 1964 [which] made discrimination illegal" (xxi). In "The Second Sermon,"
Brooks informs Black America on how to survive the whirlwind—and particularly how to deal with loss through this struggle—by understanding
that the United States is "our commonwealth" amid the inequality its democratic republic purports (52). In so doing, Brooks, in "giving a prescription
for health" by medicating her "furious flowers" through sermonic delivery,
reminds her audience that the fight for equality "is lonesome, yes. For we
are the last of the loud. Nevertheless, live" (Gabbin xix; Brooks, *Mecca* 54).

Brooks's poetical methods within both "The Sermon on the Warpland"
and "The Second Sermon on the Warpland" posits that one cannot overlook a lens of respectability politics. As stated earlier, Brooks, at one point,
calls for the community to build a Black church. Her perspective that Black
people should rebuild a church filled with love to overcome racial oppression employs a kind of respectability that Evelyn Brooks Higginbotham
contends "tapped into Christian teachings that exalted the poor and the
oppressed over the rich and powerful" (Higginbotham 191). Brooks's resurrection of the Black church symbolizes a space that Black people once used
to partake in protest. Moreover, this prophetic act of resistance that is vivid
in Brooks's "The Sermon on the Warpland" and "The Second Sermon on the
Warpland" reaches back to a time where Black people equated as Higginbotham asserts "self-respect, professionalism, and American identity with their
own intentions and interpretations" that elicit "a fluid and shifting position
along with a continuation of African American resistance" (Higginbotham
186, 187). However, through a Black Power lens, the Black church became
antithetical to ideas of Black nationalism. For instance, in an interview with
Marvin X and Faruk for *Negro Digest*, Jones/Baraka claims, "Christianity
has become a vehicle for the degenerate—it tends to cover truth rather
than reveal it'" (Marvin X, Faruk, and Jones 6).[15] In other words, because
of the Black church's political philosophy at that time based on the CRM's
integrationist agenda, Black nationalists resorted to creating organizations
such as the BPP or BARTS or joining the Nation of Islam.[16] Through these
articulations within both "The Sermon on the Warpland" and "The Second
Sermon on the Warpland," Brooks's poetry is in conversation with Baraka's

and Caldwell's plays in terms of placing the interests of radical Black culture and politics first; however, the poems still manifest a respectability politics that touts Christian values such as self-dignity and free will.

Brooks deploys a militant voice similar to Baraka and Caldwell's that invokes a poetic politics that follows a Black aesthetic. In "We Real Cool," written in 1960, she depicts Black youth participating in the harsh realities of street life and pays particular attention to the survival tactics of Black people as they try to survive the threat of death. Through the utilization of a blues motif and a Black aesthetic, Brooks foregrounds her poetry in a pivotal moment through the intensification of urban rioting in 1960s America that saw a rise in Black political militancy among young adults. The growing interest in Black Power as a political ethos in urban Black America also revived a cultural nationalism that paid particular attention to blues, soul, and funk music, which became the soundtrack to a growing movement. Brooks makes this point when commenting on Amiri Baraka/LeRoi Jones and Larry Neal, noting how their work was "supplying black poetry with some strains of black music which they feel is the authentic art of the black people. They worship [John] Coltrane and Ornette Coleman, and whenever they can, they try to push such music into their work. Sometimes the poetry seems to grow out of black music" (Brooks, *Report* 151). The BAM originators declared that a Black aesthetic must represent a "black style" that connotes what James Stewart has called the "purest expression of the black man in America" (Stewart 3). The blues became a model aesthetic and methodology that Baraka and Neal articulated as a "cultural nationalism that is rooted in the lifestyles of the Black community," its struggles, its voice, and its spirit (Neal 39).

Brooks similarly departs from writing about Black life that centered Anglo-American aesthetics. She provides a lengthy overview of her experience shadowing the Blackstone Rangers, a controversial Black youth street gang in Chicago's South Side.[17] In "After the Mecca," the teenage gang is "Black, raw, [and] ready," walking "in the city / that do not want to heal" (Brooks, *Mecca* 44). The group meanders in "their country" that "is a Nation on no map," separate from mainstream society. There are also Rangerettes, a girl gang part of the larger Blackstone Rangers, who "are sweet exotics" who wait for their Rangers to delight them with stolen jewelry and "rhymes of Leaning" (47–48). Her exploration of young men and women within the poem elicits an agency particularly for Black women, often seen but their voices silent within BAM theoretical discourse. In chapter 3, through my exploration of Sanchez's plays, I will detail more explicitly the clearly defined gender critiques that her dramas explore. In Brooks's case, in these particular poems the exploration of gender roles is subtle. Rather, my mentioning of the Rangers and Rangerettes is to make the point that Brooks revisits the Blackstone Rangers in *Riot* and they become part of the narrative. In addition, at the beginning of the poem titled "Riot," Brooks departs from the BAM emphasis on radical action through methods of violence. Instead, she invokes the language of King, in an epigraph stating "a riot is the language of the unheard" from his "The Other America" speech, to engender Black people's plight and call attention to America's overt racism (Brooks, *Riot* 9).

RIOT IS THE LANGUAGE OF THE UNHEARD: A CLOSE READING

In the poem's first part titled "Riot," Brooks begins with a quote from King: "A riot is the language of the unheard" (Brooks, *Riot* 9).[18] King's language sets the tone for what follows: an illumination of the violent and melancholic undertones displayed by the rioters that intertwine throughout the poem. Brooks's rehashing of King's quote is a social commentary about America's refusal to address poverty and unemployment in Black Chicago. Still, she also pays close attention to the riot as an entry point for uncovering the emotional turmoil Black America experienced because of the violence that killed King and the racism threatening their livelihoods.

In March 1968, a month before Martin Luther King Jr.'s assassination in Memphis, Tennessee, he delivered a speech titled "The Other America" to Local 1199 National Union of Hospital and Health Care Employees. The speech transitioned to his latest civil rights project, his Poor People's Campaign. In this campaign, inspired by King's visit to Chicago in 1966, King and his supporters petitioned the US government on behalf of poor people for better jobs and income. His vision fell short, though, as an assassin's bullet killed King at the Lorraine Motel on April 4. In his speech, King—a stalwart of nonviolence as a means for viable protest—warns listeners about the potential of rioting as an option for protest, calling it a problem that "can always be halted by superior forces" (King, "The Other America" 160). With rioting increasing in Black neighborhoods between 1964 and 1967 because of expanded white state and vigilante violence, King understood that such violence happened because white America refused to address the plight of the Black poor (*Report of the National Advisory* 91).

In several newspaper clippings published in the April 6 Chicago *Daily Defender*, Black America responded to King's death in shock but also with the warning that nonviolence will no longer demand an end to racial discrimination in American society. In one of these articles, "Threats of

Violence Hit City After News" by Donald Mosby, political organizer Doug Andrews responded to King's death, saying, "The assassination of Dr. King is very, very tragic . . . that another black brother, who had fought so firmly and honestly to alleviate the conditions and problems facing black people in this racist society. Once again, assimilation and cooperation are all but impossible. We are saying now that there must be an eye for an eye and a tooth for a tooth" (Mosby 1). In another article by Dave Potter, "King's Slaying Termed Blow to Nonviolence," a Chicago Westside resident named Robert Conda commented, "I feel this [King's assassination] is the opening of the door through which will come violence. Because of the way Dr. King died, I can guarantee it's gonna be rough here" (Potter 1). The article describes the initial impact of hearing news of King's death as it spread through the Black neighborhoods: "thousands of stunned black women and men stood in disbelief" (1). These various reactions to King's death reveal the pain and grief of Black people as well as the anticipation of a response of violence on their part to avenge the death of their fallen civil rights leader. In *African Americans and the Culture of Pain*, Debra Walker King contends, "Black people cannot be both Americans and pained. They are, therefore, the outsiders who can never be let in, the ones who do not belong but who, by virtue of their pain, are failed Americans . . . whose existence justifies the normal and stable logic of the pain-free, non-black American" (D. King 17). Walker King argues that Black pain is timeless and more often than not a metaphor for the perpetual silencing of Black voices that speak about the violence enacted upon their loved ones or members of the broader Black community worldwide.

The Kerner Commission Report, the result of an investigative committee chaired by Governor Otto Kerner Jr. of Illinois in 1968, investigated the race riots that took place in Chicago and other major cities throughout the United States. In the report, Kerner and his team admitted, "white racism is essentially responsible for the explosive mixture which has been accumulating in our cities since the end of World War II" (*Report of the National Advisory* 91). The racism described in the report pertained not only to the social and political violence imparted onto Black Americans but also to the US government's and white America's participation in denying Blacks fair housing and equal access to wealth. According to Wendy Plotkin's article "'Hemmed In': The Struggle Against Racial Restrictive Covenants and Deed Restrictions in Post-WWII Chicago," Black Americans were prohibited from owning real estate and building wealth from 1900 to 1953. Housing segregation happened because of racially coded deed restrictions, also known as racially restrictive covenants, that were legal "deeds prohibiting owners from selling or leasing their residences to members of specific racial groups" (Plotkin 39).

The effort to deny adequate housing to Black Americans was supported by the United States government's Home Owners Loan Corporation (HOLC) and the Federal Housing Administration (FHA). Both government corporations were creations of the New Deal, which meant that white Chicago real estate developers could exclusively rule "against selling or leasing housing to African Americans" amid efforts on Black Chicagoans' part to challenge restrictive covenant systems (41). Therefore, because of racism in real estate backed by the US government, Black Chicagoans were redlined to the South Side and Westside sections of the city. However, there were individual Black families (such as Lorraine Hansberry's) who won a racially restrictive covenant case in Cook County.[19]

Consequently, residential segregation, the death of MLK, and the increasing underemployment of the Black poor, is depicted in the opening of Brooks's *Riot*. The main character is John Cabot, a wealthy, affluent white man of Italian American heritage who is hobnobbing and enjoying the Chicago high life. His delighted time is interrupted when Black rioters march down his street. The rioters begin to destroy property as Cabot watches the group advancing "In seas. In windsweep. They were black and loud. / And not detainable. And not discreet" (Brooks 9). These Black people were "sweaty and unpretty / (not like Two Dainty Negroes in Winnetka) / and they were coming toward him in rough ranks" (Brooks, *Riot* 9). Brooks makes the distinction that the Black crowd charging at Cabot were not middle-class Black Americans from the elite suburb Winnetka. Instead, this Black collective were poor American citizens, "not gangs, not criminals, not even militant activists, but ordinary people [who] protest their poverty and political powerlessness through the riot" (Debo 148).

Black Chicagoans target John Cabot precisely because of his unflattering views about Black American humanity, and they want to destroy his property to protest his privileged lifestyle. When seeing Black rioters walk toward Cabot he says, "Gross, Gross . . . Don't let it touch me! the Blackness!" Black rioters respond, "You are a desperate man, and the desperate die expensively today" (Brooks, *Riot* 9–10). The Black rioters smelling of "pig foot, chitterling and cheap chili," ambush Cabot; they "malign, mocked John" in his "right linen and right wool" (9–10). Brooks makes clear that the Black rioters and John Cabot are symbols of poor and rich America.

Brooks's focus on the Black poor in "Riot" is reminiscent of such a discussion in her 1963 poem "kitchenette building," in which she describes to an unfamiliar audience the experience of living in a compacted tenement building where apartments were the size of small rooms. The Black poor living in "involuntary" conditions survived the "grayed in" walls and "onion fumes" while smelling "yesterday's garbage ripening in the hall" (Brooks, "Kitchenette" 326). While "kitchenette building" captures these unpleasant living conditions experienced by the Black poor, in "Riot" Brooks extends the plight narrative by depicting John Cabot, a symbol of white wealth, as insensitive to the unlivable conditions of Black people. He interprets poor Blackness as "beneath the nourished white" because whiteness represents economic and racial privilege (Brooks, *Riot* 10).

To reflect the dynamics of racial privilege, Brooks juxtaposes the image of Black male rioters with the portrayal of John Cabot at the opening of "Riot." Cabot's full name is a representation of Italian heritage and the Protestant Reformation. The painting by Jeff Donaldson titled "Allah Shango," which appears opposite the title page, depicts two young men with Afros holding African statues, who stand ready to rebel in the spirit of revolution.[20] Brooks describes the young Black men in the painting as looking "so alive and annunciatory" that she wanted to include their image with her written imagery of John Cabot to "wonder how a certain kind of young white man faced with such a throng . . . faced with his own confrontation with his own innards would react" (Drotning 74). In other words, Brooks introduces John Cabot not as an empathizer to Black Americans' plight but as an elite racist who had no regard for the political reform of Black civil rights. Her poem illustrates to readers how Cabot reacts to Black Americans charging at him during the riot while also having to confront his racial prejudice. In the end, Cabot does not engage with race and instead dies "in the smoke and fire" while crying, 'Lord! / Forgive these n---uhs [*sic*] that know not what they do" (Brooks, *Riot* 10). Cabot's invocation suggests that he is wrongly persecuted, but in fact he is the problem. Cabot's supposed divine image succumbs to the threat of Black resistance. Cabot dies in smoke and fire that erupts. The rioters take a stand against racial intolerance and travel through a city in flames. Cabot's death amid a Black revolution settle's the score as Black rioters seek their revenge and claim it. Moreover, his death signifies the end of white supremacy and its overt dominance over Black life. As it pertains to Black nationalism, the rioters liberate from their oppressors. At the conclusion of "Riot," the destruction among the rioters has calmed down. Black rage evolves into a moment of contemplation in which rioters begin their transformation, as Brooks remarks, like a "phoenix" (11). But this evolvement is met with white antagonism as discussed in the next paragraph.

The second part of *Riot*, titled "The Third Sermon on the Warpland," explores the Black community walking through a disjointed Chicago that is in flames and full of debris as Black people walk during darkness and confusion. It is in this moment that Black Chicagoans are in the space of rebirth—an area of being where they claim their humanity amid the turmoil. The third sermon, I contend, is a continuation of the previous two sermons discussed in Brooks's "After the Mecca." While the first two sermons stylistically appear to resemble the voices of Black preachers, in the third sermon a Black philosopher symbolizing the Black intellectual replaces them and explains the turmoil happening in the riotous area. As previously noted, the "warpland" is what Lesley Wheeler claims is the "war planned" that Black people create to make their militant presence known to the dominant society (Wheeler 231). According to Annette Debo, for the first time, "the [Black] rioters attacked real property, the symbol of prosperity that they had been denied" (Debo 147). While white America deemed Black folks' actions un-American, what they did not take into account is that the Black poor participating in the collective uprising following the death of King did so as a political response. Their actions trace back to the longstanding history of white violence against Black Americans from slavery to Jim Crow. Precisely because of this, Brooks's bluesy warpland engulfs Black imagery that operates outside of mainstream American life. The blues elements within the poem immediately appear in the third sermon when the Black philosopher proclaims that the sounds of Black folk and their physical appearance—self-reflected on "watermirrors" in a "goldenrod across the little lagoon"—remain in "chains [that] are in the keep of the Keeper" (Brooks, *Riot* 11). The reality of Black livelihood in Chicago is hidden "in a labeled cabinet / on the second shelf by the cookies, / sonatas, the arabesques" (11). It therefore remains invisible and unheard, even though Black expressivity in the mainstream society is "*Black*blues" (11). The blues motif represented in Brooks's warpland signifies a Black aesthetic. James T. Stewart contends the Black aesthetic is a dialectical method upon which Black people undergo an "essential nature of being, existence; it is the property of being and the 'feel' of being; it is the implicit sense of it" (Stewart 5). The Black Philosopher alludes that the song that Black people hear before they die is called "A Death Song for You Before You Die" (Brooks, *Riot* 11). Of such a song the Black Philosopher remarks, "You do not hear the remarkable music" because "If you could hear it / you would make music too," which is the blues (11). The blues becomes a metaphor for understanding Blackness, which for Black people is an ontological dialogue about their subjugation to racism.

The context of Brooks's poem engages in an ontological conversation about "being versus non-being" once discussed in Frantz Fanon's essay "The Fact of Blackness." Fanon, who was living in metropolitan France at the time, was forced to engage in an ontological dialogue about his Blackness when his encounter with a white woman and her young son turned uncomfortable.

The young boy, seeing a Black man for the first time in his life, shouted unconsciously, "Look, a Negro!" Fanon states he "made a tight smile" as the boy became frightened by his presence. At that moment, Fanon became paralyzed, only "to laugh [himself] to tears, but the laughter became impossible" (Fanon 258). Fanon examines his humanity, and he discovers that the mother and son he interacts with see him as subhuman. Instead, the white gaze places him in a category of non-being linked to the identification of Blacks in the Western world as "savages, brutes, [and] illiterates" (261). Seemingly, Fanon works through his essay to dismantle the belief placed on him by the white child (and others) that he is a "non-being" by rebuilding and restructuring his Blackness to become a "being," thereby disrupting the irrationality of racism that marks Blackness as otherness and nothingness. Thus, Fanon makes his presence known to white people, as the epigraph above articulates, through action.

In a similar vein, the rioters in Brooks's third sermon experience degrees of "non-being." To be whole again after the death of Martin Luther King Jr., Black Chicagoans riot as an initial response to engage the world in their humanity. The struggle for Black Chicagoans to deal with the assassination of MLK is what Blacks around the United States were experiencing at the time. Although the initial response to confront racial inequality in America in the 1960s started with peaceful, nonviolent demonstrations, this type of protest in the mid- to late 1960s turned into rebellion. Black rebellion challenges a social apparatus rooted in Western imperialism. Such a system refuses to accept Black peoples as human beings because to recognize them as such would implicate the United States in the injustice of stripping Black people of their humanity and the material necessities needed for them to survive economically in the wealthiest country in the world.

As noted, Fanon's idea of "being" argues that he had to make himself known to white people in Western society for them to see his humanity. Similarly, the Black rioters in Chicago also force America to share their pain and see their humanity, but at the same time, they also reject white acknowledgment. Brooks illustrates this by showcasing Black Chicagoans destroying symbols of white prosperity. Thereby, Black Chicagoans replace symbolic fixtures of what James Stewart contends is one "established regime and culture" to pose a dialectical opposition between Western imperialism and Black collective civil resistance (Stewart 5). Specifically, Black folks destroy Jessie's Kitchen, a restaurant that white patron frequents (Brooks, *Riot* 12). In addition, they loot a record store, stealing a radio (14).

Seemingly, Brooks's third sermon embodies the BAM's call for a Black aesthetic separate from the stronghold of a Eurocentric aesthetic and writing style. She creates this technique by identifying with her Black readership in their frustration regarding white America's lack of concern for their fallen King.[21] She intentionally targets her Black audience to engage with them about Dr. King's assassination, the primary purpose for their rioting. Still, she also engages with Black readers' mistrust of white Americans. Similar to "We Real Cool," where she depicts Black youth participating in the harsh realities of street life, Brooks's slant rhyme capitulates a cool blues aesthetic that correlates with *Riot*; both works pay particular attention to the survival tactics of Black people as they try to survive the threat of death. Through the utilization of a blues motif and a Black aesthetic, Brooks foregrounds her poetry in a pivotal moment, one in which Black writers and artists shifted their philosophies about Black resistance and began to write about Black life in a manner that was more militant and revolutionary.

Brooks similarly departs from writing about Black life that centered Anglo-American aesthetics. Instead, her poem invokes a blues sensibility that Larry Neal asserts "awaken[s] Black people to the meaning of their lives" ("Black Arts Movement" 30). As the uprising settles, Black participants in the riot begin to walk down West Madison Street, a major street in Chicago. Each pass Jessie's Kitchen, a restaurant with "perfect food" that "nobody's eating," which juxtaposes with the chili, chitterling, and pig feet that John Cabot smelled earlier when the rioters first appeared downtown (Brooks, *Riot* 12). The young men who run down the street loot record stores, stealing Melvin Van Peebles's 1968 *Brer Soul*, a spoken word jazz album, rather than taking the music of Bing Crosby. Brooks amplifies Peebles's classic "Lilly Done the Zampoughi Everytime I Pulled Her Coattail" by graphically bringing Lillie to life as she dances to the music with "twenty wire stalks sticking out of her head / as her underfed haunches jerk jazz" (13). Brooks heightens the stylization of Lillie's hair and her way of corporeal movement in a disfigured space as a means of undergirding the authentic spaces of Black performance. The sonic imagery denoting Lillie's rhythmic vibrations as her body "wiggles and trebles" to the beat of Peebles's jive-talking personifies enjoyment of life amid a dark period of racial upheaval (13).

As "The Third Sermon on the Warpland" continues, the dismal outlook for Black Americans during the riot transforms, becoming more about the power that they obtain. A scene where Black men steal a radio and listen to "James Brown / and [Charles] Mingus, Young-Holt, [Ornette] Coleman, John [Coltrane]" centralizes Brooks's emphasis on including a cultural iconography that pays homage to Black pride (Brooks, *Riot* 3). However, Black blues gets disrupted when the National Guard appears, making noise as "the law comes sirening [*sic*] across the town," and a fire erupts (15). The rioters light candles and "curse . . . the deeps of the darkness" as the outlook of their survival becomes bleak; "young men run" and "children in ritual chatter / scatter upon / their Own and old geography" (15). And although Black people try to escape the militarized police patrols, a Black mother dies surrounded by the boxes "that held the haughty hats . . . [and] Polish sausages," a woman who will never again "partake of steak on Christmas mornings" (16). Devastatingly, nine more people die, reports the *Chicago Sun-Times*, and the Black Philosopher critically analyzes America's attempt to "assure a blackless America"; but the fact remains that the rioters have succeeded in taking a stand against racial intolerance. Brooks's imagery underpins the violent consequences that happened as the riot escalated. While she recapitulates the dismal outcomes of the riot, she also highlights the resiliency of Black people. For example, the beginning of "The Third Sermon" begins with an epigraph from Webster's dictionary that reads "'In Egyptian Mythology a bird which lived for five hundred years and then consumed itself in life, rising renewed from the ashes" (11). Brooks's incorporation of the rising Phoenix as a metaphor illustrates the triumph of Black people amid those who have died. Also, the ones who remain alive will survive a period of uncertainty and rise from the ashes to create a Black politics and promote a Black pride that reflects and engages in a fulfilling spirit of community.

Brooks's inclusion of the youth street gang the Blackstone Rangers in the last part of "The Third Sermon" affirmed the need for a Black politics that engaged younger audiences who were inspired by Black Power to discuss and act on the current realities of their lives. Inspired by her meetings with the Blackstone Rangers—who, according to George Kent, "were not a monolithic group, several were responding strongly to the pressures of the streets and the crisis atmosphere"—Brooks was able to cultivate their talents through her writing workshops. The Rangers reappear, and Brooks pays homage to Richard "Peanut" Washington, a leader of the Blackstone Rangers who "will not let his men explode" (Brooks, *Riot* 18). Washington is "a gentleman," but so are the other men he leads: Rico, Sengali, Bop, Jeff, Geronimo, and Lover. The Rangers are not about rioting, hence their agreement that "this AIN'T all upinheah!" as the white onlookers mischaracterized the youth, questioning, "But WHY do These People offend *themselves*?" (18–19). Such misunderstandings that white Americans have about Black struggle, along with their necessity to stereotype Black youth, underpin Brooks's posturing of suggesting Black America's rebirth: "Lies are told and legends made. / Phoenix rises unafraid" (20). The Black Philosopher reappears, concluding that the Black rioters "came to life and exulted" for a moment and "then it was over" (20). Brooks leaves the "warpland" open-ended regarding what plan Black America will execute next in their quest for equality. She revisits her call for "love" referenced in "After the Mecca" as the solution for Black America to start new communal organizing that places Black pride first, reclaims identity, and reinvigorates "the shining joy" experienced before the death of King (22).

The final part of Brooks's *Riot*, titled "An Aspect of Love, Alive in the Ice and Fire," emphasizes the theme of "love" amongst a Black community that is waking up to a new day post-riot. The Black rage at this point dissipates. The Black and white philosophers are no longer giving their opinions about the Black plight. Instead, Brooks opens the poem exclusively detailing a new day for Black people that "is the morning of [their] love // In a package of minutes there is this We" (21). In this example is exemplified Black unity. Black people happily engage collectively with each other, knowing "the world is at the window," so they "cannot wonder very long" (21). In other words, there is limited time to bask in the glow of defeating their oppressor through the act of rioting. She is "calling black people," to echo Amiri Baraka, in this moment of sincere love and engagement to "rise" in "a moment in Camaraderie / when interruption is not to be understood" (22). The sacred time must be devoted to constructing a "belief that black people must subscribe to black solidarity and black self-consciousness" (Brooks, *Report* 150). Brooks's last section of *Riot* invokes the language of young people such as Baraka, who was "full of a new spirit" and "seemed stronger and taller, really ready to take on the challenges" (167). However, Baraka's and Caldwell's plays near the end linger with discontentment. The imagery Brooks presents, however, illustrates that Black people's rage is turning into a "shining joy" that is presumed "not-to-end" (Brooks, *Riot* 22).

As a result, Brooks presents love as a challenge within the Black community. Rioting throughout these poems has become the center of their lives, and the anger that Black rioters have borne because of King's death has removed them from the original reason why they began fighting for equality in the first place. Brooks redirects them back to "love" as a method for centering their Blackness in a new journey of civil rights activism. D. H. Melhem coins this undertaking in Brooks's poetry as "the metaphor of personal love into public action" (Melhem 201).[22] The love expressed between Black men and women is "a physical light" present "in the room" (Brooks, *Riot* 21). Since "the world is at the window," Black people "cannot wonder very long," but instead must be "direct and self-accepting as a lion / in African velvet" (21). Brooks's positioning of love as a method reignites the use of a Black aesthetic. It is a political and literary convention that illustrates her active role in contributing a response to her Black audience. For example, Black people commune in "a moment in Camaraderie" where "interruption is not to be understood" (22). This moment depicted by Brooks, of Black people joining together without interruption or distraction from white America, represents the time in which Black people must formalize their politics and continue a plan started by King and others that cost King his life. As King explained in his speech "The Other America":

> The problem with a riot is that it can always be halted by superior force, so I couldn't advise that. On the other hand, I couldn't advise following a path of Martin Luther King just sitting around signing statements, and writing articles condemning the rioters, or engaging in a process of timid supplications for justice. The fact is that freedom is never voluntarily given by the oppressor. It must be demanded by the oppressed. (King, "The Other America" 160)

He concludes that while he disagrees with rioting as a form of protest, the freedom it demands, particularly the economic independence and access to wealth that he is seeking from the United States government, will only be given if the people ask for it by marching in the streets. The "new" Gwendolyn Brooks can now see "other things that a white person might not" concerning the conditions of Black America (Brooks, *Report* 166). In "An Aspect of Love," she speaks directly to Black people "on the street" as they smile going "in different directions" (Brooks, *Riot* 22). Although Brooks does not reveal the intentions of Black people after they depart from each other, the representation of the community in this section is a continuation of the rebirth process that started in the "Third Sermon on the Warpland." The process signals a "black solidarity and black self-consciousness" invoked through Brooks's citing of Baraka's call to Black people in "SOS" and her establishment of love as the way to Black rejuvenation (Brooks, *Report* 150). Solidarity and self-consciousness in Brooks's poem are a universality of the Black experience. It is a form of politics that embraces all Black people's desires while doing away with the intraracial gender schisms that Sanchez takes up in the next chapter. Rather, the poem's focus is to interrogate the racism that oppresses Black life.

CONCLUSION

Riot is a story about Black America's response to the death of Martin Luther King Jr. Also, the poem reveals the racial tensions between Black and white America that remain unresolved. Brooks aims to identify with her Black readership in their frustration with white America's backlash to their progress gained in the earlier years of the CRM. Her poem reveals the persistent racial and economic inequality apparent in Black neighborhoods. She gives voice to the Black experience and humanizes them by confronting the gaze of non-being forced onto their lives by the fissures of racism that undergird their necessity to riot. Brooks presents the harshness of race explored through the rebellion and positions white America (through protagonist John Cabot) as racists and keepers of white supremacy rather than as saviors who are sympathetic to Black pain. Brooks's honest exploration of the darker side of Black America's fight for racial equality is revealed through their rage, discomfort, and questioning of American democracy. She allows Black America to go through their pain, but she also challenges them to work through their grief by utilizing love as a method to strengthen their reactions to racism going forward. Brooks presents rage as a necessary outlet for Black Americans to work through their pain. Additionally, she sees love as an essential expression that leads to unification. Rage and love are two different emotions that are both integral to how Black people respond to racism. Overall, Brooks's *Riot* centers a reckoning toward solving racial inequality, whereas, Sonia Sanchez's plays *The Bronx Is Next* and *Sister Son/ji* reveal the degree to which Black revolutionaries' solving of racial inequality is killing the Black poor. In addition, the quest for Black liberation is singularly through male-centered leadership, which reveals the growing chauvinistic and misogynistic undertones embedded in Black nationalist discourse.

THE CRISIS OF BLACK REVOLUTIONARY POLITICS IN SONIA SANCHEZ'S *THE BRONX IS NEXT* (AND *SISTER SON/JI*)

In Baraka's and Caldwell's plays, Black rage acts as a destructive force; in Brooks's poem it is a constructive force that leads to Black progress. Sonia Sanchez's play *The Bronx Is Next* focuses less on Black rage as a compelling force for riots and revolts. Instead, she critiques rioting as divisive and self-mutilating. In the play, the protagonist named Charles and his three henchmen Jimmy, Larry, and Roland, believe the solution to ending nihilism in Black neighborhoods is to burn down public housing in New York City. They go from borough to borough burning down tenement buildings—in some cases without even waiting for the Black tenants to vacate the premises. As the play progresses, their plan implodes, and their act of achieving liberation becomes counterproductive. Sanchez depicts New York City's predominantly Black community in Harlem in a state of emergency. As riots rage throughout the borough in response to police brutality and excess poverty, Sanchez's unflinching tale explores an array of topics delineating the militant 1960s with a specific emphasis on Black Power ideology, human rights, and misogyny.

A major topic at the helm of militant Black politics was the concept of Black Power. As noted in this book's introduction, Black Power meant, according to Ture and Hamilton, redefining the African's image in world history, politics, and culture.[1] In *Bronx*, Black Power is a central theme, but Sanchez foregrounds its negative potential for destructive outcomes. For example, the revolutionaries believe that burning down public housing might be the only dramatic course of action by which systemic racism can end, despite the threat it poses to the Black lives who live in the buildings. Sanchez, in an interview with Jacqueline Wood about the play, comments, "There are the young men [revolutionaries] who see only one direction to go in. There is a lack of patience for anything that is going to interfere with that move out of Harlem" (Sanchez, "Poetry Run Loose" 5).[2] The broader questions San-chez's play interrogates are whether the revolutionaries' approach to ending systemic racism in Harlem is realistic and whether that approach purports a type of Black Power? There is also the question of whether burning down the public housing ignores the racist systems—born of white supremacy and government policies like redlining—that restricted Black residents to tenements in the first place. The revolutionaries' actions reveal their inability to address the white supremacy that continues to maintain systemic racism in Black neighborhoods. In their minds, a deliberate act of burning down decrepit housing becomes the solution to end Black oppression. Such a model, which the revolutionaries adopt, maintains the structural domination of Anglo-America, from where the construct of white supremacy arises. Thus, Sanchez's play argues that the revolutionaries' understanding of their riotous act as an exercise of Black Power is really an act of the Eurocentric patriarchal paradigm. As Nah Dove articulates, "European patriarchy underlines the Western social inequalities that affect African women and men in equally perverse ways" ("African Womanism" 517). In other words, the Black male revolutionaries build their plan on the genocide of Black people, and instead of addressing the question of equity practices in housing, of which the poor and working-class Black people they kill or leave stranded need, the revolu-tionaries employ divide-and-conquer strategies that imbue a rearticulation of the obstruction of humanity under the guise of survival.

In addition to the rearticulation of Black Power, Sanchez's play also illus-trates that burning down public housing with Black people in it is a matter of human rights. The revolutionaries' action poses a polarizing viewpoint on how Black Americans should achieve equality in America. As I will discuss in my close reading of the play, acts of rioting and revolt have the potential to deny Blacks the right to live, as illustrated in the revolutionaries' disregard for tenants still in the buildings when they are set aflame. Sanchez emphasizes Black humanity and contextualizes it within an Africanist framework. She expresses great concern for those left behind, noting, "I think that sometimes when people are very young, as these young revolutionaries were, they don't always see the human being; they see always the ideology" ("Poetry" 5). The revolutionaries place ideology first as a way of achieving what Judson Jef-feries notes is "a fully democratic way of life for people of African descent in America" (Jeffries 298). Of course, the irony is that when ideology super-sedes humanity, that ideology becomes a destructive force rather than salva-tion. Jeffries also asserts that "not everyone agreed on how best to achieve Black Power. The tactics and ideologies employed to mitigate oppression varied greatly across organizations. These differences played a major role in preventing these organizations from embarking on a coordinated effort to alleviate the oppression of Blacks" (298).[3] Sanchez's return to humanity is through an Africanist framework; she states in a herstory interview with La Donna L. Forsgren that "[o]ur job was to put the African back on a world stage and to answer the most important question that needed to be answered: What does it mean to be human?" (Forsgren, *Sistuhs* 28). Sanchez, centering the African as the genesis of humankind, through a dramatic exploration in *Bronx* helps us understand the existential questions related to Black liberation and how to achieve it. The play reflects this lack of cohesion, as not all of the revolutionaries in *Bronx* agree with Charles's plan to eliminate the ghetto. Such an idea coming from Charles is an ideology that is void of what Dove asserts are the components of justice and humanity understood through an Africanist morality (Dove 2). For example, after scheduling the Harlem tenement to burn, Charles's sidekick Roland comments, "You think this is the right strategy burning out the ghettos? Don't make much sense to me man. But orders is orders" (Sanchez, *Bronx* 526). Sanchez's inclusion of this scene reveals a reactionism by the revolutionaries: to solve short-term problems, particularly the public housing crisis, by using destructive ends that undermined the very humanity and rights of poor Black Americans.

In addition to human rights, Sanchez's play examines the chauvinistic and misogynistic undertones embedded within the revolutionaries' reactionary approaches to systemic racism. In *Bronx*, the revolutionaries condemn a Black mother for raising children alone and making decisions that contradict their Black nationalist viewpoint. Whereas the definition of Black Power means cooperatively empowering Black people and its communities through self-determination and social responsibility, the revolutionaries, particularly their ringleader Charles, enact a reactionary type of Black nationalism that is cloaked in his disdain for single Black mothers. For example, Black Bitch (as the men call her) survives living in public housing amid the poverty-stricken isolation it purportedly engenders by creating a somewhat stable life for two sons. The other woman centered in *Bronx*, Old Sister, begins to follow the revolutionaries' orders of moving out of the tenement building until the men tell her she must leave her sentimental belongings in the apartment. Old Sister refuses to leave her items, which remind her of the Great Migration journey she made from Alabama. In response to Old Sister's unwillingness to leave her belongings behind, the revolutionaries leave her in the apartment, making her comfortable before they set the building on fire. The women in *Bronx*, Black Bitch and Old Sister, represent women who are, as Keeanga-Yamahtta Taylor argues, "disproportionately susceptible to the ravages of capitalism, including poverty, illness, violence, sexual assault, and inadequate health care and housing" (K. Taylor, "Introduction" 8). Thus, as Taylor further notes, the divisive nature of Black male-centered leadership the revolutionaries exemplify result in "interests that could not be realized in the struggles separated along lines of gender" (7). And those interests as I mentioned previously are a combination of chauvinistic and misogynistic actualities that the revolutionaries embody, particularly the leader Charles as he enacts onto the women characters, specifically Black Bitch. For instance, after an altercation with Black Bitch, where Charles enacts physical violence by slapping her, he states to his henchmen "[we] wasted enough time . . . here don't forget her passport to the white world . . . And keep your mouth shut black bitch. You hear?" (Sanchez, *Bronx* 525). Charles's egregious actions as he pontificates at the fact that he assaulted and dehumanized Black Bitch with no remorse invalidates the Black woman's experience. Furthermore, the Black woman becomes the victim of what scholar Jennifer C. Nash asserts is "gender and race as structures of domination that inflict violence on black women" (Nash 8). In other words, because of Black Bitch's womanism that makes her independent and a leader of her own quest toward liberation, Charles's prejudice activates a deep disdain and hatred for her that becomes ingrained in his psyche—so much so that he wants to give her to the "white world" (Sanchez, *Bronx* 525). Specifically, Charles wants to give Black Bitch to an anti-Black system that he believes is where she belongs. As I will emphasize later in this chapter, Sanchez illustrates in *Bronx* the discrediting of Black womanism, the ways in which Black Bitch supports herself singularly as a mother, rejecting surface, judgmental, and violent critiques of how she chooses to live and raise her children. Such an envisioning of a self-love politics, what Alice Walker termed "womanism," is what Black Bitch embodied that exists outside of Charles's hyper-nationalistic and patriarchal viewpoint.[4] Through the caricature of Black Bitch, Sanchez depicts Black male chauvinism toward Black women, which exposes the questionable dealings with the largely male-dominated BPM that defined much of the politics that emerged from this era. However, during the 1960s Sanchez has recalled that US society was sexist and that was reflected in the male-centered nature of Black movements. In a 2010 interview with La Donna L. Forsgren, Sanchez remarked that "I've never called myself a feminist, but I love the idea that Alice Walker came up with, the term 'womanist.' I believe I'm a womanist also too'" (qtd. in *Sistuhs* 176). Sanchez's recognition of Walker's term connects with her own framework of committing "to the liberation of men and women and children" (176).

Sanchez embraced womanism after the publication of her plays. However, her work reveals that she always had a consciously womanist position that centered Black women from all walks of life. Forsgren suggests that "Sanchez's dramas recover black women's silenced history, articulate the ongoing concerns of black women, and encourage unity among black men and women" (Forsgren, *In Search* 67). In agreement with Forsgren, Sanchez's plays build off a womanist framework that centers Black women and shows their strength and courage against inevitable odds. Jacqueline Wood, another scholar of Sanchez's work, suggests that her plays are an alternative "artistic expression of social protest and the condemnation of injustice" (Wood 119). Furthermore, Wood states, Sanchez "explore[s] personal anguish and spiritual transcendence" in ways her Black male contemporaries did not (119). My work builds on Forsgren and Wood's work of closely analyzing *Bronx* through a womanist lens, but I move further to locate various Black feminisms I see explored in Sanchez's work, such as womanism and Africana womanism. Clenora Hudson-Weems centers African diasporic women's roles in addressing the ongoing liberation struggle within and across the continents. She argues that Africana womanism is a paradigm concerned with identifying "the ethnicity of the woman being considered, and this reference to [their] ethnicity, establishing [their] cultural identity, related to [their] ancestry and land base—Africa" (Hudson-Weems 14).[5] Sanchez's work includes an African cosmological ethos that centers everyday women and collectively illustrates the oneness of family and community that locates Africanist values beyond solely womanist values. In a 2005 interview with Joyce Ann Joyce, Sanchez remarks "How does the African American woman compare with the Afro-Brazilian, Afro-Cuban, Afro-Britain, Afro-Caribbean, the continental?" (Joyce 187). Sanchez's linkages between African-descended women in the diaspora in understanding each of their life's paths is a womanist framework that locates the Africanity within their existence. Furthermore, her conversations with Chinua Achebe and Ngũgĩ wa Thiong'o led her to think more broadly about, as she puts it, "what does it mean to be human in the midst of greed and dislocation? How will we as Africans in the Diaspora continue to survive?" (196). The humanitarian question for Sanchez is always the focus, consciously and subconsciously. That humanitarianism evident in Sanchez's words and within her works is based on what Nah Dove argues is African people's "notions of justice and humanity from an Afrikan–based morality" (*Afrikan Mothers* 2). Moreover, Sanchez's ideas build on an Africana womanist sensibility that engages in the holism of the concept of Ubuntu. According to Stephanie Huff et al., "Ubuntu challenges the Western dichotomous perspective of the individual and the community through highlighting their interconnectivity; it also evokes the spiritual dimension of humanity and human consciousness within a collective" (Huff, 559).

Sanchez's concern with humanness in *Bronx*, especially the Black woman's ultimate well-being, rests on interconnectivity with family, community, and society. In this chapter I argue that, unlike the works of Caldwell, Baraka, and Brooks, which center revolt through a male-focused lens, Sanchez's play focuses on Black women's voices to question the efficacy of Black rage as a productive means of safeguarding Black humanity. Instead, the play challenges riots and revolts as exercises of Black liberation. Sanchez's representations of riots and revolts center the divisive and destructive capacities of Black rage that reemphasize the dehumanizing nature systemic racism engenders.

To make this argument, I first provide an overview of the play. Sanchez imagined *Bronx* as part of a trilogy but never completed the remaining parts. Instead, Sanchez wrote a second play titled *Sister Son/ji*, which I argue can be read as a sequel to *Bronx*. Both plays emphasize Sanchez's broader experimentation with Black nationalist themes, importantly, through an Africana womanist context. Thus, Sanchez demonstrates through both *Bronx* and *Sister Son/ji* that there are various routes to Black-centered feminisms. For instance, in *Bronx*, when Charles calls the single mother a Black Bitch, she replies, "Yeah. I know what I am . . . But all you revolutionists or nationalists or whatever you call yourselves—do you know where you at? I am a black woman and I've had black men who could not love me or my black boys—where you gonna find black women to love you when all this is over—when you need them? As for me I said no black man would touch me ever again" (Sanchez, *Bronx* 525). Black Bitch's response to Charles challenges his discourse and stance relative to the Black woman and her children's condition. Her response suggests what the Combahee River Collective argued against in their Black Feminist Statement, and what Nikole Alexander-Floyd and Evelyn Simien articulate as that Black women "do not advocate separation from Black men, and argue that Black feminists must work with Black men against oppression and create feminist solidarity and community with Black women" (Alexander-Floyd and Simien 103). Black Bitch centers her very humanity and vulnerability—articulating the wounds that Black men exerted on her that are too hurtful to reconcile. But in her hurt, she challenges Charles's opportunism, an advantage that is not contingent on survival and thriving of all Black people. Through a Black womanist lens, built on the notion of making Black women visible and their voices heard, Black Bitch is the personification of the Black woman's condition, what Sanchez states she writes "to offer a Black [woman's] view of the world" ("Ruminations" 15).

In *Sister Son/ji*, the protagonist of the same name is a middle-aged Black woman who is a former activist of the BPM. She retires to Mississippi to live her golden years, and she reflects on her activism while also speaking about her deceased life partner Nesbitt and their four sons, who are also deceased. Sister Son/ji's womanism is centered in Afrocentricity, the paradigm of which Daphne W. Ntiri argues that "race and class are the superordinate issues for the Africana woman who grapples with family and community survival and growth" (Ntiri 163).[6] In Sister Son/ji's solitude, she practices holism and engages with the spiritual realm, what Venetria Patton analyzes as "ancestral bonds [that] extend beyond the grave in order to maintain a sense of health and well-being in the face of a legacy of slavery and racial discrimination" (Patton 55). By embracing African traditions that link to the spiritual reminiscence of connectivity with the dead and the living—Sister Son/ji forgoes remembering the lives her partner and children once lived—instead she brings back the memories of old to inform her present future. She states "today i shall bring back yesterday as it can never be today" (Sanchez, *Sister Son/ji* 37). This hold on the past Sister Son/ji employs stands as a reflection of the consciousness of an African state of well-being, which is what she ultimately claims. Sanchez again returns to the Ubuntu concept as the axis around which Sister Son/ji survives and evolves.

Beyond the interworkings of Black feminisms in both plays, lastly, I want to emphasize that Sanchez also deals with themes in *Bronx* of poor Black Americans often marginalized for not symbolizing Black uplift and the American Dream. Civil rights leaders in their revolution were not keen to highlight this reality because they thought such aspects of Black life would diminish their appeals to white America for cultural integration and equality. In light of the themes outlined above, in this chapter I frame Sanchez's thematic illustration of the unrealized civil rights gains promised during the height of the CRM by exposing the economic inequality and limitations of Black leadership fighting for racial democracy. I argue that Sanchez presents a flaw in Black leadership when she depicts revolutionaries burning public housing as a way to end Black generational poverty. Such a fallacy on their part does not address America's failed policies with regards to racial inequality within America's poorest neighborhoods. Instead, such a framing denies the Black poor fundamental human rights, their lives threatened by the very protests their existence necessitates. The reactionary approach the revolutionaries take up causes a human rights crisis in Black neighborhoods, which in one respect manifests itself in what I illustrate earlier in the form of sexism that denigrates Black women.

In the next section of the chapter, I examine Sanchez's journey as an artist, particularly as a playwright. Most scholarly studies of Sanchez foreground her poetry. However, as I point out here, Sanchez was a playwright first. Her first play *Bronx* was omitted from the foundational BAM text, *Black Fire*.

That accidental exclusion by the editors of the anthology—Baraka and Larry Neal—effectively silenced Sanchez's play as it pertains to the lived realities of gender and sexism within the BAM. It is through her plays, specifically *Bronx*, that we see her critiques of the BPM. After discussing the politics of Sanchez as a playwright, I examine the history of Harlem and its representation in *Bronx*. Harlem is the first stop the revolutionaries make in their decision to burn down public housing. The chapter analyzes how Harlem—known as a site of social, political, and cultural uplift for Black America—is wedged between what John Henrik Clarke emphasized remaining a "nerve center of advancing Black America" and losing its status as "the most famous black city in the world" (3). Before elaborating on these themes in Sanchez's plays, I examine her journey to becoming a playwright during the BAM. That journey, marked by sexism within the BAM, made Sanchez one of the most prominent figures of the Black Power era.

THE MAKING OF A PLAYWRIGHT

Sanchez's *Bronx* first appeared in the *Drama Review*'s 1968 summer review of Black Theatre edited by Ed Bullins, a writer and playwright of the Black Revolutionary Theatre. The play was performed at the Black Theatre and the University of the Streets Productions. *Bronx* led to Sanchez's second play, *Sister Son/ji* (1969), also edited by Bullins for his book *New Plays for the Black Theatre* (1969). According to Forsgren, *Sister Son/ji* is the most produced play from the 1960s and 1970s era, appearing at Concept East Theatre in Detroit, Negro Ensemble Company at St. Mark's Playhouse in New York City, and Joseph Papp's New York Shakespeare Festival among many. In an interview with Jacqueline Wood, Sanchez recalls sending a copy of *Bronx* to Larry Neal and Amiri Baraka for their edited publication *Black Fire: An Anthology of Afro-American Writing* (1968).[7] The play never appeared in the influential book because "it got misplaced," noted Sanchez, but it did include Sanchez's poems "poem at thirty," "summary," "blues," and "to all sisters" (Sanchez qtd. in Wood 122). Baraka and Neal published Sanchez's poetry in *Black Fire*; however, the exclusion of *Bronx* in the anthology prevented her from showcasing her literary diversity in a pioneering text that would become a central work outlining the goals and aims of the BAM. Moreover, the oversight on Baraka and Neal's part points to the overlooked period in Black Arts history, where Black women's voices were marginal in comparison to their Black male counterparts.[8] Sanchez also puts sexism into perspective in an interview with Forsgren that "some people want to say that black men were really sexist . . . America was sexist!" (Sanchez qtd. in Forsgren 22). Sanchez places in a larger context sexism at its rootedness as being an American institution that everyone followed, including the men of BAM. In addition, Sanchez makes it very clear that sexism within BAM became a pronounced issue in the late sixties and into the seventies when *Bronx* and *Sister Son/ji* were published. Specifically, as Sanchez argues, "[but] what happened was at some point, organizations came about. They acknowledged that they had positions for women" (22). Similarly, Sanchez's intuitiveness about how chauvinism and sexism permeating Black discourses is expressed in her written review for *Negro World*. In an interview with *World* magazine, David Reich questioned Sanchez about that review she wrote about Eldridge Cleaver's memoir *Soul on Ice*. *Negro World*, a newspaper distributed by the United Negro Improvement Association, refused to publish it because her first lines were "Eldridge Cleaver is not a revolutionary; he's a hustler. I come from New York, and I've seen quite enough of hustlers in my time" (Sanchez, *Conversations* 81). Sanchez's honesty and her acute attention to Cleaver's vile complexities that were deeply rooted in misogyny and homophobia illustrated her unapologetic aim to call out disingenuous members of the BPM.[9] In her plays, Sanchez examines misogyny and sexism dramatized in the response from her male characters to Black Bitch, which I illustrated earlier and will elaborate on later in this chapter.

Moreover, such an example of Sanchez interrogating in her fiction and nonfiction works the gender politics of the day illustrates what Ashley D. Farmer asserts is how "gender-conscious writings" like Sanchez's "often bent the ideological and organizational trajectory of the movement toward more radical, intersectional approaches to black liberation and how [she] pushed activists and organizations to articulate a critique of patriarchy along with [her] critique of racism" (Farmer 5). In other words, Sanchez exemplified the opposite of what I mentioned earlier as the Black revolutionary artist. The term "Black revolutionary artist" became synonymous with Black male writers and critics associated with the BAM. However, Sanchez adopts the term, and scholar Ashley D. Farmer revises it, calling Black women like Sanchez the Black revolutionary woman (artist). As Farmer notes, such a persona epitomizes the "powerful, political, and militant" woman (77). Sanchez's works, particularly *Bronx* and *Sister Son/ji*, invoke her revolutionary nationalism. Sanchez's illuminating persona and contribution to the BAM is delivered in the documentary *BaddDDD Sonia Sanchez*.

Reminiscing about the BAM in the documentary *BaddDDD Sonia Sanchez* (2015), a production by Attie and Goldwater, Sanchez speaks with poet-scholar and fellow BAM colleague John Bracey about being a woman performing militant poetry at a predominantly male gathering in New York City. Sanchez was the sole recognizable female voice in a male-dominated circle where poetry, scholarship, and dramatic explanations of racism were often acknowledged only between men. Sanchez reminds Bracey, "You had just applauded them [men] saying the same thing, but the moment I got on stage, everyone's mouths dropped, the jaws dropped, and they said, did you just hear what she said? But the women were applauding and jumped up and said, 'Yay, Yay, Yay,' and that is the joy of being in the Black Arts Movement. That we had the freedom as a female to be on that stage and to use a voice that was mighty, that was loud, it was strong, it was sassy, it was mean, but it was also a female voice" (Gordon et al., *BaddDDD*). Within this moment, Sanchez reminds Bracey that her voice highlighted the noticeable sexist divide between men and women during the 1960s Black Power era. Furthermore, Sanchez's view on matters of racism were uniquely her own in solidarity with her Black brothers and sisters who stood for the cause.

BaddDDD is a documentary in which Sanchez narrates her life as an activist, teacher, and poet with a supporting cast of poets, hip hop artists, and activists who give their honest and celebratory expressions of her work. However, the film neglects to examine her work as a playwright. This oversight reflects a general trend whereby scholars study Sanchez mostly as a poet. In fact, in her essay "Poetry Run Loose: Breaking the Rules," she states, "When I am asked why I decided to write a play, I must say that it is because I actually saw the affinity between being a poet and being a playwright. . . . I saw the connection of how closely we pay attention to words as poets. That same kind of attention is paid to the dialogues that we write in plays" (3). She refers to writing a play as part of her move "out of that constriction [so that she] was able to move the language and use many different words, not just one person's voice as sometimes in a poem, but in different people's voices in a play" (3). The many voices talking at once in *Bronx* reflect Sanchez's vision when she made her poetic drama. She was able to tell these stories in a way that contextualized what Jacqueline Wood articulates as the "ritualistic action and shocking language to shatter the complacency of Eurocentric as well as African American audiences" (Wood 122). In other words, Sanchez's plays transformed the way various racial and gendered audiences perceived the Black experience in America. Sanchez's male counterparts Neal and Baraka, among others, centered the Black male's voice as synonymous with the BAM, thus often interchanging the experiences of Black men with Black themes that illuminated their ideologies on politics and culture such that they overshadowed the voices of both women and other men participating in the movement.

THE BRONX IS NEXT (AND SISTER SON/JI)

The Bronx Is Next, set in Harlem, New York, opens with Charles, a Black revolutionary conspiring to burn down all public housing within the five boroughs. The Bronx is the next borough on the list for the revolutionaries to burn to the ground. The name's significance comes from the last line of the play when Charles says, "The Bronx is next—Let's split" (Sanchez, *Bronx* 526). Before entering the Bronx, revolutionaries Charles, Jimmy, Larry, and Roland enter a Harlem apartment rented by an elderly woman named Old Sister. The men begin to move her belongings out of her apartment, without disclosing their plans to burn the building. Old Sister tells Charles about her possessions: "I brought them up with me from Birmingham 40 years ago. I always keeps them right here with me. I jest [*sic*] can't do without them. You know what I mean son? I jest [*sic*] can't leave them you see" (Sanchez, *Bronx* 520). Charles directs Old Sister back to the apartment. Her belongings are placed inside of the home; he asks his henchmen to "make [Old Sister] comfortable. She ain't coming tonight. She'll come another time" (521). What Charles means is that he is leaving Old Sister behind to die.

The story transitions to the revolutionaries' interactions with White Cop, who monitors the tenement building daily. He is supposedly paid by the revolutionaries' superiors (who are unnamed) to stay out of Harlem the night they come to transport the residents and burn the building. However, White Cop, who has been secretly having an intimate relationship with the other female character Black Bitch, begins to question the revolutionaries. He yells, "What are all the people doing out in the middle of the street? What's happening here? There's something going on here I don't know about and I have a right to know" (521). The men do not respond to White Cop, causing a verbal confrontation between them. The revolutionaries and White Cop begin a heated debate about poverty and Black rioting. White Cop says, "Poverty of the mind and spirit . . . things are so much better . . . but these riots. It's making good people have second thoughts about everything" (522). White Cop and the revolutionaries place the blame of poverty on the Black tenants instead of addressing how systemic racism has played a factor in their plight. The play also addresses police brutality. In one scene the men role-play; the revolutionaries are cops, and the White Cop is a revolutionary. The purpose of the role reversal, which the revolutionaries initiate, is to teach White Cop a lesson about police brutality. White Cop gets beaten, and instead of understanding how his pain is a reflection of policemen abusing their power against Black people, he instead tells the men, "Enough is enough. I'm ready to stop—I'm tired" (523). To begin with, he does not empathize with

Black people's pain because he does not see himself in their position. The scene transitions to a Black woman the revolutionaries refer to as Black Bitch, who is also White Cop's mistress. In order for Black Bitch to make ends meet, Sanchez explains, "[Black Bitch] had White Cop supplementing her income" (Sanchez qtd. in Forsgren, *Sistuhs* 179). Black Bitch becomes a prototype (as Sanchez calls her) illustrating how many poor Black women who made below minimum wage found alternatives such as prostitution to financially support their families. Sharon Harley describes such work Black women considered taking as an underground economy and adds, "most women and men in the underground economy (illegal and extralegal) needed their jobs as attractive alternatives to the vast majority of low-paid menial jobs reserved for blacks or as the only alternative to homelessness or starvation" (Harley 53). Black Bitch describes her relationship with White Cop as "I am surviving. This dude has been coming regularly for two years—he stays one evening, leaves and then drives on out to Long Island to his white wife and kids and reality" (Sanchez, *Bronx* 525).

The relationship between the Black woman and cop serves as a microcosm of sorts that brings into focus the blighted realities that Black women living in tenement buildings experience, such as marginalization and exploitation. The revolutionaries see Black Bitch as a social deviant and play into the behavioral stereotypes about Black women posed in the 1965 Moynihan report. For instance, Roland sarcastically says, "Another black matriarch on our hands—and with her white boyfriend. How you gonna teach them all this great stuff when you whoring with some white dude?" (Sanchez, *Bronx* 524). But the scene also brings up another set of social realities, described by Anneka Henderson as the "fragile relationship between African American women and wedlock" (Henderson 4). Black Bitch chooses not to marry a Black man because of previous abuse and solely uses White Cop to supplement her income. Her singlehood and motherhood conflicts with conservative and patriarchal notions of family and marriage. As Henderson further explains, "the private sphere, often through the guise of patriarchal family, is venerated as a form of empowerment and 'Black Power' against unwieldy systemic hurdles in the public sphere" (10). Therefore, the revolutionaries' Black Power, their overt normalization of patriarchy, and disdain for an unwed Black woman further perpetuates the chauvinism and misogyny that undermine their purpose to alleviate Black people from oppression. For example, there is a rift between Charles, the other revolutionaries, and Black Bitch in a scene in which Black Bitch interrupts the commotion going on between the men by running to White Cop's aid. The revolutionaries, visibly upset, yell at her. Charles shouts explicitly, "Now is that any way to act bitch?

We just want to talk to you for a minute" (Sanchez, *Bronx* 524). She refuses to address the men while inserting herself in the debacle. The confrontation that emerges between the Black woman and revolutionaries is undergirded by a more complex narrative that has to do with race and class. Charles expects Black Bitch to stand in solidarity with him and the other men because of an unuttered solidarity that is connected to the issue of poverty in the United States, where Black men's being barred from the labor market and Black women's relegation within the labor market contribute to these hostilities. Barbara R. Bergmann argued in 1971 that Black people were crowded into low-wage jobs in America due to racial discrimination. Bergmann's "crowding" hypothesis sought to reveal the underlying reasons for such bias when referring to Black workers. Her conclusions were that "of the eighteen deficit occupations, fifteen had deficits of non-whites of more than 50 percent. Two occupations, service workers and nonfarm laborers, accounted for 82 percent of the surpluses" (Bergmann 297). Thus, "black workers' low wage reflects at least in part their low opportunity cost'" (298). Michelle Holder asserts that "Bergmann also recognized that extreme occupational segregation can depress wages of subaltern groups given opportunity costs; if a member of a subaltern group is unwilling to accept lower wages for the same job as that done by a favored group member, then the only choice left is to seek a lower-level, lower-paying job" (Holder 683).

The revolutionaries choose not to take lower-level jobs in a biased job market, but their alternative still comes at an expense—that is, splitting up communities and families, leaving some to die or treat with cruelty, and provoking violence on women. For instance, Charles hits Black Bitch in the face in front of her son. She hits back and they get into a violent dispute. Black Bitch says to her son: "No. watch this boy. You still young. Watch me. Don't touch me. Watch me get up. It hurts. But I'll get up . . . Here I am, a black bitch, up for grabs. Anyone here for me. take your choice—your pick—slap me or fuck me—anyway you get the same charge" (Sanchez, *Bronx* 525). No one comes to the Black woman's aid, and it is not until she leaves that Charles stops his plans to burn down the tenement building where Black Bitch lives to apologize. He says "All 'cept No. 214—we have some business there. Give us ten minutes then light it up" (526). While Black Bitch and her son's lives are spared, the mistreatment that she experiences is everlasting. According to Shondrah Nash, "African American women are 1.23 times more likely to experience minor violence and more than twice as likely to experience severe violence as are white women" (Nash 1421). Black Bitch normalizes the physical violence from Charles and the sexual exploitation from White Cop and manages her mistreatment by fighting back or accepting payment. Black

Bitch internalizes the chauvinistic and misogynistic oppression by normalizing the chaotic episodes through a womanist ethos. Black Bitch exemplifies a womanist resilience, what Alice Walker describes as "outrageous, audacious, courageous, or willful behavior" that is "committed to survival and wholeness" when she stands up to all men when she says "anyway you get the same charge" (Walker 22; Sanchez, *Bronx* 525). But her actions also invoke what Shawn Arango Ricks terms *normalized chaos*: "a defense mechanism used by Black women to minimize daily hassles and life situations, viewing them as part of their 'normal life'" (Ricks 343).

Sanchez's creation of a character such as Black Bitch contests the universality of Black men who use Black Power as part of their agenda to define themselves as leaders of their communities. Black Bitch's character exposes the real intentions of this set of supposed revolutionaries who are invested in setting the conditions by which Black women should participate in Black Power. The Black male characters in *Bronx*, as revealed through their actions in the play, have a conservative sort of values relative to the Black experience: Black women such as Black Bitch must stand by and only have intimate relations with Black men; Black single mothers cannot raise their children independent of marriage or co-habitus relationships; the elimination of public housing will eliminate Black poverty. Thus, the Black revolutionaries, notably Charles, play into Western, patriarchal, conservative, male viewpoints of poor Black women. Overall, Charles treats poor Black people inhumanely. He says to White Cop: "It's hard working with these people. They like cattle you know. Don't really understand anything" (Sanchez, *Bronx* 522). Charles and White Cop have similar views when referring to poor Black people. In agreement White Cop remarks, "But the hardest thing for me to understand was that all you black people would even live in these conditions" (522). Charles's conversation with White Cop and his opinions about poor Black people play into old stereotypes that historically classify them as subhuman. He uses Black Power as a buffer that conceals his internalized racism. Janeé M. Steele defines internalized racism as "a negative view of self, based on the perceived inferiority of one's own culture or race" (Steele 202). Charles's negative core beliefs about poor Black people as chattel illustrate a belief held in Western societies that people of African descent are unintelligent and bestial. These generalizations that Charles feeds into and that White Cop accepts as universal perpetuates oppression and prolongs a violation of human rights. The play ends with all the revolutionaries rushing out of the building to move forward with planning their next arson attack in the Bronx. The fate of the remaining characters is absent from the play; however, the implication is that Old Sister is left in her apartment to die while Black

Bitch along with her children might have survived. White Cop tries to run from the revolutionaries. Roland hits White Cop, knocking him unconscious.

Another major theme highlighted in *The Bronx Is Next* is police brutality. Sanchez recalls that she wrote the play after reading "in the newspaper about a cop chasing a kid down the street" (Joyce 199). Sanchez explains further: "I wrote the play because I wanted to show how urban cities were killing Black folks, how death permeated our souls as it is in these ghettos, in the tenements, in these houses that people didn't care about, and I wanted to show also how the possibilities of organizing people to take them South where they had come from and to begin to rebuild'" (199). Within the play, she offers a solution to end police brutality by suggesting that police officers participate in role-reversal training. Sanchez offered a role-reversal scenario in her play, between the Black men and white police officer, to provide a solution in police training in impoverished neighborhoods where the Black American working class and poor reside. Later in the chapter, I will examine more specifically the ways in which Sanchez deals with themes such as police brutality and the didactic nature of *Bronx* to proactively address police misconduct and ways to end such societal problems.

As mentioned previously, *Bronx* initially was to be a trilogy. Sanchez describes two other plays of her originally proposed trilogy that would portray Black Americans' "trek south and their final settlement" (Sanchez, "Poetry" 3). In other words, the play intended to examine the Great Migration narrative. While some Blacks were fortunate to have a better quality of life in American cities such as New York and Chicago, others, as depicted in *Bronx*, became confined to segregated housing, low wages, and concentrated poverty. Sanchez's trilogy would have chronicled a reverse migration of Blacks returning to the South, but those other two plays never were written. However, Sanchez's second play, *Sister Son/ji*, published in 1969 by Ed Bullins, fits well as a sequel to *Bronx*.

Revealingly, Mississippi is the backdrop of the one-woman play *Sister Son/ji*. The drama follows a middle-aged Black woman named Sister Son/ji. She engages the audience in a story about her emigration to the South after being a Black Power activist and raising four sons, described as "brave warriors." The men are all deceased (Sanchez, *Sister Son/ji* 37). Her return to the deep South is a nostalgic return to a past that mourns Black people and points to the hurt and pain that "engage the ritual of death and dying" (Holloway 655). Karla F. C. Holloway coins "black mourning stories" to describe narratives within Black American culture that represent the dead speaking directly to the present. Sister Son/ji cannot deny her past because the acts of remembering "are for the near/dead/dying," and "death is made up of past/actions/

deeds and thoughts" (Sanchez, *Sister Son/ji* 37). She remembers the man in her life, Nesbitt, and the sons she raised. Thus, Sister Son/ji often refers to her early days as a college student at Hunter College and the discrimination she experienced. She reminisces about her Black Power activism, the deceased men in her life, and the need to unite with them while "letting them move in tall/straight/lines toward our freedom" (39). Sister Son/ji believes she shares with Nesbitt a mutual respect grounded in love and Black Nationalism that removes white supremacy's "sadistic/masochistic/society that screams its paleface over the world" (39). Whereas Black Bitch invests in a womanist viewpoint that centers her humanity and how to answer to chauvinistic abuse from the revolutionaries and sexual exploitation from White Cop, Sister Son/ji responds to race, class, and gender oppression from an African-centered womanist perspective. Sister Son/ji built her community on what Jasmine A. Mena and P. Khalil Saucier argue is "based on racial identity and as a survival strategy against oppression" (Mena and Saucier 251). For instance, when Sister Son/ji recalls one conversation she has with Nesbitt about her former political science professor at Hunter College failing to acknowledge her enrollment in the course, she exclaims, "do you know nesbitt that that ole/bitch in my political theory course couldn't remember my name and there are only 12 of us in the class—only 3 negroes—as different as day and night" (Sanchez, *Bronx* 37).

The tenets of Africana womanism center race and gender as contextual frameworks based on how women and men, for example Sister Son/ji and Nesbitt, live their lives. Sister Son/ji in that particular moment experiences racial oppression as a dominate identifier that she shares with Nesbitt as they communally fight against racism. Hudson-Weems contends that "the chief role of the Africana woman is to aid in bringing to fruition the liberation of her entire race" (Hudson-Weems 33). Sister Son/ji seeks to eliminate the stigmatization of otherness in her political science classroom by taking a stand against racism. She exclaims, "she showed me no respect. none of the negroes in the class was being respected as the individuals we are. just three/big/blk/masses of blk/womanhood . . . i'll write the reason i lost these three credits is due to discrimination" (Sanchez, *Bronx* 38). Sister Son/ji's choice to drop the course instead of enduring the subconscious racial bias exhibited by the white woman professor illustrates her Africana womanist sensibilities. In other words, Sister Son/ji processes the problematic dealings of racism/white supremacy through heightened alertness to the professor's inhumanity toward the Black students in the course. Sister Son/ji says, "i'm a human being to be remembered just like all these other human beings in this class" (38). By leaving the course, Sister Son/ji keeps her humanity intact. Through interlocking approaches such as courage and fervor, her Africana womanist sensibilities act as a holistic method toward wholeness. Conversely, in *Sister Son/ji*, as I will illustrate later on, Sister Son/ji builds on the Africana womanist framework throughout her life based on her desire to create healthy Black families. Her framework connotes an African-centered philosophy that, as Wade W. Nobles argues, promotes "unity, cooperative effort, and mutual responsibility, [that] influence[s] every aspect of Black social reality" (Nobles 133). Sister Son/ji's centering of Nesbitt and their sons, supporting their efforts to fight in a race war that ultimately claims their lives—"Chausiku. Mtume. Baraka. Mungu./brave warriors. DEAD"—enlists the core values of a community grounded in liberation.

Seemingly, I seek to demonstrate the efficacy of Sanchez's variegated womanisms in both *Bronx* and *Sister Son/ji* to expand a conversation on the meaning of race and gender oppression beyond Westernized constructions of feminism that are in response to patriarchal maltreatment, among other things. I further want to illustrate the complexity of Black women's experiences in handling racism and gender oppression by highlighting the interconnectivity of interracial and intraracial conflict. To solidify my point, as Jacqueline Wood notes, in both *Bronx* and *Sister Son/ji* Sanchez "portrays black female characters as images of black women who are struggling to just survive, yet do not hesitate to courageously protest against their abusive experiences" (Wood, "To Wash My Ego" 21–22). As illustrated in examples mentioned earlier in this section, while Black Bitch deals with her physical abuse from the revolutionaries directly by fighting back, Sister Son/ji suppresses her feelings about the lack of conviction from Nesbitt in supporting her efforts to combat racism. Sanchez complicates Black women characters by moving beyond the stereotypes such as Sapphire or the Strong Black Woman that often accompany Black women's actions. Rather, Sanchez spotlights Black women's vulnerabilities in the thick of a collapsing movement politics centralizing their resilience and self-determination.

In the same way as Brooks's *Riot*, Sanchez's first two plays engage Black people in a conversation about love being a primary unifier; just as it builds healthy families and mutual respect between people, love should also focus on building Black nationhood. Before the construction of Black nationhood can begin, Sanchez suggests that in the struggle for Black freedom Black women and men have to work as equals, side by side, and respect one another in the process. In her plays, Sanchez illustrates how the lack of respect between Black women and men and generational poverty can have dire consequences on the Black family and its communities. Sanchez highlights economic genocide as a systemic problem in poor Black communities—one that perpetuates acts of violence from both within and outside of the community that reflect larger systems of oppression and that magnify through the terrors of racism. In the next section of the chapter, I examine how the Black Power revolution began to materialize, while at the same time Harlem's obvious social, economic, and political pitfalls come to the fore. Such an analysis of Harlem is significant as it pertains to addressing the racial, gendered, and class realities of Black people—particularly those that represent families ravaged by economic inequality. Insightfully, in her play, Sanchez focuses on Harlem as the epicenter of the Black experience. She emphasizes the importance of Harlem to the development of Black culture and politics but also showcases its decline and impact on the citizens who remain in the borough. Harlem poses a dilemma as a space reflecting Black potential but also a hub of racism that oppressed a growing Black underclass. Generational poverty is a significant concern for the revolutionaries in *Bronx*, and it is the reason they believe burning public housing is the definitive solution. Sanchez illustrates that such a fallacy on the revolutionaries' part does not address America's failed policies on racial equity regarding wealth and prosperity for Black Americans living in impoverished neighborhoods.

THE HISTORY OF HARLEM AND ITS
REPRESENTATION IN *BRONX*

Harlem, the setting of *Bronx*, has a complicated Black history. Between the 1880s and early 1900s, white landlords who desperately wanted to keep the neighborhood exclusively white collectively formed racially restrictive covenant laws. Such a plan on the part of white Harlemites would maintain their real estate property at a high value and attract other owners interested in purchasing the property. In "Harlem: The Making of a Ghetto," Gilbert Osofsky notes that Blacks were historically considered the "most depressed and traditionally worst-housed people" (Osofsky 20). In other words, Black Harlemites were seen more as a liability than an asset in terms of wealth building. Why were they seen as a liability? What did they do to drive down property values? This prejudice stemmed from the historical nature of African descendants in the United States. For Black people, regardless of their national affiliation—whether they migrated north to New York or immigrated from the Caribbean or South America—racism limited their opportunities to own property or work in sectors where they could earn higher wages. Redlining and other methods for restricting Blacks to particular areas in Harlem became so pronounced that, as Osofsky points out, some covenant agreements "even put a limitation on the number of Negro janitors, bellboys, laundresses, and servants that could be employed in a home" (21). Such organizations as the Harlem Property Owners' Improvement Corporation and the West Side Improvement Association were adamant about dismantling "the Negro's steady effort to invade Harlem," as many whites perceived it (21). In some sections of Harlem, landlords placed whites-only signs in their apartment buildings. A movement had begun to keep the growing population of Blacks, particularly in Upper Manhattan, at low or relatively nonexistent levels. As Osofsky notes, "Negro realtors were contacted and told they would be wasting their time trying to find houses on certain streets" (22). By 1917 the New York state government confirmed that "racially restrictive housing covenants were unconstitutional" in Harlem, and Black people were afforded the opportunity to purchase, rent, and sell the property to other Black tenants (22). Although Black Americans could access a plethora of housing in Harlem, they were still conscious of racial violence happening throughout America.

On July 28, 1917, W. E. B. Du Bois, who was living in Harlem at the time, organized a silent march of Black children, women, and men down New York's Fifth Avenue to protest lynching and anti-black violence exhibited in East St. Louis. Soyica Diggs Colbert argues that this kind of protest signaled "an act of enfranchisement that called attention to black citizens' disenfranchisement" (Colbert, *Black Movements* 144). In many ways, the protest coalesced the mass demonstration for Black Harlem residents to equally protest against other forms of disenfranchisement, including housing segregation that continued in Harlem amidst unconstitutional housing laws.[10] Through the subtle removal of racially restrictive covenants in Harlem, a prominent Black middle class grew and made Harlem an artistic and ethnically vibrant community, home to a New Negro/Harlem Renaissance. Still, Black property owners remained a minority, primarily due to a lack of economic and social resources (Osofsky 24). With white flight inevitable and "relatively few Negroes" who "were wealthy enough to buy," Harlem became known as "New York's equivalent of the Negro ghettos of the nation" (23–24). Because of the concentration of Black populations, the lack of wealth, and their isolation in Harlem, Black Harlemites, who created their covenant, were met with struggle and strife. Still, it became the epicenter of cultural and political nationalism. Harlem was an ideal place to live regardless of the lack of financial resources.

In the mid-1960s, the Black Power revolution began to materialize. Scholars, writers, and sociologists such as John Henrik Clarke, Langston Hughes, Hope R. Stevens, and Kenneth B. Clark wanted to revive Harlem's Black history—specifically, exploring Harlem's obvious pitfalls that caused many Black writers and artists to migrate further west.[11] Clarke frames Harlem as a once vibrant "city" that had become a "ghetto" by the early 1960s (3).[12] In the introduction to his edited collection titled *Harlem: A Community in Transition*, Clarke describes Harlem as "the cultural and intellectual capital of the black race in the Western world" (Clarke 8). Clarke foregrounds Harlem's history within the context of the Great Migration, Marcus Garvey's Back to Africa movement, and the artistic and political richness that had taken place during the Harlem Renaissance, where scholars such as Alain Locke coined the term "the New Negro" (8). Clarke reveals the noticeable decline in Harlem during the post–World War II years, when "many old residents, now successful enough to afford a better neighborhood moved" and others "died or moved away," making Harlem a non-self-sufficient community (9). Harlem was distinct as a leading Black metropolis because of its self-sufficient roots—what activists of the BPM termed self-determination—and collective action.

In 1934 the implementation of public housing through the New York City Housing Authority (NYCHA) initiated an aggressive push to build tenement buildings in the greater New York City area to refashion the city as an attractive, wealthy metropolis. It also was a means of providing affordable housing to a Depression era population. According to *Toward the End to Be Achieved: The New York City Housing Authority, Its History in Outline*, a report compiled by the NYCHA under the leadership of Mayor Fiorello LaGuardia, "the war, however, and its aftermath of social unrest and a stirred social conscience, accelerated the process of elimination of slums and the construction of new houses" (New York City Housing Authority 5). The federal government funded the housing authority to place citizens in desirable cost-efficient housing. However, the document does not make clear how this was to apply to citizens who participated in NYCHA across racial or ethnic lines, given the rise of racial zoning practices and the fact that Black residents were relegated to racially segregated areas. Black residents largely did not benefit from this type of affirmative action. Instead, Black Americans were displaced and zoned to public housing in Black neighborhoods that, according to Douglas S. Massey, "dramatically [increased] the geographic concentration of black poverty" and magnified the deteriorating growth of Black America's most prized metropolis (Massey 574).

Clarke shares that in the 1960s Harlem became "a black community with a white economic heartbeat" (Clarke 9). The determination of Black people to hang on to their handful of businesses, combined with the national surge in integration as a protest campaign made by those in the CRM, shifted Harlem from a self-sustaining economic, political, and artistic Black metropolis to a locale where Blacks "fight to gain control of their community" (9). The shift from being a cultural site to becoming a ghetto—where Sanchez's revolutionaries would rather move Black residents and burn the borough down than reclaim control from outsiders—created a crisis point within Black nationalism. Once a promising hub of Black consciousness and unity, Harlem by the 1960s had become a deteriorating site of Black despair marked by conflicts and poverty. Harlem's limited economic and political resources prevented it from assuming "its proper place in the Negro Revolution" (10). Many, including Daniel P. Moynihan, understood the Black revolution to exemplify the growing demand for civil rights among Black people as "distribution of achievements among Negroes roughly comparable to that among whites" (Moynihan 3). Harlem became a test study for Moynihan. In his controversial document, *The Negro Family: The Case for National Action* (1965), he explains that Harlem was experiencing "mass deterioration" within its institutions (Moynihan 4). Basing his statistics on the decline of the Negro family and the downfall of Harlem, Moynihan makes the point that "what is true of central Harlem can be said to be true of the Negro American world in general" (4). In other words, Harlem, once a model site for Black excellence, by the 1960s mirrored the rest of Black America, as many other Black cities were experiencing high unemployment and poverty. Not only does he use grim language to describe Harlem, calling its poor population a "disturbed group," but Moynihan also blames a cycle of poverty and behavioral attitudes on the "tangle of pathology" caused by matriarchal heads of household (4).

Narratives about Black plight continued, through an economic-historical lens. For instance, in *Dark Ghetto: Dilemmas of Social Power*, published in 1965, Kenneth B. Clark contends:

> With the growth of the civil rights movement, Negroes have won many footholds earlier forbidden to them, and it would seem logical to conclude, as many do, that Negroes are better off than ever before in this gradually desegregating and generally affluent society. But the fact is that in many ways the Negro's situation is deteriorating. The Negro has been left out of the swelling prosperity and social progress of the nation as a whole. He is in danger of becoming a permanent economic proletariat. (K. Clark 34)

Clark gives a blunt analysis of the conditions of Black people living in ghettos in Harlem during the 1960s. Although the Civil Rights Act of 1964 guaranteed Black people the freedom to pursue employment in any sector within the

United States void of discrimination, the act did not address the fact that Black people were growing into a permanent underclass.[13] Clark supports his argument with statistical data on the income of Black men and women living in public housing as well as of those in the Black middle class. According to his statistics, in 1965 "one out of every seven or eight adults in Harlem [were] unemployed" (34). Also, Black unemployment grew faster than white unemployment. For example, young men between the ages of 18 and 24 were "five times as high for Negroes as for whites . . . [and] for the girls, the gap was even greater" (34).[14] Clark concluded that college did not place Black men and women into a higher income bracket. His data, supported by Herman P. Miller's 1964 book *Rich Man, Poor Man*, revealed that a Black college graduate "will expect to earn only as much in a lifetime as whites who have not gone beyond the eighth grade" (35).[15] Clark's research revealed the racial caste burden reserved for Black Americans, inadequate income and non-steady job accumulation in Black communities, and a continuous cycle of poverty in concentrated Black cities. Regardless of civil rights laws that were in place to protect Blacks and garner them living-wage jobs and income, the reality for the Black people who protested for economic gains was far from the ideal of a racially equal society.[16] The final section of this chapter provides a close reading of *Bronx* to highlight these issues of poverty, racism, and sexism.

A CLOSE READING OF *BRONX* AND *SISTER SON/JI*

The opening scene in *Bronx* involves Charles, Roland, Jimmy, and Larry attempting to burn down a tenement building in Harlem. In an effort to maximize time and vacate residents from the building, Charles tells Old Sister, a longtime Harlemite and resident of the building, that she cannot take all of her belongings, only "things [she] would grab and carry out in case of a fire" (Sanchez, *Bronx* 520). Old Sister seeks understanding, pleading with Charles, "I always keep them right here with me. I jest can't do without them. You know what I mean son?" (520). Charles responds by telling Old Sister to return upstairs to her apartment and that he will come back another time. Old Sister is unaware that the revolutionaries will make her comfortable because she will die in the fire with her belongings. Situating Old Sister in *Bronx* is gripping. When asked about Old Sister, Sanchez describes her as a relic of the past. She exclaims, "She couldn't make the trek. She would have never made the trek all the way, and they were moving. Also, she was symbolic of the old way of looking at things that had to die out" (Forsgren, *Sistuhs* 188). According to the timeline Sanchez writes in *Bronx*, Old Sister spent forty years living in Harlem after migrating from Birmingham, Alabama, in 1928. That means she arrives in Harlem toward the end of the New Negro/Harlem Renaissance era. She lived in Harlem for forty years and saw firsthand the deterioration of the community. Specifically, she lived through the riots of 1935 that were instigated by mounting Black unemployment and police brutality. The sociopolitical climate deteriorated further as Black Harlem residents post–Depression era demanded representation in America's labor and political markets. Black leaders created, for example, the "Don't Buy Where You Can't Work" (DBWYCW, also known as "Jobs for Negroes") campaign. This initiative was led by the New Negro Alliance in Washington, DC. From 1933 until the early 1940s, civil rights activists, such as A. Phillip Randolph, sought to push forth an agenda where Black workers would not only obtain employment but also work in upscale white-collar jobs. In Harlem, DBWYCW meant that the unemployed would demand and win "clerical positions" by qualification "in white-owned Harlem businesses" (Greenberg 114). The campaign, initially a middle-class Black protest in DC, shifted to a mix of middle-class and working-class-poor protest in Harlem that jobs for Blacks were scarce and limited. As Cheryl Greenberg asserts in *"Or Does It Explode?": Black Harlem in the Great Depression,* "the displacement of black workers by [whites] all over the city intensified black frustration with the inequality of economic opportunity" (114). The campaign incentivized Blacks across metropolises to "buy black" and to "hire black" as the solution to Black collective progress in Harlem.

Reprising Black campaigns such as DBWYCW did not occur in 1960s Harlem, and Old Sister, whose apartment was filled with sentimental possessions that tied her to the American South. These belongings foreground what Sanchez illustrates as a struggle between the "Old Negro" and "New Negro" ideology epitomized during the New Negro/Harlem Renaissance era. In many ways, Old Sister's belongings (which are unnamed possessions in the play) represent a memory of the past. Old Sister's southern possessions symbolize for Charles what Chad Williams describes as "the conservatism, parochialism, and political accommodationism of the Old Negro" (C. Williams 348). Charles instead defines a "New Negro" mentality for Blacks who are migrating or re-migrating South and whose exemplary liberalism, militancy, internationalism, and self-organization would define their new America. Charles plans to migrate South. His new South represents a return to ancestral grounds minus the strife that marks the historical legacy of racism among Blacks in America. In a new era where Black Americans have acquired their civil rights by law, the remigration south will permit greater prosperity for them than remaining in the North where jobs are scarce, and

the living conditions continue to deteriorate. Although Old Sister's determined death rests upon what Sanchez suggests is an idea that "even in a
motion and movement towards change sometimes people die, some people
get hurt, and some people don't make it," what remains critical to the story
is the way in which the revolutionaries determine whose life matters (Forsgren, *Sistuhs* 188).

Conversely, while removing the residents, they encounter White Cop
(his name is not revealed). White Cop symbolizes white liberal America. He
proclaims not to hate Black people and does not participate in the brutality
and racial prejudice some of his law enforcement colleagues subscribe to
regularly (Sanchez, *Bronx* 526). White Cop and Charles have a conversation
in which White Cop explains to Charles that "the hardest thing for me to
understand was that all you black people would even live in these conditions . . . everybody has had ghettos but they built theirs up and there was
respect there. Here. There is none of that" (522). White Cop is perplexed
about Black people and their living conditions, in part, because he makes a
false comparison between them and immigrant Irish, Jewish, and German
communities. Those immigrant communities were segregated from mainstream Anglo-American communities in New York City but not from the
economic opportunities that would afford them better living conditions than
their Black counterparts.[17] Charles responds to White Cop that it "is a color
thing—I mean even though the Irish were poor they were still white—but
as long as white people hate because of a difference in color, then they ain't
gonna let the black man do too much" (522). Charles maintains that the
Black man's plight and his restriction to the ghetto are pervasive because of
color discrimination.

White Cop does not accept Charles's answer. Instead, White Cop reverts
to a conversation of nihilism, arguing that Black Americans believe in "hopelessness. Poverty of the mind and spirit. Why? Things are so much better.
All it takes is a little more effort by you people. But these riots. It's making
good people have second thoughts about everything" (522). White Cop fails
to understand that despite the civil rights gained by Black Americans, those
living in the ghetto are becoming a permanent underclass. Instead, he is
troubled by the riots enacted by Black folks and sees this as an assault on
white America. White Cop's commentary points to the idea that "[Blacks]
should choose only those techniques, tactics, and demonstrations which do
not inconvenience the dominant white society" (K. Clark 16). In other words,
any form of revolt against the status quo inconveniences white people. The
conversation continues with Roland intervening, "It's a long time going—
man—this hopelessness—and it ain't no better. Shit. All those good thinking

people changing their minds never believed in the first fucking place" (Sanchez, *Bronx* 523). The longstanding nihilism that Cornel West examines and
that I explore in chapter 1 recurs, as Roland makes clear.

In Roland's opinion, white America never believed in equity for Black
people, and the cause of hopelessness is attributable to the continuation of
second-class citizenship. However, they migrated north to have better economic opportunities and quality living accommodations. His analysis also
hints at the failure of the 1968 Fair Housing Act, which promised to deseg-
regate the housing market by outlawing discrimination against Black people
seeking to rent, buy, or sell a property. The FHA, which successfully passed
after the assassination of Martin Luther King Jr. and was intended to address
the riots that followed it in ghettos throughout the United States, came too
late to redress housing inequality among Black communities. Many Black
Americans became a permanent underclass with little to no essential means
of achieving equity as the Nixon administration stalled on the civil rights
legislation that Lyndon B. Johnson's "Great Society" promised. Johnson's commitment "to bring the Negro American to be full and equal sharing in the
responsibilities and rewards of citizenship" was what Black Americans had
all along believed they would achieve by migrating North (Moynihan 48).[18]
As noted in *Bronx*, the composition of the ghetto isolated Black communities. It relegated them to tightly knit, close spaces that became surveillance
quarters where police were able to exert their brutality onto Black citizens
who stepped outside of the confined boundaries of the ghetto.

There is a scene in *Bronx* where Charles, Jimmy, and Roland become
cops, and White Cop becomes a revolutionary. The role reversal among the
revolutionaries is to teach White Cop a lesson about police brutality. To help
him understand their perspective better, Charles, Jimmy, and Roland decide
to teach White Cop a lesson on racial intolerance and humanity. After chasing White Cop, the revolutionaries accuse White Cop of stealing. Sanchez
draws upon several problematic exchanges between the men and White
Cop. Charles, Jimmy, and Roland try to dehumanize White Cop by calling
him a n----r and kicking him excessively to make him understand that these
are prime examples of how Black men are treated when encountering law
enforcement. However, the abuse they inflict on White Cop provides no
adequate understanding of how Black Americans are shamed and harassed
in police misconduct situations where high levels of bias are involved. The
men instead resort to violence, and, as Soyica Diggs Colbert maintains, "the
black men demonstrate how easy it is to assume the inhumane role of an
oppressor" instead of drawing attention to how police officers should solve
conflicts maturely and peacefully (Colbert, "Pedagogical" 81).

Moreover, what White Cop fails to learn from this lesson are the aggressive ways some cops exert their authority over Black men. He never embodies what it might feel like to be a Black man enduring such harassment that denies his civil liberties. White Cop maintains his whiteness and pleas to the revolutionaries to end the abuse. He insists, "But, I'm white! I'm white! No . . . This can't be happening—I'm white!" (Sanchez, *Bronx* 526). White Cop's choice to end the role reversal immediately illustrates his recognition of whiteness as an advantage that privileges his livelihood. In assessing the benefits of whiteness and heteronormativity, Alison Bailey contends that "privileges are a special class of advantage . . . [t]he benefits granted by privilege are unearned and conferred systemically to members of dominate groups; capriciously and unjustifiably granted to those groups by virtue of their membership; and are invisible to those who have them" (Bailey 2). White cop renders invisible the unearned prerogative he demands from the revolutionaries to end their abuse. He fails to connect the brutality he endures with the routine cruelty Black men experience from police by virtue of the endemic nature of racism.

Sanchez further explores police brutality in *Bronx*, exposing the profane reality that Black residents faced when patrolled by police regularly and the mental anguish it created. Jimmy, one of the revolutionaries, describes experiencing police brutality by two white cops: "I was running down my ghetto street and these two white dudes stopped me and asked what I was doing out so early in the morning—and cuz I was high off some smoke—I said man—it's my street—I can walk on it anytime. And they grabbed me and told me where everything was" (Sanchez, *Bronx* 523). Jimmy does not have a street. The dominant society owns the road that the cops protect. Jimmy can only be free in his tenement buildings that are "dark ghettos . . . social, political, educational and—above all—economic colonies" that restrict people "to a special area and [limit] their freedom of choice on the basis of skin color" (K. Clark 11). This type of confinement causes the hopelessness that White Cop cannot seem to understand.

What cannot be overlooked in *Bronx* is the revolutionaries' misogynistic and chauvinistic actions toward Black Bitch. She is the mistress of White Cop. When the revolutionaries and White Cop enact a role reversal for White Cop to experience and understand police brutality, and White Cop wants the enactment to stop, the revolutionaries ignore his request, and from a distance, Black Bitch intervenes and "stands defiantly" in front of the men (Sanchez, *Bronx* 524). Black Bitch's stance causes the revolutionaries to direct their attention to her instead of White Cop, ending their role reversal. The conflict between Black Bitch and the men takes place in the tenement building. White Cop is present during the debacle, but Black Bitch's two sons are not. Black Bitch is controversial because, as Jacqueline Wood asserts, she audaciously expresses "her courageous criticism of black militant hypocrisy and sexism" (Wood, "To Wash My Ego" 22). For instance, when Jimmy calls her a "Smart—assed—bitch," she walks up to him and responds, "That's right kid. A smart—assed—black—bitch that's me . . . Yeah, I know all about black men. The toms and revolutionary ones" (Sanchez, *Bronx* 524). Black Bitch's response to Jimmy and the other revolutionaries' examples of activism resembles Sanchez's characterization of Eldridge Cleaver as a hustler in her unpublished review of *Soul on Ice*. The men degrade her based on her relationship with White Cop, which is none of their business. Moreover, they repeatedly stereotype her, questioning "how many kids [she] got" and "another matriarch on [their] hands" (524). Black Bitch responds to the revolutionaries: "Yeah. I know what I am . . . But all you revolutionists or nationalists or whatever you call yourselves—do you know where you at? Where are you gonna find black women to love you when this is over—when you need them?" (525). She goes on to say that she would never date Black men again; her treatment by the revolutionaries alludes to what Alice Walker notes in "In Search of Our Mothers' Gardens": "We have also been called . . . mean and evil Bitches . . . When we have pleaded for understanding, our character has been distorted" (Walker, "In Search" 405). Black Bitch's dialogue in Sanchez's play and Walker's comments represent the hypocrisy of Black male militants (or self-defined revolutionaries).

The men's attitude toward Black Bitch reflects the idea that Black women were invaluable to the Black nationalist cause. Because of a general disregard for Black women as political agents within the BPM, a group of Black feminists, calling themselves the Combahee River Collective, issued a statement, published several years after *Bronx*, that charged Black women to commit their politics against "racial, sexual, heterosexual, and class oppression" and to develop an "integrated analysis and practice based upon the fact that the major systems of oppression are interlocking" (Combahee River Collective 3). As Jacqueline Wood notes, "Sanchez portrays black female characters as images of black women who are struggling to just survive, yet do not hesitate to courageously protest against their abusive experiences" (Wood, "To Wash My Ego" 21–22). Black Bitch and Old Sister are abused by Black men who claim to be revolutionaries fighting racism and declaring liberation for Black people. Sanchez refrains, however, from positioning the revolutionaries as anti-woman. She states that if they "had really been anti-woman, they would have killed the Black Bitch, but they didn't" (Sanchez, "Poetry Run Loose" 5). Sanchez's comments resonate with the fact that her "early plays, like her poetry, were ostensibly intended, published, and produced as representations of black militant nationalist discourse, addressed directly to blacks and meant to arouse anger and violent response toward white racist oppression from within the black community" (Wood, "To Wash My Ego" 5). Similarly, as Sanchez explains clearly to Forsgren, she remarks "I don't think this Black Bitch was a person that was put in there to show how much black men hated black women. No, she was a person put in to remind them of their humanity" (qtd. in Forsgren, "Sistuhs" 188). After all, Sanchez, more acutely addresses the human rights issue illustrated in *Bronx* by centralizing Black Bitch's voice to challenge the revolutionaries' actions that call into question their motives for helping Black communities achieve liberation, because of their tactics that really jeopardize Black humanity.

However, Sanchez's refraining from labeling the revolutionaries anti-woman suggests that she wrestled with themes of hypermasculinity and misogyny. For example, although Sanchez does not extensively problematize the different relationships between Black men and women of that era in *Bronx*, she does so in *Sister Son/ji*. In Sanchez's second play, particularly when it comes to addressing the Revolutionary Black Woman, she illustrates how Black women, such as herself who were part of the Black Arts and Black Power Movements, navigated structurally racist and sexist spaces within them. As Jacqueline Wood points out, "Sanchez attempted to expose the hypocrisy of the rhetoric proffered by many black males of the period by demonstrating a womanist philosophy centered on respecting all individuals and reflective of an inclusive African worldview" (Wood, "To Wash My Ego" 20–21). I go beyond Wood's analysis to argue that, while womanist philosophy is clearly articulated in *Bronx*, in *Sister Son/ji* the type of feminism exemplified more closely aligns with Africana womanism. For instance, there is a scene in the play where Sister Son/ji challenges Nesbitt to stand by his words and actions. She begs Nesbitt to "stay home with [her] and let [them] start building true blk/lives—let [their] family be a family built on mutual love and respect" (Sanchez, *Sister Son/ji* 40). The core values suggested by Sister Son/ji are in line with the rhetoric of Black Power, but her words also rely strongly on an Africana womanist philosophy that champions connectivity and holism. According to Joelle M. Cruz, "holism illustrates how women's lives need to be considered in light of the entire society" (Cruz 27). Sister Son/ji sees the Black family as interconnected with the community, and connectivity means that Africana women must "often consider the group rather than the individual as unit of analysis" (27). Henceforth, Sister Son/ji's outlook on the tenants of Black Power is an example of what Obioma Nnaemeka terms "nego-feminism." Through an Africanist framework practiced among African and African diasporic women, she "knows when, where, and how to negotiate with or negotiate around patriarchy in different contexts" (Nnaemeka 378). For example, Sister Son/ji outright commits to promoting Black Power, stating to Nesbitt that she "will talk to sisters abt/loving their blk/men and letting them move in tall/straight/lines toward our freedom. Yes [she] will preach blk/love/respect between blk/men and women for that will be the core/basis of [their] future in white/america" (Sanchez, *Sister Son/ji* 39). Sister Son/ji emphasizes to Nesbitt that without unity "they'll fall into the same traps their fathers and mothers fell into when they went their separate ways and one called it retaining their manhood while the other called it just plain/don't/care/about/family/hood" (40). Her rhetoric urging Nesbitt to stay with her and the family exposes that "issues of community are never secondary; the interaction between black men and women is primarily framed within a discussion of a need to unify the black community towards a common goal of economic and social liberation" (Wood, "To Wash My Ego" 21). The ability to unify between Sister Son/ji and Nesbitt never materializes because he dies along with their four sons for the revolution. But while Nesbitt is alive, he does not hold up his end of the bargain of keeping the family together. For instance, Sister Son/ji says to Nesbitt: "u've been out all this week to meetings. can't we have some time together. The child is in bed . . . i'm afraid that one day we'll have nothing to say to each other" (Sanchez, *Sister Son/ji* 40). In this example, Sister Son/ji negotiates the right time to address patriarchy and call into question Nesbitt's commitment to building a stable family unit. Nesbitt participates in movement work, but he also engages in recreational "drugs, weed, whiskey and going out on Saturday nites" (40). His actions trouble Sister Son/ji; she asks, "shouldn't we be getting ourselves together—strengthening our minds, bodies, and souls" (40). Nesbitt's actions illuminate a male posturing that centers on his prowess rather than his responsibility as partner to his wife. Revealingly, through the above examples, Nesbitt's activities belie his commitment to building a Black nationhood, through Sister Son/ji's understanding of protection, stability, and intimacy from a loving partner.

Instead, Sister Son/ji is the last woman standing as she continues to fight the race war. She says, "My family is gone. All my beautiful children are buried here in Mississippi" (37). Similar to Walker Vessels in Baraka's play, who at the beginning of *The Slave* is an old field slave reminiscing and trying to make sense of his life after the revolution is long gone, Sister Son/ji (who is also old and grey and telling her own story) recalls her commitment to Black Power. Her loyalty to reproduce Black nationhood is interrupted when she questions why her sons allow a white woman among their ranks, exclaiming, "if he keeps the devil/woman then he shd be made to leave" (43). Unlike Walker Vessels, who before leading a race war in *The Slave* wants to align with white liberals such as Easley, Sister Son/ji disavows liberalism, arguing "if she's so good, so liberal, send her back to her own kind. Let her liberalize them" (43). Through Sister Son/ji's recollection, Sanchez invokes her past, affirming her commitment to Black Power while also connoting her marginalization within the movement as she stands firm in her convictions. Furthermore, Sanchez incorporates women characters such as Sister Son/ji to discuss complex topics such as integration that are often seen in Black nationalist literature as part of male-centered conversations. Recalling a conversation with Nesbitt, Sister Son/ji says "my son[s]/our son[s] did not die for integration" but "they died for the right of blk/children to run on their own land and let their bodies explode with the sheer joy of living" (43). Sister Son/ji refuses to let her motherhood become part of a conversation about racial unity; rather, her agreeance to sacrifice her son's lives in the race war is built upon a radical reimagining of transformative justice and ensuring that generations of Black children can experience the possibilities of living joyful lives void of racial terrorism. Black motherhood, as Dana-Ain Davis puts it, "challenges the erasure of Black children and their exclusion from societal concern" (D. Davis 9). By committing to the Black nationalist cause, Sister Son/ji refuses to lose sight of its initial tenets of self-determination that undergird the way in which Sanchez deals with difficult questions about Black humanity by centering Black women's voices.

In conclusion, the linguistic devices displayed by Sanchez capture the linguistic overtones that engage conversational and free-flowing diction. Thusly, such abbreviations within Sister Son/ji's dialogue, Jacqueline Wood asserts, is "[wrenching] the language visually away from standard written form through fractured spelling and punctuation, through a dramatic infusion of backslashes, through inconsistent capitalization" (Wood, "To Wash My Ego" 10). Sanchez is one of the critical architects within the BAM whose literary technique contributes to the changing shift of intracultural communication between Black people that represented existing parallels within hip hop culture.[19] It is through the creative writing of Sanchez that a Black revolutionary womanist voice is personified. *Sister Son/ji* and *The Bronx Is Next* are two plays that "refined protest language" by problematizing the rhetoric of Black Power and nuancing it to showcase the courageous and often devastating experiences of Black women who were either part of the movement or challenging it (Wood, "To Wash My Ego" 3). Through the examples of Old Sister, Black Bitch, and Sister Son/ji, Sanchez exposes the hypocrisy within Black male militant rhetoric that belies Black liberation. She did so in a way that shined a light on the crisis of Black politics and Black male revolutionaries' failures to resolve gender discrimination with the female characters as they try to overcome systemic racism. In addition, Sanchez exposes the dismal realities of Black politics at a crisis point, as the CRM waned and the BPM took off. Sanchez dramatized the polarizing ideologies of Black Nationalism while also highlighting the heightened racism and poverty in Harlem that had been brewing since Blacks migrated north to escape Jim Crow segregation. Sanchez also examines sexism and how Black male revolutionaries acted in chauvinistic ways that undermined Black women's leadership, their contributions to Black collective action, but also the prevailing ways their voices question the efficacy of Black rage as a productive means of safeguarding Black humanity. The next chapter, covering Henry Dumas's short story "Riot or Revolt?" will continue to examine various manifestations of Black resistance through the ever-shifting dynamics of US politics.

Chapter 4

BLACK POLITICS AND THE NEOLIBERAL DILEMMA IN HENRY DUMAS'S "RIOT OR REVOLT?"

Sanchez critiques rioting as a divisive tool in *Bronx* and exposes the polarizing beliefs associated with reactionism in Black politics and the enduring crisis it creates within Black working-class and poor communities in Harlem. She also analyzes counter-responses to police brutality, the decline of Harlem as an epicenter of Black progress, and Black male chauvinism and sexism. Like Baraka and Caldwell, she emphasizes the destructive nature of riots and revolts and focuses on Harlem as a physical and ideological space. In this last chapter, I turn to Henry Dumas, who also focuses on Harlem as an epicenter of Black politics. However, unlike Sanchez (and Baraka and Caldwell), Dumas adopts a more optimistic approach to riots and revolts. Similar to Brooks, he argues that Black protest is a necessary step toward racial reconciliation. He is chiefly concerned with how Black communities move through the protest to arrive at a resolution. Rather than critiquing Black protest, however, he focuses more on the obstacles that impede Black America's efforts toward racial progress. The biggest hurdle is neoliberal politics, the idea that racial uplift is a matter of individual agency rather than structures of white supremacy that have, for centuries, conspired to strip Black Americans of personal agency and financial independence.

In his short story "Riot or Revolt?" set in 1960s Harlem, Dumas depicts a riot that ensues following the deadly shooting of a Black male teenager by a white police officer. When white city leaders turn to the story's Black, male protagonist, Micheval LeMoor, to quell the violence and calm Harlem's Black residents, he refuses. LeMoor tells the governor of New York, "I am not a Negro leader. Do you think that the people know me as a Negro leader? I speak as a private citizen, who comes in contact with the people" (Dumas, "Riot or Revolt?" 378). Micheval understands that Harlem residents are protesting as a result of systemic oppression. Because they do not control those systems, they cannot be responsible for ending the violence produced by them. Individual acts of intervention on the part of Black Harlem residents like Micheval won't assuage Black rage. White city officials, Dumas argues through the story, must be made to acknowledge the systemic injustices and dismantle those systems. With this short story, Dumas looks past the Black rage that is the focus of the other BAM writers discussed in previous chapters and emphasizes the cause of that rage through systems of white supremacy.

Dumas's dramatization of a riotous protest differs from the depictions provided elsewhere in this book. I contend that "Riot or Revolt?" preempts a vital examination about riots through the lens of neoliberalism. Dumas's short story challenges the state's plan on civil rights and thus anticipates the rise of neoliberalism. That concept arose in US policy in the late 1970s. According to Jodi Melamed, neoliberalism "refers to a set of economic policies that include financial liberalization (deregulation of interest rates), market liberalization (opening of domestic markets and the dismantling of tariffs), privatization, deregulation, and global economic management through international institutions and multilateral agreements" (Melamed, *Represent* 146). Since the 1970s, scholars such as Wendy Brown and Thomas Biebricher have examined neoliberalism within and beyond free-market capitalism to explore its political manifestations.[1] As Melamed makes certain, "[neoliberalism] is a world-historical organization of political governance" (147). I apply Melamed's analysis to understand how neoliberalism has decentralized Black politics from the end of the 1960s through today. Because of such political governance, Black Americans' past and present are vulnerable to structural inequalities and state-sponsored violence. Jordan T. Camp notes, "the insurgent demands of Black freedom labor movements for dignity, freedom, and the redistribution of social wealth have been conversely characterized as disorder" (Camp 4). As a result, neoliberalism is responsible for exacerbating gender, race, and class inequalities, so much so that it is meant "to refuse the social wage (public housing, education, health care, employment, and other essential social programs), and violently enforce consent to this refusal" (4). Specifically, as it relates to this chapter's discussion about race, neoliberalism compounds race relations and necessitates racial conflict. For example, even though reports such as the Kerner Report, discussed throughout this book, acknowledge racial inequality and the poor living conditions for Black Americans, government structures have failed to redress those issues or dismantle the systems that produce them. Instead, they point to Black Americans as individual actors complicit in their own suffering through personal life choices. As a result of this inaction produced by neoliberal idealism, even today Black communities continue to protest through grassroots movements such as #BLM. Like their BAM predecessors, activists participating in #BLM address police surveillance within the working class and poor Black communities as well as unresolved harassments and murders of Black citizens in the United States.[2] I discuss the present-day movement in more detail in this book's epilogue.

In this chapter, I argue that Dumas represents riots and revolts in his fiction to illuminate the primary obstacle to overcoming racial oppression: neoliberalism, which provides a cover for state-sanctioned violence and surveillance to prevail. Focusing less on Black rage or critiquing the tenets of Black nationalism, Dumas aims to dismantle the ideology of neoliberalism that situates racial solutions within the purview of Black American agency. I begin the discussion with an overview of "Riot or Revolt?" Next, I discuss Dumas's untimely death. He was killed by an off-duty policeman in a Harlem subway station. It is vital to understand why he died because it is an example of state-sanctioned violence—the same state violence he explores in "Riot or Revolt?" Moreover, his death points to the increased risk of discrimination Black Americans face when encountering law enforcement.[3]

Next, I explore the politics found within the story. I include discussions about the importance of "political education," as represented by Black bookstores that played a central role in Black protest politics. The term political education refers to people collectively gathering to read qualitative and quantitative data that anchors social, cultural, and economic issues most pertinent to an interest group. Civic education includes book readings, town halls, and social media virtual dialogues, among others. Dumas's protagonist Micheval uses his bookstore as the basis to promote to his patrons and the community a political education about racism and how it informs the social conditions Black people faced in Harlem.

"Riot or Revolt?" centers on a fictional Black bookstore that rioters do not destroy because it is a symbol of Black pride and resistance. When the governor of New York asks Micheval to describe his bookstore, he responds, "Pride dressed in knowledge!" (Dumas, "Riot or Revolt?" 375). Additionally, the short story interrogates the act of revolt as a method for Black politics and as a creative muse that gets represented in Black art. Dumas also comments on racial integration, its legacy within civil rights politics, and the rifts it created within Black communities across the United States. I discuss the residual effects of the integration debate (merging a racial minority into a desegregated America). I conclude the chapter with a close reading of "Riot and Revolt?" illustrating Dumas's critique of neoliberalism through themes of police brutality, political education, and integration.

"RIOT OR REVOLT?"

Henry Dumas's short story "Riot or Revolt?" is set during a riot in 1960s Harlem, New York, following news of a white policeman killing a Black male teenager. The story presents dialogue from various characters in Harlem amid the emotional tension and the civilian-police conflict that gave way to the riots. It features Micheval LeMoor, a Black American bookstore owner in Harlem, and Harold, a Black male teenager whose life is spared by LeMoor in what would have been another police murder. Micheval is a charismatic and outspoken elder in the Black community; he is respected by his peers and patrons who visit his store. When the riot erupts, protestors leave untouched Micheval's bookstore, which then becomes a central space where Black Americans strategize their next act of resistance in response to police brutality and government intrusion. LeMoor and his brother Carib protect Harold from police violence by hiding him in the bookstore's basement. In the cellar, Harold learns about Black Americans' longstanding tradition of protest and resistance in the Western hemisphere. He becomes the next generation in line to participate in the Black freedom struggle.

"Riot or Revolt?" addresses the continuities between violence, social protest, and civil resistance happening at the onset of a radical formation in 1960s Black America. Also, the short story calls attention to the vast contradictions arising from the Black American community regarding issues of integration, economic empowerment, and racial inequality. The story's title "Riot or Revolt?" questions whether we should understand Black protesters' rage as a riotous act or as an act of revolt. As I explained in this book's introduction, the term "race riot" in twentieth-century America initially referred to white people attacking and destroying Black people and property but by the 1960s was used in reference to Black people, often destroying white property to address a moral grievance (police and vigilante brutality). Black America's complaints during a riot, even today, are seen as reactionary moments of unruly behavior and disorderly conduct. To emphasize the righteousness of Black protest, Dumas differentiates between the terms *riot* and *revolt* and their implications. For example, the character named the Mayor tells Micheval during a conversation at his bookstore that, "You gentlemen living in the area must have some theories about why the people are so easily aroused . . . [w]e apprehend criminals everyday, and we don't have riots because of it. All kinds of criminals, colored, and white. I for one want to get to the bottom of this thing. Our citizens are aroused now" (Dumas, "Riot or Revolt?" 375). In this example, the Mayor comprehends the riots happening in his city as acts of agitation, lack of self-control, and an absence of civil leadership to circumvent the destruction and potential violence that might escalate because of the upheaval. Furthermore, the Mayor states to Micheval, "If there's going to be trouble like this just because . . . the police department is doing its duty, then more measures will have to be taken" (375). The city official recognizes this instance of unrest as a moment of trouble instead of questioning the very reason why the people riot in the first place, which is in response to the unethical and immoral behavior of police brutality. Dumas complicates the idea of rioting by insisting that the reader think about it differently, as an act of revolt. In the short story, Black people riot in response to a white policeman killing a Black adolescent. By examining this civilly disobedient response as a form of "revolt" implies a different interpretation. That is the Black protesters' denunciation of the policeman's alleged act and a refusal to comply with state and government actors. As Micheval denotes, "The people get tired of dying. Just because you have other problems, doesn't mean they die less . . . That's a smoke screen to let you know that ain't nothing going to be done. The people know that" (377). The revolt that happens is an act of affirmation by Black people who defy authority to make a statement about the humanity of the Black male youth killed by the policeman. What Micheval insinuates with his comments to the Mayor is that the revolt that is happening is justified because there is a challenge to state and government officials to recognize and affirm Black people's humanity.

Also, Micheval's acts of revolt are his Africana bookstore, which I will discuss later in the chapter, and his art collection, which professes a radical Black subjectivity. For instance, Harold, the young man Micheval saves from police brutality, hides in the LeMoor brothers' basement as protection away from the unrest. Harold sees a portrait of himself in the LeMoors' art studio alongside other notable people who have entered the bookstore. The unnamed paintings are beautiful images of "Negro, Africans, and Asians" who have come to the bookstore to seek knowledge and truth (381). It is Black political art commissioned by the LeMoor brothers.

Dumas also invokes Black art as a form of revolt, in addition to the actual rebellion taking place among the protesters, as a tool for Black American political speech. His creative move reflects BAM's emphasis on liberation rather than civil rights. Keeanga-Yamahtta Taylor defines Black liberation as "a world where Black people can live in peace, without the constant threat of the social, economic, and political woes of a society that places almost no value on the vast majority of Black lives. It would mean living in a world where Black lives matter. [. . .] Black liberation is bound up with the project of human liberation and social transformation" (Taylor, *From #BlackLives-Matter* 194). Larry Neal echoes the point, asserting, "It is no longer a question of civil rights for Negroes; but rather, it is a question of national liberation for black America . . . our struggle is one with the struggles of oppressed people everywhere, and we alone must decide what our stance will be" (Neal, "Black Power" 137). The portraits that the LeMoor brothers describe as "knowledge" and "truth" are the language of the oppressed, who, for centuries, have fought and rebelled against a white supremacist power structure that continues to infringe on their liberty, well-being, and pursuit of happiness. The paintings symbolize the liberation-transformation that Harold and others will embark upon as they rise together in protest.

"Riot or Revolt?" offers a different way of moving toward liberation. For example, among the characters art and grassroots activism are a method of revolt, one in which collective group action is the goal rather than action compelled by single leaders. In this way, Dumas anticipates the philosophy and activism of present-day grassroots organizations like #BLM. As I will argue in this book's epilogue, since 2013 the #BLM movement has adopted a leaderless strategy. Activists such as Alicia Garza and Patrisse Cullors argue that "a movement with a singular leader or a few visible leaders is vulnerable, because those leaders can be easily identified, harassed, and killed, as was the case with Dr. King" ("11 Major"). For the movement to survive it has to be bigger than one person, because the ultimate goal is freedom for the multitude. In "Riot or Revolt?" Micheval rejects the New York governor's plea for him to serve as the local leader in Harlem and call for an end to the rioting. He tells the governor, "If you want to talk to leaders, then you must find them among the people" (Dumas, "Riot or Revolt?" 378). He resists this leadership role because he believes that it is his duty as a private citizen to report issues of crime and civil disturbance, even when police officers are at fault. In addition, he rejects the notion that the responsibility for resolving the differences between Black Americans and the police must solely rest upon Black people. Micheval's statement above argues for a comprehensive way for local governmental officials to handle violent acts committed by law enforcement that involve racial bias. Dumas's story spotlights violence and systemic racism happening in Black American communities in northern cities, civil-police conflict, and the current deaths of Black leaders. Fittingly, Dumas addresses the efficacies of a leaderless movement. Malcolm X and Martin Luther King Jr., who were considered revolutionary and critiqued white supremacy in its most salient forms, succumbed to vigilante violence because of their protest. Dumas's fictional character, Micheval LeMoor, teaches us that a leaderless movement is not doomed to fail because of disorganization; rather, a multitude of people strengthens the advocacy against oppression. While a leaderless strategy goes against the kind of charismatic leadership that characterized the civil rights activism of the 1960s, it is representative of the political ethos within Black communities today. The influence of Malcolm X and King, as I mentioned in chapters 1 and 2, fed into the mythic narrative that their leadership was singular, rather than representative of a cadre of people coming together to demand societal change. Erica R. Edwards describes this kind of leadership as the charismatic scenario, "a series of extemporaneous bodily, spiritual, musical, and rhetorical affections as well as the performance of an idealized, narrative of liberation that is rooted in history" (Edwards 18). The charisma in Black leadership places "the positioning of the leader in front of, in the center of and/or above the collective ethos of resistance" (19). Micheval is a charismatic leader more than his brother Carib. Micheval raises his voice to advocate for the collective concerns of Black Harlemites but does not give speeches as a leader would in the traditional sense. Women are seldom represented; the only women present are the wives of the LeMoor men, who help their husbands run the bookstore. Dumas's minimizing the visual and aural spaces of Black women within "Riot or Revolt?" emphasizes the male-centered orientation I discussed in the book's introduction. Moreover, what Brittney Cooper argues is "the subordination of Black women's political issues to the more pressing concerns of a Black male-centered liberation narrative" (Cooper 121). The examination of political activism in response to police brutality mainly becomes the fight that Black men fight—the LeMoor brothers, and later, Harold. Black female voices are silenced, leaving inaudible their concerns regarding state-sanctioned violence in their communities. In the next section, I discuss Dumas's exploration of racial violence and how (mainly) Black men fight against it in his texts. Also, I discuss racism from the perspective of Dumas's death as a result of police violence.

THE AFTERLIFE OF DUMAS: CIVIL UNREST AND THE WILL TO FIGHT POLICE BRUTALITY

On May 23, 1968, Dumas was shot and killed by New York City subway transit cop Peter Bienkowski in Harlem. According to the *Amsterdam News*, Dumas was in a heated confrontation with an unidentified man when Bienkowski approached both men about disturbing the peace. The transit cop alleged that Dumas "slashed" him, and he shot and killed Dumas in self-defense ("Bury Man" 13). As told by Dumas's biographer Jeffrey Leak, "Henry's death did not make it to the obituary desk at the *New York Times*, but it was broadcast over the radio" (Leak 152). The Black newspaper *Amsterdam News* printed the obituary, and a (Black) radio station announced his death. The questions about Dumas's death in later accounts of it remained unanswered. As noted by Leak, the evidence detailing Dumas's death "was destroyed in a bureaucratic merger in the 1990s" (2). Neither the cop nor the State of New York ever answered for Dumas's death. He became another statistic, or in the words of Huey P. Newton, "a thing, a beast, a nonentity, something to be ignored or stepped on" (Newton, "Fear and Doubt" 78). The cop's claim of self-defense portrayed Dumas within the mythology of the "the super-predator." This myth "not only acts to legitimize the violence responsible for black male deaths . . . [but] [Black] male death is necessary and an indispensable strategy for the safety and security of American society" (Curry, "Michael Brown" 3–4). Social media was not around in 1968 at the time of Dumas's death. Today, grassroots protests that spread through social media challenge the super-predator myth, as was the case, for example, in 2014 when black youth Michael Brown was gunned down by a cop in Ferguson, Missouri. The cop alleged he feared for his life—although there is ample evidence that Brown was running away when the encounter occurred. As Barbara Ransby notes, "Michael Brown was not a saint. [However], in the resistance that followed his death, organizers insisted he did not have to be" (Ransby 49). Black Lives Matter protesters deemed Brown's life worthy of recognition, deserving of justice because he was an American citizen. For Dumas, there were no public protests and calls for justice. His family was left to mourn his fate and question the account of how he died. As his aunt Mary Gillens noted, "[Dumas] became a civil rights activist after serving in the Korean War with the Air Force, but it's hard for me to believe he would fight a cop" ("Bury Man" 13). During the CRM's early years of advocating for civil rights, Dumas was a member of the NAACP's New Brunswick chapter and served as publicity chairman in 1961 (Leak 60). During that time, Dumas advocated against funding school segregation during John F. Kennedy's administration. In addition, he supported Black Tennessee sharecroppers who lost their homes, and employment while protesting two years for voting rights. According to Jeffrey Leak, Dumas visited Somerville, Tennessee, "to interview and deliver much-needed items he had collected from the black community surrounding New Brunswick to black families displaced from their homes" (60). Dumas took an interest in supporting racial injustice; however, when it came to his life, to the world at large, his life seemingly did not matter.

Following the death of Dumas, his widow Loretta Dumas appointed BAM poet Eugene B. Redmond, a writer and friend of Dumas, as literary executor of her late husband's estate. In 1970 Redmond oversaw the publication of many of Dumas's writings, including the poetry collections *Ark of Bones* and *Poetry for My People*, both co-edited by Hale Chatfield.[4] Other books such as *Play Ebony, Play Ivory* (1974), *Rope of Wind and Other Stories* (1979), and *Goodbye, Sweetwater* (1988) would follow in a resurgence of Dumas's work. In 1988 the *Black American Literature Forum* published a special issue titled "Henry Dumas," which Redmond edited. The issue featured celebrated writers and poets of the 1960s and 1970s such as Margaret Walker Alexander, Maya Angelou, Baraka, and Toni Morrison, and an essay by Russell Atkins titled "Henry Dumas: An Appreciation." Atkins criticizes Dumas for being too political and argues that politics obscured Dumas's true literary talents. He asserts that "[Dumas] chose to be too responsible and expended time on directions diverging somewhat from his real talent but in line with feelings that interfered" (Atkins 159). He goes on to say that "[When] you feel strongly about injustices, it may be better sometimes not to allow them to distract the art" (159). Atkins condemned Dumas's participation in the civil rights movement as a distraction from his "real talent" but never thinks to connect Dumas's keen interest in Black politics with his literary works.

A year before Dumas's tragic death, he lamented that he "was very much concerned about what is happening to [his] people and what we are doing with our precious tradition," in *Black Fire: An Anthology of Afro-American Writing* (Dumas, "Biography" 661). This "precious tradition," according to Clyde Taylor, was "the mythic vision of Dumas's art," which would lay the foundation for a new "concept of Black writing that was emerging" (C. Taylor 354). As a result, toward the end of his life Dumas realized that he was deeply affected by the assassination of King. During one of his last known poetry performances before his untimely death, he performed "Our King Is Dead" at the Celebrity Room in East St. Louis (Redmond 152). Dumas laments the void that widens as the death toll of Black American leaders rises:

> you killed our prophets
> our princes and our warriors
> Marcus, Malcolm, and Martin
> you do not want us to have a king
> I am ready to die if dying
> means that we have our king. (Dumas, "Our King" 20–25)

Leak posits that Dumas had experienced immense turmoil by the time "Our King Is Dead" was recited in front of Redmond and other poets at the Celebrity Room. Despite Dumas's pain, he successfully translates his civil rights activism and social work experience into Black American literature. Atkins must not have anticipated any more unpublished writings from Dumas's arsenal. But Amiri Baraka hints at it in his tribute to Dumas, asserting "[he] was an underground deity, glowing in ascension into post-material recognition" (Baraka, "The Works" 161). In fact, "Riot or Revolt?" was published in 2003, in a short story collection edited by John S. Wright titled *Echo Tree: The Collected Short Fiction of Henry Dumas*. As Baraka explained decades before the release of *Echo Tree*, "art is the life of people, society, and nature. The theme is always our real lives in actual society" (Baraka, "Henry Dumas" 165). What Baraka taps into that Atkins overlooks is how Dumas's experiences within Black political circles affected his attention to it in his art, exemplifying what the BAM stood for in the mid-1960s and 1970s. It relates to what Neal referred to as the "concern with the relationship between art and politics" (Neal, "The Black Arts Movement" 55). Part of Dumas's work, as reflected in *Echo Tree*, was about racial violence specifically as it related to police and (white) vigilantes. Dumas's short story "Riot or Revolt?" advocates a Black politics that unearths prominent themes among Black literary and social circles past and present. Seemingly, the next section analyzes the pride and reverence of Black bookstores as the primary locus of intellectuality and social consciousness during the Black Power era. Additionally, the section examines integration, its contentious presence within Black politics, and how it culminates in both fictive and non-fictive Black discourses.

THE POLITICS OF INTEGRATION AND EDUCATION

The 1954 *Brown v. Board of Education* decision by the Supreme Court ended legal segregation in American schools. However, by the end of the 1960s, little had changed in Black America in terms of educational improvement for Black youths. Segregation still operated post-*Brown*, and the uptick in white violent extremism against integration and police brutality in Black communities surged. As noted by Elizabeth Anderson, "white Americans, while claiming to agree in principle with its goals, in practice vigorously resisted policies that would achieve more than token integration of their neighborhoods and schools" (Anderson 1).[5] Some Black Americans, fed up with the United States' broken promises of equality and inclusion, resisted the practice of nonviolence led by the CRM. Instead, they responded to white supremacy militantly, opposing segregation by protesting frequently and participating in racial uprisings in reaction to the violence and murders of Black people committed by white vigilantes and brutal police.

Malcolm X conveyed America's history of violence as a template for Black America to "get independence" and justice by seeking revolution. Shabazz's charge was not through accommodation or integration, but by resisting American colonial power and taking their grievances to the United Nations, an authority that would serve as the best tactic for Black folks to guarantee their human rights in the United States. He argues in his speech "The Black Revolution" that "revolutions overturn systems" (Malcolm X, "Black Revolution" 48). Thus, because 1964 would be an explosive year met with "much racial violence and much racial bloodshed," the Black revolt will be uncompromising in their Black nationalist goal of achieving full repair of Black America (50). As noted by Errol A. Henderson, "In 1964 [Malcolm X] championed the mainstream CRM's efforts toward desegregation and offered support to SNCC's initiative in the South. During that time, he also promoted black electoral participation and an independent black political party" (E. Henderson 3). Malcolm X's ideology veered slightly away from black separatism and integration. The central tenets of his Black nationalism remained—resistance through armed struggle and self-defense as a means of overthrowing the American "colonial power" that undermined Black Americans' access to "freedom, justice, equality, or human dignity" (Malcolm X, "Black Revolution" 51). Malcolm's readings of self-determination and armed struggle in Africa, Latin America, and Asia against European colonial powers crystallized his argument for a Black revolution that should not "be confined to the shores of America" but actualized through an international context. As Henderson further asserts, "the *black* revolution was part of an international struggle against white supremacy—especially against Western imperialism—which was evident in anti-colonial struggles through Africa, Asia, and Latin America" (E. Henderson 8). Black nationalism within the US context was trivialized as a separatist political philosophy, particularly by those who believed that militant Black nationalists were setting back the momentum for racial equality by engaging in practices of alienation and isolation from the larger CRM, whose aim was for further integration into US society. Malcolm X refuted these perceptions about Black nationalism, suggesting instead that the real Black revolution is a revolt carried through by nonwhite people to remove the European "colonizing powers" from their countries (Malcolm X, "Black Revolution" 50). Including Black American liberation within this internationalization of the Black revolution, Malcolm X positioned Black nationalism as the cornerstone of revolution.

In 1964 the US government's efforts to suppress Black America's right to claim full citizenship had been made fully evident to Malcolm X. After his departure that year from the Nation of Islam, Malcolm X toured the United States before making several trips abroad, first to the Middle East, where he made his pilgrimage to Mecca, then to Africa and Europe. Through his campaign of Black nationalism, his first effort would be in the form of a voter-registration drive in Harlem, to attract masses of Black voters to vote independent rather than voting through the established two-party system (Republican or Democrat). He believed, as stated in his speech "Ballot or the Bullet," that Black people must unify and vote in their own best interests as independents, because the current political system is corrupted and controlled by white liberals who "have controlled the civil rights movement" (Malcolm X, *The Militant* 1). Malcolm X's ideology ran contrary to many in the CRM because their solution for guaranteeing the equality of Black America meant the full inclusion of Black Americans within US democracy without limitations based on race. Civil rights leaders such as King, Bayard Rustin, Whitney Young, and others believed that the only way to achieve Black inclusivity in white America was to form interracial coalitions, particularly coalitions with white liberals, in order to appear nonthreatening and to guarantee financial support to maintain their civil rights causes. Between 1954 and 1963, the successes of *Brown v. Board*, the Montgomery Bus Boycott, the sit-ins, and the March on Washington for Jobs and Freedom catapulted the momentum for racial equality in the United States among an interracial coalition of civil rights leaders who made substantial progress in claiming full citizenship for Black Americans. Conversely, Malcolm X argued that "the entire civil rights struggle needs a new interpretation, a broader interpretation" ("The Ballot or the Bullet" 31).

In practice, Malcolm's brand of Black nationalism would unify various Black people with different political and ideological tactics for realizing freedom. In particular, coalition-building between Black integrationists and separatists, Christians and Muslims, and southerners and northerners was essential to the success of his Organization for Afro-American Unity (OAAU). Black people would organize and protest together in the interests of Black America in "support of such things as rent strikes, school boycotts, [and] repeal of frisk and no-knock laws" that were regulated by the US government in the interest of white racists' backlash to Black progress (Malcolm X, *The Militant* 1). Malcolm's attempt to unite Black leadership from many different vantage points through the OAAU was his way of igniting a call for Black action to demand the US government act upon redistributing wealth and power to Black Americans denied to them during slavery and Jim Crow. Accordingly, as William Sales Jr. puts it, "The OAAU's strategy was to achieve the unification of all people of African descent in the world and use this unity to create an organizational structure that could impact on the world on behalf of Black people" (Sales 254). As Malcolm X asserted, the United States had repeatedly failed to repair Black America economically through reparations or politically through full voter representation. As stated previously in chapter 1, Malcolm X aligns Black struggle not with civil rights but with human rights. Also, he demands that Black America bring forth their case to the United Nations because "whenever you are in a civil-rights struggle, whether you know it or not, you are confining yourself to the jurisdiction of Uncle Sam. No one from the outside world can speak on your behalf as long as your struggle is a civil rights struggle" ("The Ballot or the Bullet" 34). Malcolm X pinpoints precisely the limited advocacy, or the lack thereof, of actual civil rights. Black nationalism's tenets of self-determination and self-defense served as the impetus for Malcolm X's call for Black America's proactive response to (white) America, and a sect of Black Americans agreed and followed suit. Some Black Americans would tread the line of nonviolent and Black nationalist ideologies that would characterize the remainder of the 1960s.

But 1964 was a volatile year met with racial division, contentious national politics, countless acts of police brutality, and vigilante violence. It was the year that President Lyndon B. Johnson signed into law the Civil Rights Act, which prohibited individuals and organizations from discriminating against American citizens based on race, color, religion, sex, or national origin and guaranteed full protection under the law. On July 16, 1964, two weeks after Lyndon B. Johnson signed the bill, a riot occurred in Harlem following the death of fifteen-year-old James "Jimmy" Powell. Off-duty Lieutenant Thomas Gilligan shot Powell. Gilligan claimed that Powell, a Bronx native, was following and harassing an apartment superintendent who had sprayed him and fellow students with a water hose. Powell attended summer school at Robert E. Wagner Sr. Junior High School in Manhattan's Upper East Side—an upper-middle-class white neighborhood and business district (Abu-Lughod 171). Gilligan shot Powell three times. When Black folks in Harlem learned about the fatal shooting, protesters gathered for a rally against police brutality. Riots followed in Harlem; Bedford-Stuyvesant, Brooklyn; and Rochester, New York. These riots were in response to the shooting and the city's failure to arrest and charge Gilligan (174). The circumstances surrounding the riot left an unprecedented tension between Black Americans and police officers. Henry Dumas's "Riot or Revolt?" takes elements of the murder and riot that followed, informing readers on the first page, "a youth had been slain by police in Brooklyn" (Dumas, "Riot or Revolt?" 362).

The Harlem–Bedford Stuyvesant riot lasted two days and became a pivotal moment during the CRM. King argued for an increase in Black law enforcement to alleviate the mounting racial tension between white officers and Black Americans, contending that the New York City riots were "not so much . . . an anti-white revolt as . . . an anti-police revolt" (King, "WSB-TV").[6] He further contended that Americans "have failed to grapple with the depths of discontent and resentment where the Negro is concerned toward police forces and particularly police brutality" (King, "WSB-TV"). His solution to end police brutality and discontent in Black communities was to increase Black employment in law enforcement. Based on King's comments from the WSB-TV interview, he assumes that the increase of Black police in law enforcement will address systemic racism by making police departments fair and accountable for how they police Black citizens. But King's assertion presumes that increasing Black representation in law enforcement will address the anti-Black racism in policing that is endemic in police culture. King's audacious approach neglects to consider that Black police in the 1960s, as Beryl Satter contends, "were used as a 'colonial guard' to contain crime within black communities, smooth police-community tensions, infiltrate black organizations, and feed information about black life to white police" (Satter 1111). In contrast, Malcolm X, who was in Cairo, Egypt, during the 1964 riots, stated that the New York Police department's quelling of the riots in Harlem was a "case of outright scare tactics" that could "escalate into something very serious" if not resolved (Malcolm X, qtd. in Peter Kihss 17). More precisely, Malcolm X's call for a Black revolution pinpoints Black America's impatience with the CRM's methods of integration into mainstream US society.

As a result, Malcolm X's speeches about integration within Black America raised concerns about the conflicts between middle-class and working-class Black Americans. In his speech "Twenty Million Black People in a Political, Economic, and Mental Prison," Malcolm X tells his audience:

> There are two types of Negroes in this country. There's the bourgeois type who blinds himself to the condition of his people, and who is satisfied with token solutions. He's in the minority. He's a handful. He's usually the handpicked Negro who benefits from token integration. But the masses of Black people who really suffer the brunt of brutality and the conditions that exist in this country are represented by the leadership of the Honorable Elijah Muhammad. (Malcolm X, "The Last Speeches" 37)

Malcolm X's speech recited in 1963, a year before he left the Nation of Islam, not only pushed a Black agenda, of which white America disapproved, but it also placed the middle and working classes of Black America at odds with one another. His criticism of integration was that all Black Americans who are better off economically, regardless of their religious beliefs, will likely benefit from integration over those who are working class, and especially poor. The implication here is that integration becomes a divisive tool within the Black American community that separates each person based on their social, economic, and political status. Kwame Ture and Charles V. Hamilton reach similar conclusions but advance Malcolm X's point by addressing white liberal society's hand in the matter. They go on to say, "we are not now speaking of whites who have worked to get black people 'accepted' on an individual basis, by white society . . . [too] often those efforts are geared to the same false premises as integration; too often the society in which they seek acceptance of a few black people can afford to make the gesture" (Ture and Hamilton 81–82). In other words, integration becomes a site in which the ethnic-racial order is maintained. As Elizabeth Anderson notes, the fact remains then and now "that blacks live several years less than whites, that 13 percent of black men are disenfranchised due to a felony conviction, and that more than one-third of black children live in poverty" (Anderson 2). "Riot or Revolt?" interrogates this politics of integration; the characters exhaustively debate whether merging into the dominant society is beneficial to Black America or whether it will hinder the social justice causes toward racial equality.

Symbolically, the integration laws of the 1960s changed the understanding of race relations in America today. For example, Barack Obama, the first Black president, cemented large voter turnout from liberal white Americans. As Farah Jasmine Griffin notes, the fact that "large numbers of white Americans voted for a qualified, intelligent black candidate certainly is evidence of progress. It is proof that large portions of white America are becoming less racist. But less racist does not mean post-racial" (Griffin, "At Last . . . ?"133). According to Clarence Lang, President Obama appeased these voters by lecturing to poor and working-class Black Americans "about their overreliance on government and their dysfunctional childrearing, especially with regard to undervaluing education, allowing the television set to babysit children" (Lang 81).[7] Lang analyzes Obama's critique as an ethos of racial uplift and respectability that bypasses the central issues of mass incarceration, mass unemployment, substandard education, and inadequate housing and healthcare that disproportionally affects these communities (79).[8] Overall, Obama's commentary on Black Americans' behavior reasserted racial stereotypes that fit within the social fabric of American race relations. During President Obama's second term, he continued this line of commentary when giving a speech at the fiftieth anniversary of the March on Washington for Jobs and Freedom. He reflected:

We'll admit that during the course of 50 years, there were times when some of us claiming to push for change lost our way. The anguish of assassinations set off self-defeating riots. Legitimate grievances against police brutality tipped into excuse-making for criminal behavior. Racial politics could go both ways, as the transformative message of unity and brotherhood was drowned out by the language of recrimination. And what had once been a call for equality and opportunity, the chance for all Americans to work hard and get ahead, was too often framed as a mere desire for government support—as if we had no agency in our own liberation, as if poverty was an excuse for not raising your child, and the bigotry of others was reason to give up on yourself. (Obama, "Barack Obama's Speech")

Here, President Obama praises the nonviolent CRM for their moral protest and respectable ways of advocating for equality, but condemns the BPM for rioting, government dependency, and evoking a "language of recrimination." Although President Obama stated that protests against police brutality in the quote above could be legitimate, using Black Americans' behavior as a scapegoat for police misconduct presents a benign neglect approach to anti-Black violence. Obama's words illustrate what Lester K. Spence and Clarence Lang point to earlier within a neoliberal America that blames Black Americans for their Blackness, as opposed to confronting how systemic racism normalizes Black oppression.

In addition to the integration discussion and how it manifests in Black life then and now, Black bookstores during the 1960s became important sites where young activists came together to cultivate their grassroots ideologies. As the need for Black political education became increasingly important, bookstores served as the home base for community discussions. When the governor asks Micheval in "Riot or Revolt?" what he hopes to achieve from owning a bookstore in Harlem, Micheval answers, "Pride dressed in knowledge" (Dumas, "Riot or Revolt?" 375). The slogan includes two concepts promoted throughout the mid-1960s during the rise of the Black Power Movement. Black pride was a celebration of culture and a counter-hegemonic response to the Anglo-American culture that was the social fabric of US identity. Knowledge, or education, was always valued in Black American communities but especially so during post-emancipation, when education became legal for Black Americans to pursue.[9] Black people used intellectualism as a strategy to gain citizenship and become American.

For example, the Black Panther Party for Self-Defense, founded by Huey P. Newton and Bobby Seale in 1966, developed what David Hillard called "liberation schools" for youth as "an opportunity to be amongst the children and start a conversation, and stimulate their minds to seeing clearly the state of repression that [they] are living in" (Hillard 36). Former Panther Ericka Huggins and scholar-activist Angela D. LeBlanc-Ernest assert that "community education, specifically education for young people, was central to its vision" (Huggins and LeBlanc-Ernest 161). The liberation schools based their curriculum on revolutionary action and culture. This curriculum meant that youth participants often read newspapers and wrote essays about various social and political happenings in the United States and abroad. Also, students were tasked with reciting orations about poor people, exploitation, police brutality, political prisoners, and the worldwide struggle for freedom (Hillard 36). Such education for these children ages ten to thirteen often supplemented their underfunded public education. The liberation schools grew throughout California and later transformed into community schools in Oakland.[10] These schools were instrumental in cultivating young minds to think critically about the social and political disadvantages of marginalized people throughout the world.

The Black Panthers' liberation schools and the uptick in Black bookstores during the 1960s coincided with the rise of Black political consciousness. As Joshua Clark Davis notes, "black booksellers promoted African American political reeducation and knowledge of self through books, pamphlets, and journals on black nationalism and pan-Africanism" that would "empower black Americans to recover their lost heritage and history as proud peoples of the African Diaspora" (J. Davis 37).[11] Similarly, Colin A. Beckles contends that "certain black bookstores functioned as institutional 'Pan-African sites of resistance' in order to politicize the Black community" (Beckles 63–64). In contrast, some other Black bookstores were created for economic opportunity or both. The fictional LeMoor bookstore in Dumas's short story functions as a site for economic growth. Also, the bookstore serves as space where Micheval and Carib can cultivate political education. The fictitious bookstore paid homage to the impact of Lewis Michaux's National Memorial African Bookstore, which was central to grounding patrons in Black politics, championing Africana history, and building community.[12] The LeMoor bookstore is a public space known as a knowledge hub where Black Harlemites discuss and practice politics, to achieve a radical transformation of self and community. Deborah Atwater and Sandra Herndon define the use of public space, Black American museums in particular, as sites that "can display and reveal the intersection of race and culture in the recovery of a society's historical and cultural memory" (Atwater and Herndon 69). Moreover, as Joshua Clark Davis asserts, the Black bookstore also functioned as space for "activist groups wishing to hold meetings and distribute their own locally produced media and flyers, authors and poets who gave public readings, and reading groups that met to discuss books" (J. Davis 38). Micheval's mission for the bookstore to be "pride dressed in knowledge" is an example of how the slogan transforms the public space into a site of knowledge exchange.

The bookstore is a sacred space, where owners such as the LeMoors built community and made their patrons critically aware of the issues of the day, such as integration and police brutality. The bookstore is also a building where knowledge is cultivated and disseminated to people who want to learn about Black history. Maisha T. Fisher alludes to this point when she says, "the method of sharing and exchanging knowledge through culturally distinct literary practices is considered as important as the knowledge itself" (Fisher 84). When the riot erupts in Harlem, Harold notices that the bookstore "had not been touched by the crowds" (Dumas, "Riot or Revolt?" 362). He remembered a person shouting not to touch the bookstore. LeMoor's bookstore goes unscathed not because it is merely a Black bookstore, but because it is a conduit for conveying culture, heritage, and tradition and is the very symbol of protest.

As Black Power began to decline, so did Black bookstores. According to Joshua Clark Davis, "Only at the end of the 1980s did a new wave of black radical writings help black bookstores rebound" (J. Davis 39). However, with the growth of monopoly supply chains such as Barnes & Noble and Amazon by the late 1990s, according to Davis, "just 17 percent" of independent bookstores, both Black and white, survived (J. Davis 79). With that said, only 54 Black bookstores remain today.[13] The centrality of bookstores within Black radical politics of the 1960s becomes evident through an examination of Dumas's "Riot or Revolt?" In the next section, I provide a close reading of the story that not only illuminates the significance of black bookstores but also highlights Dumas's major political concerns with police brutality, integration, and political education. He deploys his creative art as a tool to advocate for Black liberation and challenge the neoliberal social order.

"RIOT OR REVOLT?": A CLOSE READING

In Dumas's short story, art and grassroots activism is the solution to ending state-sponsored violence in Harlem. As a response to police brutality that resulted in the harm or death of Black men, women, and children, civil unrest occurred through the mid- to late 1960s in predominantly Black-urban neighborhoods, which was thoroughly documented by the Kerner

Report. "Riot or Revolt?" signals this will to fight against police brutality through rioting as the shift in nonviolent practices of protest transitioned to militant protest in Black communities. The short story highlights this shift while dramatizing how the act of resistance liberates and activates a radical sensibility to fight oppression. At one point, Micheval tells state and city leaders:

> I must say that no amount of persuasion is going to convince me that the city and state officials don't know what's going on. When a Negro boy is shot and killed by policemen who do not check the situation before pulling their guns, the people get angry. It is simple. I have no special message from God about the thing. I'm not a preacher. It is a simple law of nature. The people get tired of dying. (Dumas, "Riot or Revolt?" 377)

Micheval addresses the local and state officials by telling them why Black people are angry and why their actions have led them to riot in protest. The Mayor overlooks Micheval's point and instead understands "that the rioting is spontaneous, and the mobs have no organized leadership" (376). Similarly, rather than focusing on the causation of the rioting, the governor focuses on "all of the damage [that] seems to be done to targets that seem to be patterned. But the white merchants are bearing the brunt of the attacks" (376). The state officials' responses raise points I observe in secondary inter- pretations of rioting in this book's introduction. For instance, Peter LaBrie observes that "[t]he white business and political leaders of the cities cannot stand for widespread looting and rioting because it means the destruction of their properties and disturbing their political and social positions" (LaBrie 75). Furthermore, Mehrsa Baradaran examines Black rioters' ending of debts with white creditors by burning and looting their stores (Baradaran 143). The actions that the fictional characters describe do not center the infraction that Black Harlemites are making. Micheval raises the social and political concerns of the community and the recurring nature of police brutality. During the 1960s, when a riot would break out, many government leaders believed that chosen leaders were in place to address the concerns of Black Americans during racial conflicts that involved Black American residents and the predominantly white police force. Ben Caldwell makes a precise observation of this fact in *Riot Sale, or Dollar Psyche Fake Out*. Because of this perception, Gail Williams O'Brien cogently states, "there were ways that black people, including leaders, were supposed to conduct themselves around whites, and that deportment extended to speech" (O'Brien 148).[14]

Black Americans were treated as second-class citizens, even in situations where civil rights politics were at the forefront of the agenda.

Micheval, adamant about the local and state officials recognizing his citizenship, assumes no responsibility for leading the effort to eradicate violence or hate crimes in his community. As the bookstore owner, he makes sure that he sells books but also converses with citizens in the community about life in Harlem. The scene between Micheval and the governor points to the reasons that state officials want to intervene. Micheval is exercising his American right to choose what he will, or will not, do in this particular racial incident. His response to the governor provides an answer to the public's outcry. The Black majority is tired of compromising their civil liberties against violent cops. Micheval's unwillingness to continue his participation in solving the matter places the responsibility on government officials, who should handle the issue reasonably. His reluctance to participate in reform by placing the blame on local and state officials reverses the neoliberal tactics of what Lester K. Spence refers to as "secondary governmentalization," which "is the attempts of African Americans to problem solve their own conduct" (Spence, "Neoliberal Turn" 140). Placing such responsibility on Micheval, and the rest of the community, suggests that police brutality is mostly a Black issue that the Black community has to solve. Local and state officials fail to take responsibility and ownership of the structural racism at work; Dumas's short story is an example of how Spence argues "neoliberalization starkly increases inequality," and leaves police brutality against Black Americans unchecked (141). While the police's actions go unchecked, the LeMoor Bookstore is an alternative space where concerns surrounding integration, inequality, and its effects on Black living spaces, such as Harlem, are openly expressed. One particular conversation in the bookstore shifts to a contested debate about integration and economic instability among Black Americans in Harlem. When Micheval shows that people only gather in his bookstore when there is trouble, a customer responds, "cause ain't nothing in Harlem or any other black ghetto but trouble! . . . You got to have trouble and riots for us to get what rightly belong to us" (Dumas, "Riot or Revolt?" 369–70). Micheval disagrees with him and argues that the economic and class divide between Black Americans and non-Blacks in Harlem is the reason that Black Americans have not progressed in society. He supports his opinion with a personal anecdote about entering into business at the same time as his Jewish counterpart:

Thirty years ago I moved into this goddam store; we moved in and a Jew moved in next door. We went into business on the same goddam day! Mind you! Now here I come like a damn fool selling n----rs a little knowledge. Do you know what that Jew was selling? Today that man has got a million n----r's dollars in his pocket. He wines and dines on the French Riviera, goes off on long vacations. I haven't seen him in Harlem in fifteen years, but he still owns the place. (370)

The Jewish storeowner was selling "hair grease, pomades, and conk juice" (370). As a result of the Jewish storeowner's successful business venture, he established a manufacturing company for Black hair care in downtown Manhattan and Chicago. The larger concern brought forth by Micheval is twofold. On the one hand, it is the economic control that Jewish storeowners have over Black buying power. On the other hand, it is Micheval's articulation of the Jewish owners' embodied whiteness and how it operates in his pre-dominantly Black neighborhood. Since the 1890s, when the size of the Black American middle class in northern cities increased, class has been at the center of these debates. According to Joe Williams Trotter Jr., "Ordinary black workers responded to exploitation and racial discrimination in a variety of ways . . . [t]heir responses also recognized limitations of cross-class alliances" (Trotter 67).[15] In line with these observations, since the early 1900s, Jewish immigrants, and their descendants, purchased housing, rental, and retail properties throughout Harlem. The Jewish community was able to establish economic control in Harlem by the time Black Americans began living in the borough. Jonathan Kaufman asserts that after 1966, Jewish and Black American relations became intense and conflicting: "Federal studies after the riots were over indicated that Jews owned 30 percent of stores in these ghetto neighborhoods" (Kaufman 111).[16] Because of Jewish economic control, Black American business owners had a smaller share of the market. Moreover, the Black American consumer became reliant on Jewish businesses. While Black Americans were appreciative, they "had a far more ambivalent view of Jews, shaped by economic contact that almost always put Blacks one step below Jews on the urban economic ladder" (109). Eric L. Goldstein underscores Kaufman's point: "[i]n a society where the color line played a major role in determining social status, Jews had been able to achieve a high level of success and integration by the 1960s, while African Americans were often still fighting for basic freedoms" (Goldstein 1). Such a point does not overshadow the struggles with racism Jewish Americans experienced in the late nineteenth and early twentieth centuries. However, Micheval's position raises the complicated way racial minorities that could access whiteness often gained access to American wealth in ways that Black Americans were denied. For example, Langston Hughes addressed the economic imbalance that Black

Americans experienced in 1960s Harlem. He raised concerns about economic injustice, questioning why "the prices for food in Harlem are higher than anywhere else in Manhattan. A 3-cent lemon downtown is a 5-cent lemon uptown. Why? On 125th Street's long business artery, less than half a dozen shops are owned by Negroes" (Hughes 215).[17] Hughes's example points to Black Americans paying more for fruit than non-Blacks living in other parts of Manhattan. Moreover, the nominal businesses that Black people own in Harlem at the time diminishes their ability to make wise economic choices about purchasing fruit if they choose to buy in their neighborhood. Black entrepreneurs competing with white businesspersons for a Black market in a capitalistic society become what Manning Marable once called "the linchpin of underdevelopment and capital accumulation within the Black community" (Marable 123). Black business owners were the foundation to the economic enterprises in urban cities throughout the twentieth century and, as noted by St. Clair Drake and Horace R. Cayton, "constituted almost half of all the businesses in Negro neighborhoods, [but] they received less than a tenth of all the money spent by Negroes" (Drake and Cayton 438). Moreover, Black business owners were discriminated against in lending practices by paying predatory loans and rents, so that the higher prices required by Black business owners in order to turn a profit were shifted to the Black consumer. As noted in chapter 3, although Harlem is the world's largest Black empire full of artistic expression and political engagement, Sanchez in *Bronx* and Dumas in "Riot or Revolt?" reveal in their texts that Black Americans living in the Black Mecca experienced economic injustice and police brutality that diminished their quality of life, thus overshadowing the contributions they made decades prior.

In addition, Dumas explores the effects of integration using the LeMoor bookstore as a site of contestation by having their Harlem community members debate whether or not the United States should be integrated. On the one hand, some Black Harlemites argue that integration is necessary for social and political advancement in the United States. On the other hand, Micheval contends that while integration will promote Black Americans to full citizenship, inequality in education, entrepreneurship, and access to wealth will remain the same. As Mehrsa Baradaran denotes, "ending segregation was not the same as integration" (Baradaran 137). In the bookstore, a Black male in support of integration exclaims, "as soon as integration comes, the American dream will be the truth and not a dream" (Dumas, "Riot or Revolt?" 373). He believes that integration will bring true equality to Black Americans. However, Micheval argues that integration is a ploy, an "interest convergence" whereby "the interest of blacks achieving racial equality will be accommodated only when it converges with the interests of whites," as defined by Derrick Bell (Bell 22). Micheval's comments support Bell's claim when he states:

The Negro preachers have been spitting that brainwashing powder out to baptize n----rs' heads since 1954. What integration? You can't legislate and regiment this thing. If you want to be swallowed up by the majority in this country, then go ahead with your integration. I wouldn't want it if it could work. It's only a trick my friend, a trick. The man knows he's on the downgrade and he's letting everything go into the war now. He'll even stoop down and let a few n----rs into the melting pot. But it's all a trick. The whole concept of democracy ain't integration. It is brotherhood, and the rule of the majority, and the right of each individual to his own. (Dumas, "Riot or Revolt?" 373)

Micheval's critiquing of integration rest on his disagreement with the involvement of the Black American clergy and the middle class advocating for it. He decidedly calls integration a "brotherhood" and a "rule of the majority," implying that integration is white male brotherhood—where the white majority still controls the American system. Much of Micheval's opposition to integration is that it cannot truly achieve racial equality because it will impact the societal privilege of white America. And Derrick Bell's comment alludes to Micheval's point, claiming that "whites may agree in the abstract that blacks are citizens and are entitled to constitutional protection against racial discrimination, but few are willing to recognize that racial segregation is much more than a series of quaint customs that can be remedied effectively without altering the status of whites" (Bell 22). In the 1940s, Drake and Cayton arrived at the same points made by Bell in the late 1970s that when white America is challenged with Blacks' demands for full participation in the US economy, Blacks are met with strong pushback.[18] As a result, "Negro businessmen and community leaders stress the dogmas of racial solidarity in an effort to amass capital and patronage" (Drake and Cayton 437). The economic limitations of this business model illustrated that within a capitalistic society, Black Americans do not achieve the privileges of economic success for the long term because they are still competing with enterprises owned by whites that have more capital and credit due to systemic racism. While democracy is about the individual's right to own, buy, and live freely, integration does not close the gap in Black America's wealth deficit. As Bell states, it "fails to encompass the complexity of achieving equal educational opportunity" (22) as well as business and ownership opportunities for Black Americans who were denied access for so long.

In the LeMoor bookstore, Micheval and Carib give every famous Black woman, man, girl, and boy visiting the bookstore a portrait. Each painting symbolizes pride in Black life and culture that will last for generations. Harold is waiting to display his portrait in the bookstore. At this moment, Harold is in the bookstore basement and walks with Carib LeMoor while the riot erupts outside. To protect Harold, Carib whisks him away while sirens wail, and shots are fired (Dumas, "Riot or Revolt?" 380). As Harold runs down the steps to the LeMoor basement, a customer asks Carib, "are they rioting outside, Mr. Lemoor?" (380). Carib does not respond to the patron. When Harold enters the room in the basement, he is happy about what he sees. In the cellar, "Harold heard the sounds from outside, but saw all the paintings, all the photographs of the famous Negroes, Africans and Asians, all the various black people who had visited LeMoor's since the store was opened, saw them all swirling in the masses of people yelling loud under the August sun" (380). During this commotion, "all the black voices shouting in blood and sweat, lifting their souls up in a mighty wave, a mighty fervor, all syncopated" (381). After Harold and the protesters rise up the story ends, leaving readers to assume that this new generation of freedom fighters will follow in the spirit of activists who preceded them.

The history of rioting in Black American history, or revolt as Dumas has framed it, cannot be separated from the goal of freedom. Black America's insistence on revolution is part of the Black freedom struggle that is about civil rights and liberties that all people should have. Henry Dumas made clear in *Black Fire: An Anthology of Afro-American Writing* that he was concerned with the future of Black life and its tradition. In whichever way Dumas believed the circumstance of Black Americans and its history were in some form of crisis, "Riot or Revolt?" is a poignant story about art and grassroots activism as a method of revolt and that cooperative group action should be the goal. This type of activism requires Black American pride and knowledge of political education to confront police brutality and racial violence.

EPILOGUE

Young, or middle-aged Black men being shot by police . . . what
astonishes me is . . . not so many because there has always been a lot
just never been newsworthy . . . is the obvious cowardice of the police,
not all police but the ones we hear about . . . how are you afraid of a
man running away from you? How are you afraid of someone standing in
the grocery store on a phone or with a toy gun you could buy in
the store . . . how could you be afraid of a little boy?

—TONI MORRISON, ON BALTIMORE: "TROUBLING AND COWARDLY" *TIME*, 2015[1]

In my book, I have highlighted the critical works of BAM artists and writers that examine civil unrest. Precisely, how these artist-writers understand riot as an explorative site to address the unresolved remnants of social justice claims from the CRM and BPM eras—issues that continue to reappear in present-day US politics and discourse. I also examine how the BAM's artistic production was and is a pathway for recognizing parallels within systemic racism, including poverty, police violence, and state surveillance, which have remained strong within many Black communities in America. In so doing, the Black Arts period engages us and, in particular, demands that we utilize literature as a resource to decode the fractures of neoliberalism and racism that strip Black lives of safety, comfort, and benevolence. Morrison's recollection of tragic police killings of Black men and boys, specifically during Baltimore's civil unrest after the death of Freddie Gray, echoes Langston Hughes's statement he made in the book's introduction about the death of James "Jimmy" Powell, who also died as a result of police violence. Morrison's questioning of actions made by actors of the state recalls the discontent that lingers from the Black civil unrest of the 1960s: Why are police officers afraid of unarmed civilians who are really afraid of them? Or, why are Black children viewed as threats when their bodies and maturity show that they are not adults, but are still violently treated as such? Tamir

Rice, a twelve-year-old from Cleveland, Ohio, was shot to death for waving in his hand a toy gun that appeared to police to be a real gun. Walter Scott, from Charleston, South Carolina, was shot dead after fleeing a traffic stop in fear of not only being charged for a ticket but, as his family claimed, for owing back child support, which would authorize an arrest. Not mentioned in Morrison's statements (she passed away in August 2019), but relevant to the discussion is the police killing of George Floyd in Minneapolis, Minnesota, which reignited an ongoing and more consistent act of riot and revolt that spans across the world. Similarly, Black women and girls who have died at the hands of the state, as recently as the police killing of Breonna Taylor, an emergency room technician whose home was sprayed with bullets after a no-knock drug warrant gone wrong;[2] Rekia Boyd, who was fatally shot by an off-duty police chief in Chicago; or Sandra Bland, who died alone in a Texas county jail after being arrested and racially violated by a policeman for a routine traffic stop that went wrong.

Such tragic incidents inform my aim to analyze BAM works and also to emphasize, as other BAM researchers have before me, how politics played a critical role in shaping the artistic development of the movement. In the twenty-first century, it has become abundantly clear that the drama, fiction, and poetry discussed in this book are committed to exploring Black art that is unapologetically radical and raw in terms of experimenting with topics that are still polemical in today's society.

I convey the same arguments about white businesses in Black neigh-borhoods in chapter 3 covering Sanchez's *The Bronx Is Next*; and the fight over property and Black human life is still a reality. As the Kerner Report of 1968 sought to "help understand and control the surge of uprisings that occurred in 1967 . . . to understand the problem with black people," the sentiment reemerged in the twenty-first century with President Obama's President's Task Force on 21st Century Policing, which also issued a report (Bentley-Edwards et al. 21). As Keisha Bentley-Edwards et al. argue, both "reports overlap in their focus on the causes, consequences, and the solutions for managing black rage" (21). Also, the reports overlap in terms of the task forces of each document not being proactive in making sure that such recommendations be implemented to prevent future riots from happening. As we knew in 1968, riots erupted after the assassination of Martin Luther King Jr. as outlined in Gwendolyn Brooks's *Riot*; and riots occur in 2015 through 2020 in Baltimore, Milwaukee, and Minneapolis-St. Paul, as indicated earlier. The treatment of riots in BAM texts, particularly Brooks's and Baraka/Caldwell's extensively examining Black rage, speak to Black

Americans' legitimate concerns when it came to a discussion about police and vigilante violence.

The legacy that BAM protest aesthetics leaves with us is exposing the condition of people's lives through racial and religious contexts. For example, the artist-writers featured in this book use art as a method to engage in the political difficulties that challenge our everyday freedoms past and present. The mid-1960s brought about a moment of contention within Black America in terms of delineating the failed promises of social, political, and economic upward mobility through the implementation of civil rights bills that were supposed to change the lived conditions of Black citizens—particularly the Black poor. Amid the internal frustration among Black Americans, many wrestled with ideologies of integration and revolution. At the same time, civil unrest undergirded the dissent looming out of Black communities reflected in riot-stricken cities. All of the artist-writers take up the discussion of race relations, particularly within Black America, in terms of addressing the origins of racism in US society and how Black people should connect that history to the contemporary realities of their existence in the 1960s—for example, Baraka's articulation of art acting as a method through which Black writers and artists must resist an urge to "merge with the oppressor for solace" (Baraka, "The Revolutionary Theatre" 21). Instead, Black people must embody a Blackness that is spiritually affirmative, rooted in revolution, and centered as a bridge between generations and must continue to deliver political messages that confront or overturn anti-Black sentiment in Western society. Black artists since the 1960s have responded to anti-racism by articulating social and political messages through their art that examine issues at the forefront of our current society. Such responses to anti-racism are a way these artist-writers continue to remake their identities to fit within the existing political moments that are shaping Black lives. As indicated by Margo Natalie Crawford, "black art (in its most innovative forms) is always a remaking of 'black' and 'post-black' within the layered circle of black post-blackness" (Crawford 2).[3] Crawford assesses that this refashioned Blackness is part of how Black artists and writers responded to the evolving growth of Black culture. I would add that within Black culture there remains a Black aesthetic that engages in a repeated conversation about citizenship, justice, and how Black people can lay claim to American identity. In chapter 4, examining Dumas's "Riot or Revolt?" I illustrate that the connection between the fictional representations of Black protest and present-day illustrations of #BLM protest is consistent, as each makes a direct point to redress the democratic wrongs that continue to be inflicted on the lives of Black Americans.

This book interrogates the ideological conflicts that divided Black communities' perspectives about civil unrest. Foregrounding the assassinations of Malcolm X and Martin Luther King Jr. and their ideological impact on the psyches of Black Americans, I pay particular attention to how their leadership and unfortunate deaths shaped the political content embedded within the literature. Also, I emphasize the racial uprisings that served as markers for addressing the revolutionary nationalism that artists and writers united around in their work. Malcolm X's influence in BAM works, as Carolyn Gerald notes, was a "growing status as the source at which to renew" Black America's "faith in [their] destiny" (Gerald 49). Malcolm X became a hero in Black communities, who followed his politics of self-determination and transformation through consciousness-raising of Black identity independent of Westernized constructions of Blackness. In 1964, following his departure from the Nation of Islam, Malcolm X formed the Muslim Mosque, Incorporated, and the Organization for Afro-American Unity (OAAU) to implement a Black nationalist agenda. This agenda intended to bring Black Americans together regardless of their religious, political, and social affiliations to combat racial oppression in American society and to internationalize the Black freedom struggle according to Malcolm X "by indicting the United States government before the United Nations" (Malcolm X, "The Black Revolution" 45). Such an audacious act by Shabazz put pressure on the US government to act on a civil rights agenda that would most effectively help Black Americans demand their full rights as US citizens. However, his untimely death cut short his vision for Black politics that would require human rights recognition. The impetus for a Black Arts Movement began in response to Malcolm X's assassination, in order to continue his mission in promoting self-determined Black people who would unapologetically celebrate their Blackness and claim self-defense in response to white violence. The death of Malcolm X inspired writers during the BAM to use art as a method to address Black America's rage and to argue for social change that would require America to admit its endemic racism. Analyzing Baraka's and Caldwell's plays pinpoint themes within BAM texts such as the meaning of Black rage to highlight how police brutality and vigilante violence were (and still are) threats to Black American life.

At the same time, Black Americans also identified with Martin Luther King Jr.'s philosophy of nonviolence and advocating for integration as a method to obtain economic and social resources that would improve the lives of Black men, women, and children. As noted by Clarence Lang, King's image and what he stood for in recent times became "a potent symbol of moral authority surpassing that even of US presidents . . . King's transformation into a civic saint" has eclipsed his own rage and fear that he may have integrated his people into a burning house (Lang 74).[4] In public memory, King's legacy has been remembered for his nonviolence rhetoric during his thirteen-year career as a public figure and leader of the CRM against racial injustice and economic inequality. He is the only Black American in history to receive a national federal holiday, and his 1963 *Time* magazine Man of the Year designation, as well as his 1964 Nobel Peace Prize, make King an undeniable figure in American history.[5] King's most played speeches on popular news media outlets such as CNN and MSNBC are "I Have a Dream," recited at the March on Washington for Jobs and Freedom, and "I've Been to the Mountaintop," recited in Memphis, Tennessee, in support of sanitation workers striking against unequal pay. Those speeches in 1963 and 1968, at the height of his career and nearing his assassination, are minimized to selected words—particularly the classic lines in which he envisions that his four children "will one day live in a nation where they will not be judged by the color of their skin but by the content of their character."[6] While King may have seen the promised land watching Lyndon B. Johnson signing the 1964 Civil Rights Act, he would fall short of getting to the mountaintop of seeing racism eliminated from American society. King's prophecy optimistically believed in the power of humanity, telling his fellow audience, "[b]ut I want you to know tonight . . . that we as a people will get to the promised land" (King, "To the Mountaintop" 195).[7]

In 2013, the modern-day CRM—#BLM, founded by Alicia Garza, Patrisse Cullors, and Opal Tometi—began as a Twitter hashtag as a call to action to address the murder of seventeen-year-old Trayvon Martin by neighborhood watchman George Zimmerman. Sybrina Fulton, the mother of Martin, characterized her son as an average teenager. In 2015, during a panel conversation sponsored by the Syracuse University National Pan-Hellenic Council, Fulton remembered Martin as a loving teenager, a young man who always protected his mother, listened to music, skated at the skating rink, and found an interest in girls.[8] Fulton's paints a picture of her son that is the opposite of his most well-known image in social media, his hooded sweatshirt, which unfairly reinforced negative stereotypes about Black males. According to bell hooks in *Killing Rage*, she argues that "television does not hold white people responsible for white supremacy; it socializes them to believe that subjugation and subordination of Black people by any means necessary is essential for the maintenance of law and order" (hooks 112).[9] The image of Martin in his hooded sweatshirt taken from his social media page sensitized whites' fear and suspicion of Black youth through television and social media, which ultimately validated George Zimmerman's alibi and led to his acquittal. However, during the student panel, Fulton rejected the pejorative characterization of her son in a hooded sweatshirt. She exclaims, "he was wearing a hoodie. It does not make sense, but the police tried to justify the murder of Trayvon, who was a 17-year-old minding his own business" (Fulton).[10] Fulton's counterexample humanizes the incident from the standpoint of a mother trying to make sense of what happened to her teenage son but also realizing the detrimental role racial profiling played in her son's murder. Patricia Hill Collins argues for a critical examination of what she terms controlling images targeting Black womanhood. The stereotypical images of Black women such as mammy, the matriarch, and welfare recipient "are designed to make racism, sexism, and poverty appear to be natural, normal, and an inevitable part of everyday life" (P. Collins 77).[11] The controlling images that exploit Black womanhood are also apparent among stereotypes that characterize Black men, women, and children who become victims of racial violence. Fulton's example defends her "right to define [her] own reality, establish [her] own identity, and name [her] history" in a society that is slow to acknowledge Black women's voices (P. Collins 79).

Fulton paints a vivid picture of the worst day of her life, in which she remembers seeing Martin in his white casket, dressed in white, with a smirk on his face signaling to her that he was at peace—painful imagery that still haunts Fulton today. Reciting this moment in Fulton's life, she mentions that telling this story to people at her speaking engagements is part of her healing and restores the broken pieces of where she comes from since processing her son's murder. This level of pain and grief that Fulton expresses is channeled into strength to live life and to define who Trayvon Martin was in a world that has demonized her son.

In 2016, artist Nikkolas Smith edited Trayvon's hoodie onto a Martin Luther King Jr. portrait to illustrate the parallels between racial violence then and now.[12] Smith's artistic work reinserts King into a conversation about the murders of Black children killed because of racial violence. Amid King's rise to public notoriety in 1955, Black Americans and their allies were protesting the inhumane murder of fourteen-year-old Emmett Till. White supremacists murdered Till after he allegedly whistled at a white woman. Mamie Till Bradley, Till's mother, allowed mass-media outlets to photograph her son's disfigured body and to show the world in her words "what they had done to [her] boy"; this laid the groundwork for the CRM (qtd. in Green 179).[13] Fast-forward to September 15, 1963: one month after King recites his "I Have a Dream" speech, he gives a eulogy for four young girls killed in the 16th Street Baptist Church bombing in Birmingham, Alabama.

King's image is reconfigured in Ava DuVernay's 2014 film *Selma*. A critical scene that connects to my discussion of Black lives mattering is when King, played by David Oyelowo, eulogizes twenty-five-year-old Jimmie Lee Jackson, played by LaKeith Stanfield. On February 18, 1965, Jackson, a follower of King and activist in the CRM, attends a rally in Marion, Alabama, where clergy and civil rights activists sing freedom songs in protest of their fellow civil rights workers incarceration in the county jail. About five hundred people participate in this rally. Alabama state troopers, city police officers, and sheriffs opposed to the rally end it by hitting protesters with billy clubs and chasing them with dogs. Jackson, his grandfather Gager, and his mother Viola all flee to a nearby restaurant called Mack's Café. Police officers rush into the café and begin to flip over tables and disrupt the peaceful ambiance. When Viola is attacked, Jimmy rushes to her aid but is struck with a gunshot wound to the stomach. Eight days later, Jackson dies. His shooter, James Bonard Fowler, was unidentified during the debacle.

Selma chronicles King and other civil rights leaders' participation in civil rights protests in Alabama. Their efforts to protest a southern state notorious for its segregationist practices under the leadership of then-Governor George Wallace were courageous. Jackson's death provokes King to march from Selma to the state capitol in Montgomery to continue fighting for voting rights. It also fortifies Delphine Letort's observation that "Jackson is literally silenced when shot to death in a scene of police brutality" (Letort 204).[14] In the first and only interview given by James Bonard Fowler, he states that his shooting of Jackson was in self-defense. He argues vehemently that "[h]e was trying to kill me. I have no doubt in my mind that, under the emotional situation at the time, if he would have gotten complete control of my pistol, he would have killed me or shot me" (qtd. in Fleming).[15] Fowler would go on to contend, "don't think legally I could get convicted for murder now no matter how much politics they got [be]cause after 40 years they ain't no telling how many people is dead" (Fleming). In 2007, forty-two years after killing Jimmie Lee Jackson, Fowler was charged with first and second-degree murder. Fowler surrendered to authorities in 2010 on the second-degree murder charge and stated that he killed Jackson in self-defense, believing that Jackson was grabbing his gun during the time the shooting took place. Fowler was convicted of Jackson's murder decades after it happened, but only served six months in prison and was released early. He died in July 2015 of pancreatic cancer. Despite the state of Alabama's attempt to correct their judicial wrong, Fowler was not remorseful. The former policeman's morality is an illustration of how while America believes that we live in a post-racial society, there is still the inherent belief that killing unarmed Black men and women is an act of self-defense because they always pose a threat. Today, there is still no correcting of this language in our national conversations about racism in the United States.

To address a continual racial divide, King discussed the plight of Black Americans. As noted in Brooks's poem *Riot*, King argued, "A riot is the language of the unheard" (qtd. in Brooks, *Riot* 3). I discuss at length how in Brooks's *Riot* King's words inspired her political poem as a method to address Black rage. In 2014, King's famous sentence was used repetitively during media commentary, for example, on CNN, MSNBC, and C-SPAN in explaining the riots in Ferguson, Missouri. In addition, the quote reappears in a tweet written by the Martin Luther King Jr. Center in Atlanta and retweeted by his adult children.[16] The riotous language during the Ferguson and Minneapolis-St. Paul uprisings and within Brooks's fictional poem becomes one foregrounded in Black political speech that addresses the discontent of Black America from several areas, including mass unemployment, segregated housing, and a substandard educational system.

Toward the end of King's life, he embarked on a campaign for the poor people's movement, in which he argued that the "giant triplets of racism, extreme materialism, and militarism" would consume American society to very low morale. In his "Beyond Vietnam" speech, given April 4, 1967, at Riverside Church in New York, he argues: "I am convinced that if we are to get on the right side of the world revolution, we as a nation must undergo a radical revolution of values. We must rapidly begin the shift from a thing-oriented society to a person-oriented society. When machines and computers, profit motives and property rights are considered more important than people, the giant triplets of racism, extreme materialism, and militarism are incapable of being conquered" (King, "Beyond Vietnam").[17] King proposes that the United States end the war in Vietnam, offering a final solution that would lead to peace talks between both the US and Vietnam as leading examples of how to form a truce. King's reference to "giant triplets" points to his dismay that profit and property feed racism, materialism, and militarism, which assume precedence over human life. In US global relations as it relates to the Iraqi war, Afghanistan war, conflict in the Israeli-Palestine state, Occupy Wall Street, ISIS, and how we should respond to Russia, all relate to King's conversation as we continue to think about our own giant triplets. In Henry Dumas's "Riot or Revolt?" I illustrated how King's thesis manifests through the United States' focus on neoliberalism. As I stated in chapter 4, Dumas shows us how Black politics (through examples of riotous protest) are undermined by free-market capitalism. While Dumas and other BAM writers argued for Black liberation and wrote about it in their fictitious works, the overwhelming flow of neoliberal policies from the late 1960s into the 1970s prohibited Black activists from eliminating racism and white supremacy. The growth of wealth inequality that I discuss throughout the book makes it difficult for Black politics to thrive in the twenty-first century without dramatically changing neoliberal politics. Despite the United States Department of Justice report released in 2014 that illustrated proof of Black Americans in Ferguson, Missouri, being stopped and arrested at higher rates than whites, the rise in police and vigilante murders against Black Americans continues to soar.[18] The continued protests against racial bias and police brutality demonstrated by a multiracial coalition of #BLM protesters undergird pervasive manifestations of social and civil unrest in modern-day society. The current conversation about civil unrest nationwide must be discussed as a necessary dialogue on how to address the effects of race and racism. The works examined in this book written by artist-writers during the BAM allows us to create, engage, and take action in this dialogue that must be discussed by all citizens who value our democratic belief in being equal and just. *Start a Riot!* builds on an established and growing body of literature seeking to frame civil unrest as a critical form of study in Black American literature, and in particular, BAM literature, to give relevant meaning to Black uprisings and protests that continue to permeate US society.

NOTES

INTRODUCTION

1. See Barbara Sprunt's article from NPR, "The History Behind 'When the Looting Starts, the Shooting Starts,'" to read Donald J. Trump's tweet and its origin story.

2. See Janet Abu-Lughod, *Race, Space, and Riots in Chicago, New York, and Los Angeles,* 11–12. I also realize that "uprising" and "rebellion" are more commonly used to define Black resistance. However, I am keeping the term "riot" to maintain a seamless link between BAM fictive works and historical information.

3. *Death beyond Disavowal: The Impossible Politics of Difference.*

4. See 2015 final report titled *The President's Task Force on 21st Century Policing.*

5. See *The Myth and Propaganda of Black Buying Power* by Jared A. Ball. I reference his work to raise attention to how the global economy at large and the US economy in particular continues to exploit Black people alive or in death on the basis of their capitalistic strength either through their commoditization or buying power.

6. See *New York Times* article "U.N. Panel Condemns the President's Response to Racial Violence in Charlottesville."

7. See Josh Penrod, C. J. Sinner, and MaryJo Webster, "Buildings Damaged in Minneapolis, St. Paul After Riots," Minneapolis *Star Tribune.*

8. See Kenneth W. Warren, *What Was African American Literature?*

9. Khari "Discopoet" Bowden is the son of the renowned woodwindist Mwata Bowden, who is the director of jazz ensembles at the University of Chicago. The younger Bowden in his own right serves as artist-in-residence at Purdue University, where he teaches, creates, and performs original spoken word performances with the ensemble Haraka Writers. Recognized by Gwendolyn Brooks for his extraordinary talent as a spoken word musician, Bowden has performed around the world, has released three studio albums, and in 2019 released *Haiku 4 Justice: A 365+ Day Commentary of (In)Justice in America & Abroad.*

10. See Womack, *Post Black: How a New Generation Is Redefining African American Identity.*

11. "Start a Riot" by Khari "Discopoet" Bowden is a song from his 2016 album *The Revolution Has Been Compromised: Honoring the Words and Works of Gil Scott-Heron.*

The performance of this song at Hamilton Park in Chicago was a commissioned project funded by the Jazz Institute of Chicago.

12. See Cheryl Finley, *Committed to Memory: The Art of the Slave Ship Icon.*

13. See Gerald Horne, *The Counter-Revolution of 1776: Slave Resistance and the Origins of the United States of America.*

14. I want to clarify my intentions for terming underrepresented Black neighborhoods as "ghettos." I am specifically discussing how Black neighborhoods in the twentieth century are constructed by US state governments as underdeveloped economic spaces that as Mehrsa Baradaran points out "were cut-off from the outside economy." In other words, "the ghetto" was purposefully made to stifle Black wealth and to segregate Black communities within these neighborhoods from the larger US economic infrastructure. Because of the lack of economic resources, these communities still exist today as the principal site where much of the civil unrest took place, from Chicago to New York City, Ferguson, Missouri, and Baltimore, Maryland. These spaces have been locations where Black uprisings repeatedly have occurred in response to proletarian conditions and police violence. Also see Dunbar S. McLaurin's 1969 Ghetto Economic Development and Industrialization Plan "Ghediplan," the description of which can be found in Baradaran, *The Color of Wealth: Black Banks and the Racial Wealth Gap,* 173.

15. See SNCC, "Position Paper on Black Power."

16. See Ture and Hamilton, *Black Power: The Politics of Liberation.*

17. See Tony Bolden, *Afro-Blue: Improvisations in African American Poetry and Culture,* 21–22.

18. Also see Houston A. Baker Jr., *Blues, Ideology, and Afro-American Literature: A Vernacular Theory,* 5.

19. This is also to emphasize that Bolden's point extends to understanding the depth of which Black music is a staple within the Black American literary tradition. However, specifically I am discussing the BAM here to situate how it connects back to the ethos of Black Power.

20. Kenneth B. Clark, the famed sociologist credited with unearthing the racial wealth gap in his 1965 book *Dark Ghetto: Dilemmas of Social Power,* revealed that Black Americans post–World War II comprised a fifth of the public housing population in Harlem, New York. In addition, only half of the Black population in Harlem between 1920 and 1960 made less than $4,000 compared to overall New Yorkers making $4,000 or more. The Harlem Riot of 1943 that is depicted in Ann Petry's novella, *In Darkness and Confusion,* exposes the racial animus of wealth inequality while at the same time Black American private citizens and veterans were denied the right to live freely as citizens.

21. In addition to *The Fire Next Time,* also read *James Baldwin: Living in Fire* (2019) by Bill V. Mullen.

22. See Langston Hughes's essay in John Henrik Clarke's edited collection *Harlem: A Community in Transition.*

23. The story of James "Jimmy" Powell's death and the coverage of the 1964 Harlem–Bedford Stuyvesant rebellion that happened in response is found in three important historical and sociological accounts: Janet L. Abu-Lughod, *Race, Space, and Riots in Chicago, New York, and Los Angeles* (2007); Michael W. Flann, *In the Heat of the Summer:*

The New York Riots of 1964 and the War on Crime (2016); Ann V. Collins, *The Dawn Broke Hot and Somber: U.S. Race Riots of 1964* (2018).

24. Ira Katznelson, in *When Affirmative Action Was White: An Untold History of Racial Inequality in Twentieth-Century America* (2005), discusses the mechanisms of unequal legislation that economically disadvantaged Black Americans and continued a cycle of poverty or low-income status even when the federal government under the FDR administration created the New Deal to circumvent destitution within American society. While white Americans were able to achieve wealth and prosperity because of the institutionalized subsidization of the New Deal, Black Americans were either denied participation in such government policies or had to settle for public government subsidies such as low-income housing as a means of survival that denied the possibility of creating wealth.

25. See Martin Luther King Jr., *"All Labor Has Dignity,"* edited by Michael K. Honey.

26. See James Smethurst, *The Black Arts Movement: Literary Nationalism in the 1960s and 1970s*; GerShun Avilez, *Radical Aesthetics and Modern Black Nationalism*; Jonathan Fenderson, *Building the Black Arts Movement: Hoyt Fuller and the Cultural Politics of the 1960s*.

27. See Amiri Baraka, "The Black Arts Movement: Its Meaning and Potential," *Nka: Journal of Contemporary African Art* (2011), in which he outlines the origins of what became the Black Arts Movement and speaks about Malcolm X's influence and seeking redress for his murder.

28. See Kenneth B. Clark, *Dark Ghetto: Dilemmas of Social Power*.

29. See Toni Morrison, *Playing in the Dark: Whiteness and the Literary Imagination*.

CHAPTER 1: THE INABILITY TO COMPROMISE: EXAMINING BLACK
RAGE AND REVOLT IN THE REVOLUTIONARY THEATRE OF
AMIRI BARAKA AND BEN CALDWELL

1. See Amiri Baraka (LeRoi Jones), "The Revolutionary Theatre," *Negro Digest* (April 1966): 23.

2. See National Humanities Center, "The Making of African American Identity: Vol. III, 1917–1968," http://nationalhumanitiescenter.org/pds/maai3/protest/text12/barakatheatre .pdf. Also see James Smethurst, *The Black Arts Movement: Literary Nationalism in the 1960s and 1970s*; Howard Rambsy II, *The Black Arts Enterprise and the Production of African American Poetry*.

3. See Harold Cruse, *Rebellion or Revolution*. In this collection of essays and reviews, Cruse discusses Black music and vernacular as the cornerstone of United States' aesthetics and culture.

4. In the summer of 1968, *Riot Sale, or Dollar Psyche Fake Out* was published by *Drama Review* in a special issue titled "Black Theatre." This special issue, volume 12, no. 4, featured other notable BAM plays such as Sonia Sanchez, *The Bronx Is Next*, and Larry Neal, "The Black Arts Movement."

5. See Orlando Patterson, *Slavery and Social Death*; Lewis R. Gordon, *Bad Faith and Antiblack Racism*; Christina Sharpe, *In the Wake: On Blackness and Being*.

6. See "Amiri Baraka's Theatre of Ritual: from Staging Rituals of Unfulfillment to Performing Rituals of Political Praxis."

7. See Margo Natalie Crawford, "The 'Atmos-Feeling' of Resurrection: Feeling Black (Not Slave) in Black Arts Movement Drama."

8. See Amiri Baraka (LeRoi Jones), *The Motion of History and Other Plays*. In this compilation, Baraka includes the script for *Slave Ship* and program notes of the first performance at Spirit House in March 1967.

9. Ben Caldwell is referring to Baraka's essay "The Revolutionary Theatre" that was rejected by the *New York Times* and several other mainstream newspapers. Baraka's essay would go on to appear in major Black publications, including the well-known *Negro Digest*. In addition, Caldwell's acknowledgment of Larry Neal's influence on his work, connecting Black art and politics, is in reference to "The Black Arts Movement" essay published alongside his play *Riot Sale* in *Drama Review*.

10. See Kenneth Bowman's interview with Caldwell, "The Revolution Will Not Be Televised Nor Staged"; Soyica Diggs Colbert, "A Pedagogical Approach to Understanding Rioting as Revolutionary Action in Alice Childress's *Wine in the Wilderness*."

11. Several authors discuss the transition of nonviolent action to more militant forms of action that would become known in the Black Power Movement: Mary L. Dudziak, *Cold War Civil Rights: Race and the Image of American Democracy*; Peniel E. Joseph, *Waiting 'Til the Midnight Hour: A Narrative History of Black Power in America*; Charles E. Cobb Jr., *This Nonviolent Stuff'll Get You Killed: How Guns Made the Civil Rights Movement Possible*; and Errol A. Henderson, *The Revolution Will Not Be Theorized: Cultural Revolution in the Black Power Era*.

12. Howard Rambsy II, author of *The Black Arts Enterprise and the Production of African American Poetry*, notes that the memorialization of Malcolm X "came to represent a significant element in the aesthetics of black poetry and the formation of the Black Arts Movement" (104).

13. See Baraka, "November 1966: One Year Eight Months Later," in *Raise, Race, Rays, and Raze: Essays since 1965*.

14. The Civil Rights Act of 1964, signed into law by President Lyndon B. Johnson, prohibited individuals and organizations from discriminating against American citizens based on race, religion, sex, or national origin and guaranteed full protection under the law. However, two weeks after the bill was signed into law, a riot ensued in Harlem, as Black citizens reacted to the death of fifteen-year-old James Powell, who was killed by an off-duty police officer. Racial conflicts between Black citizens and police would continue well into the 1960s. Baraka's framing of the Civil Rights Act as a symbol, rather than a piece of legislation meant to protect Americans, particularly Black Americans, is a response that is steeped in apprehension about the ways in which civil rights policies failed Black people rather than protecting them, because the dominant society can always overturn those laws. As an example, Baraka uses the Reconstruction period in US history as evidence to support his point.

15. See Malcolm X's speech titled "The Ballot or the Bullet," delivered April 3, 1964, in Cleveland, Ohio, in which he explains the essential difference between civil rights and human rights. In this speech he makes clear that civil rights only allow American citizens,

particularly Black citizens, to present racial grievances within a US jurisdiction. Because of America's racists history, Black citizens' "civil rights" are judged by a biased regime. However, human rights are all people's "God given rights" that are recognized by planet Earth.

16. See Malcolm X's speech titled "The Black Revolution," delivered April 8, 1964, at a socialist gathering coordinated by the Militant Labor Forum. In this speech, Malcolm X declared Black oppression in the US a human rights struggle and acutely framed Black nationalism as a philosophy for Black Americans to demand human rights. A new generation of Black Americans would no longer only use nonviolence as a protest tactic for demanding full citizenship and equality in the United States. Instead, the Black Power generation would practice resistance through armed struggle and self-defense as a means of overthrowing the American colonization that undermined Black American equality. Malcolm X's "Black Revolution" speech describes self-determination and armed struggle in Africa, Latin America, and Asia against European colonial powers. He believed that a Black revolution should be not only an American protest but an international protest. Black nationalism within the US context was trivialized as a separatist political philosophy, particularly by those who believed that militant Black nationalists were setting back the momentum for racial equality by engaging in practices of alienation and isolation from the larger civil rights movement, whose aim was further integration into US society. Malcolm X refuted these perceptions about Black nationalism, suggesting instead that the real Black revolution is a revolt carried through by nonwhite people to remove the colonizers from nonwhite nations. Including Black American liberation within this internationalization of the Black revolution, Malcolm X positioned Black nationalism as the cornerstone of revolution.

17. See *A Nation within a Nation: Amiri Baraka (LeRoi Jones) and Black Power Politics.*

18. In an interview with Kenneth Bowman titled "The Revolution Will Not Be Televised Nor Staged" published in 1999, Caldwell reveals that he rented a house together with the Baraka family. This house was called "The Spirit House" and operated as a culture center for the Black Revolutionary Theatre.

19. *The Black Arts Movement: Literary Nationalism in the 1960s and 1970s.* See also Kenneth Bowman, "The Revolution Will Not Be Televised Nor Staged: An Interview with Ben Caldwell," where Caldwell discusses Baraka's move from Harlem to Newark, which was forced because of his surveillance from the FBI, and several disagreements he had with other BAM artists that eventually led to BARTS's demise.

20. See Rick Rojas and Khorri Atkinson, "Five Days of Unrest That Shaped, and Haunted, Newark," *New York Times.*

21. See Saul Gottlieb's interview with Baraka, "They Think You're an Airplane and You're Really a Bird." Details of Baraka's hospitalization during the Newark uprising and subsequent arrest are featured.

22. Read Julia Rabig, *The Fixers: Devolution, Development, and Civil Society in Newark, 1960–1990.*

23. See Saul Gottlieb's 1967 interview with Amiri Baraka, "They Think You're an Airplane and You're Really a Bird," *Evergreen Review.*

24. See Amiri Baraka's (LeRoi Jones), *Arm Yourself, or Harm Yourself! A Message of Self-Defense to Black Men.*

25. On April 6, 1964, Malcolm X's "new" Black nationalist politics materialized in a speech titled "The Black Revolution," which was delivered in front of a largely white crowd composed of members of a leftist-socialist organization whose newspaper, *The Militant*, gave a balanced reading of the multivalent Black Liberation Movement (BLM) as a whole and specifically vocalized Malcolm X's political ideology. He called the Black oppression in the United States a human rights struggle and acutely framed Black nationalism as a philosophy for Black Americans in the United States to demand human rights, which was in opposition to its characterization as a separatist ideology in mainstream American society, as well as among some civil rights leaders and white liberals.

26. See Errol A. Henderson, *The Revolution Will Not Be Theorized: Cultural Revolution in the Black Power Era*.

27. See Shermaine Jones, "Presenting Our Bodies, Laying Our Case: The Political Efficacy of Grief and Rage during the Civil Rights Movement."

28. Such dissent concretizes what bell hooks posits in *Killing Rage: Ending Racism* as "transformative revolutionary action" (19). The resistance to the normalization of racism among the characters capitulates grassroots activism that insights transformative political coalitions. Thus, Mako Fitts-Ward, in "Theorizing Transformative Revolutionary Action: The Contribution of bell hooks to Emancipatory Knowledge Production" states that "collective organizing becomes a site of clarity, broad-mindedness, accountability, and potentially where resistance in thought and action are possible" (118).

29. See Shanna Greene Benjamin, "The Uses of Anger: Wanda Coleman and the Poetry of Black Rage," 64.

30. See Aida Hussen, "'Black Rage' and 'Useless Pain': Affect, Ambivalence, and Identity after King."

31. See *The Counter-Revolution of 1776: Slave Resistance and the Origins of the United States of America*.

32. In *From Here to Equality: Reparations for Black Americans in the Twenty-First Century*, William A. Darity Jr. and A. Kirsten Mullen make a case for why Black reparations is imminent as it is a means to end the racial wealth gap in the US as a result of slavery, Jim Crow apartheid, and mass incarceration. Specifically, the book explains the economic caste system in the United States and how Black Americans are at the bottom of the system while their European counterparts across ethnicities remain at the top.

33. See Michael Cade-Stewart, "A Satyric Paradise: The Form of W. B. Yeats's 'News for the Delphic Oracle,'" in *Writing Modern Ireland*, edited by Catherine E. Paul.

34. See *Black Rights/White Wrongs: The Critique of Racial Liberalism*.

35. Inge Nielsen, *Cultic Theatres and Ritual Drama: A Study in Regional Development and Religious Interchange between East and West in Antiquity*.

36. See *Taking It to the Streets: The Social Protest Theatre of Luis Valdez and Amiri Baraka*.

37. See *Afro-Blue: Improvisations in African American Poetry and Culture*.

38. See *Furiously Funny: Comic Rage from Ralph Ellison to Chris Rock*.

39. See Robin DiAngelo, *White Fragility: Why It's So Hard for White People to Talk About Racism*.

40. Thornhill's study "Racial Salience and the Consequences of Making White People Uncomfortable: Intra-Racial Discrimination, Racial Screening, and the Maintenance of

White Supremacy" analyzes racial discrimination within American institutions. Using a sociological approach, and a legal studies methodology, Thornhill argues that Black Americans native to the United States through ancestry and lineage are evaluated by their white superiors through an intraracial coded system. Essentially, Black Americans who apply for college admission or for a job within corporate America are often overlooked if their appearance, attitude, and written work reveals a Black-affirming sensibility. Such an identity appears to white superiors as a strong proponent of racial pride and attention to racially related concerns. Thornhill's research examines how this centuries-long practice of discrimination continues in twenty-first-century American life.

41. See Thornhill, "We Want Black Students, Just Not You: How White Admissions Counselors Screen Prospective Black Students."

42. See the essay "On the Question of Nigga Authenticity."

43. In 2005, Stephen Best and Saidiya Hartman edited a special issue of the University of California at Berkeley journal *Representations* titled "Redress." The collection of essays was inspired by the Redress Project, a reading group gathered by the editors for the purpose of bringing scholars together across disciplines to open up critical discussions on questions about injury, justice, and closure in regards to remedying slavery.

44. On February 7, 2005, the US Senate presented Resolution 39 (S. Res 39), at the 109th Congress titled, "Apologizing to the victims of lynching and the descendants of those victims for the failure of the Senate to enact anti-lynching legislation." While an apology was publicly acknowledged, compensatory payments given to the descendants of victims' families were not offered. Some fifteen years later, the US senators Kamala Harris, Cory Booker, and Tim Scott, all minority senators, passed the Justice for Victims of Lynching Act. The 2020 bill, an extension of the 2005 bill, notes the racist legacy of lynching while also including a list of federal hate crimes that affect other marginalized communities.

45. See "Blood Debt: Reparations in Langston Hughes *Mulatto.*"

46. In *Riot Sale*, the rebellious crowds' rejection of civil rights leadership, exemplified in their reaction to the police, confirms what Baraka's claim in 1984 that "the black bourgeoisie had forfeited leadership of the black liberation movement" (Baraka, "Black Liberation" 212). In other words, the Black middle classes' leadership attempted to undercut American imperialism through compliant opposition, whereas in *Riot Sale* the Black working classes are tired of acquiescing to the ruling regime, including a Black middle class. Thereby, the call for restitution made by Baraka through a socialist framework epitomizes the Black underclass moving toward revolution in order to recoup land that was stolen during Reconstruction following emancipation, a self-determined Black Belt South, and equitable distribution of materiality to the historically oppressed (218). All claims Baraka pertinently states come from a revolution led by the Black working underclasses. See "Black Liberation/Socialist Revolution" in *Selected Plays and Prose of Amiri Baraka/LeRoi Jones.*

47. H.R. 40, "The Commission to Study and Develop Reparation Proposals for African-Americans Act" is a bill led by Congresswoman Sheila Jackson Lee. The study of the bill is comprised of understanding slavery, the role the federal government played in upholding institutional slavery, and how its detrimental effects still impose onto Black American life. The bill remains stagnant and has not been voted on by the US Senate.

48. See *From #BlackLivesMatter to Black Liberation*.

49. See Soyica Diggs Colbert, *The African American Theatrical Body: Reception, Performance, and the Stage*.

50. See *The Color of Money: Black Banks and the Racial Wealth Gap*.

51. In the late 1890s, Callie House, a Black woman and ex-slave from Tennessee, led the unsuccessful but commemorative movement for reparations called the National Ex-Slave Mutual Relief, Bounty and Pension Association. See a full-length study of House's efforts in My Face Is Black Is True: Callie House and the Struggle for Ex-slave Reparations by Mary Frances Berry.

52. In an article titled "In 1870, Henrietta Wood Sued for Reparations—and Won" in *Smithsonian Magazine*, W. Caleb McDaniel states that Wood's $2,500 settlement is worth nearly $65,000 in 2019. That money helped her son Arthur purchase a house and pay for his schooling. He became the first Black American to graduate from Northwestern University's School of Law and became a successful lawyer. Wood's successful reparations case illustrates that if all formerly enslaved Blacks received restitution that their lives would be fundamentally changed. Moreover, economically, Black Americans would have more opportunities to build generational wealth, as did Wood and her son.

53. See *Sweet Taste of Liberty: A True Story of Slavery and Restitution in America*.

CHAPTER 2: "BLACKBLUES": THE BAM AESTHETIC AND BLACK RAGE IN GWENDOLYN BROOKS'S *RIOT*

1. A literary moment from the 1930s–50s, in which Black American writers such as Brooks, Lorraine Hansberry, Richard Wright, and Langston Hughes, as well as artists, scholars, and musicians, wrote about social protest and discrimination as it related to race, class, and gender through the Great Depression, World War II, and migration into cities such as Chicago during the Great Migration.

2. For further information, see Brooks's autobiography *Report from Part One*, 22.

3. See Jane Abu-Lughod, *Race, Space, and Riots in Chicago, New York, and Los Angeles*, 93.

4. Broadside Press was founded by Dudley Randall in 1965. The press became a significant component to the growing of BAM literature and culture. Brooks's decision to publish *Riot* with Broadside instead of with longtime publisher Harper and Row illustrated her commitment to the growth of black-owned publishing and to standing in solidarity with Black freedom movements.

5. I am saying this with the exception of Cheryl Clarke, *After Mecca: Women Poets and the Black Arts Movement*.

6. See Annette Debo, "Reflecting Violence in the Warpland: Gwendolyn Brooks's *Riot*"; and Raymond Malewitz, "'My Newish Voice': Rethinking Black Power in Gwendolyn Brooks's Whirlwind."

7. See Brooks, *Report from Part One*, 183.

8. See "'My Newish Voice': Rethinking Black Power in Gwendolyn Brooks's Whirlwind."

9. See Evelyn Brooks Higginbotham, *Righteous Discontent: The Women's Movement in the Black Baptist Church, 1880–1920*. I use the term respectability in this instance to illustrate that although Black Americans try to morally and ethically rise above white supremacy's modes of racism, they still succumb to it because white racism pervades and is adverse to Blacks' practices and attitudes of Victorian-American social norms. Instead, Blacks are always defined by their stereotypes and caricatures.

10. See the Gwendolyn Brooks Papers 1917–2000, at the University of California at Berkeley's Bancroft Library.

11. The Fisk University Writers' Conference was also a contentious space where poets such as Robert Hayden, for example, were challenged by Baraka (then LeRoi Jones) and others about the meaning of calling oneself a "Black poet." Hayden surmised that a Black aesthetic is reductive and does not evoke the fluidity of Black culture or experience. Further examples of these accounts can be found in *Report from Part One*; Derik Smith, "Quarreling in the Movement: Robert Hayden's Black Arts Era."

12. The 1969 poem "SOS" reads as a chant in which Baraka calls every Black person regardless of race, gender, and class affiliation to come together. See *SOS—Calling All Black People: A Black Arts Movement Reader*, edited by John H. Bracey Jr., Sonia Sanchez, and James Smethurst.

13. The poem is a symbolic appraisal of the rise and decline of the rich cultural, political, and social foundations of Black Chicago of the early twentieth century. The poem is about the Mecca, a luxury apartment building in Chicago. Built in 1892, it was once known for housing patrons of the World's Columbian Exposition. In the early 1910s, particularly during the Great Migration period, the Mecca became a fixture of the Chicago Black Renaissance, where artists and writers would meet for various gatherings, particularly during the jazz era. But in the 1930s, the Mecca began to deteriorate, and became a tenement building for the working poor. The building was torn down in 1952.

14. See "Heralding the Clear Obscure: Gwendolyn Brooks and Apostrophe."

15. See "Islam and Black Art," *Negro Digest* 28, no. 3 (January 1969). The interview was conducted by BAM and BPM participants Marvin X and Faruk.

16. For a more elaborate discussion about this topic, see Errol A. Henderson, *The Revolution Will Not Be Theorized: Cultural Revolution in the Black Power Era*, 39.

17. The Blackstone Rangers, formed in the late 1950s, are a youth street gang from Chicago's South Side. In 1967 Brooks met with the gang during her many free poetry workshops.

18. See "The Other America" speech in "*All Labor Has Dignity*," edited by Michael K. Honey.

19. See Natalie Y. Moore, *The Southside: A Portrait of Chicago and American Segregation*.

20. Jeff Donaldson is a member of AfriCOBRA, or the Coalition of Black Revolutionary Artists, which formed in Chicago in 1968.

21. See Malewitz, "'My Newish Voice': Rethinking Black Power in Gwendolyn Brooks's Whirlwind," 532. He discusses in length Brooks's intentional move to part ways with the mainly white printing press Harper and Row to Dudley Randall's Black-owned Broadside Press. This transition was an effort to connect with her Black readership, but also to increase the sales of a fairly young Black-owned press.

22. See *Gwendolyn Brooks: Poetry and the Heroic Voice*.

CHAPTER 3: THE CRISIS OF BLACK REVOLUTIONARY POLITICS IN SONIA SANCHEZ, *THE BRONX IS NEXT* (AND *SISTER SON/JI*)

1. See *Black Power: The Politics of Liberation*, chapter 2.

2. See Wood's edited collection of plays by Sonia Sanchez and selected interviews, *I'm Black When I'm Singing, I'm Blue When I Ain't and Other Plays*.

3. See *Black Power in the Belly of the Beast*.

4. See Alice Walker, *In Search of Our Mothers' Gardens: Womanist Prose*.

5. I acknowledge that Weems's theorization is controversial because it rejects other feminisms. Africana womanism at its core focuses on race issues, the Black heterosexual family, and Black empowerment. My interest in including Africana womanism is to illustrate how various feminisms embodied by the Black women characters are explored in both *Bronx* and *Sister Son/ji*. Thus, I contend that Sanchez recognizes that womanist ideologies from a narrow or multidimensional viewpoint are part of Black women's epistemologies.

6. I also use this term to highlight Molefi Kente Asante and Ama Mazama's emphasis on an African sense of totality, wholeness, and perspective.

7. See "'This Thing Called Playwriting': An Interview with Sonia Sanchez on the Art of Her Drama."

8. See Colbert's discussion of sexism in BAM art and politics in "A Pedagogical Approach to Understanding Rioting as Revolutionary Action in Alice Childress's Wine in the Wilderness," in *Theatre Topics*.

9. See Farmer, *Remaking Black Power: How Black Women Transformed an Era*. On pages 76 and 77, she discusses Cleaver's evolvement from a misogynist to a reformed advocate of gender equality while being a minister of information with the Black Panther Party.

10. See Gilbert Osofsky, "Harlem: The Making of a Ghetto." He notes that there were a minority of white landlords that attempted to maintain their restrictive covenants.

11. Notably referring to the Chicago Black Renaissance, which took off in the 1930s as the Harlem Renaissance/New Negro movement began to decline.

12. See the 1964 book *Harlem: A Community in Transition*, a collection of essays by Harlem's finest writers, artists, and social critics edited by Clarke.

13. See Mehrsa Baradaran, *The Color of Money: Black Banks and the Racial Wealth Gap*. She upholds Clark's argument well into the twenty-first century.

14. See William Darity Jr. et al., *What We Get Wrong about Closing the Racial Wealth Gap*. In it, Clark's statistical data holds true. Black Americans continue to hold less wealth than white Americans and other racial and ethnic groups that have immigrated since the 1980s.

15. Again, this data holds true in the twenty-first century. Read "The Color of Wealth in the Nation's Capitol" by Kilolo Kijakazi et al. http://www.urban.org/sites/default/files /publication/85341/2000986-the-color-of-wealth-in-the-nations-capital_1.pdf.

16. Clark's argument is still accurate in the twenty-first century when discussing the economic plight of Black Americans. See Darrick Hamilton and William Darity Jr., "The Political Economy of Education, Financial Literacy, and the Racial Wealth Gap," 62.

17. See Noel Ignatiev, *How the Irish Became White*.

18. See also Baradaran, *The Color of Money: Black Banks and the Racial Wealth Gap*, especially chapters "The Decoy of Black Capitalism" and "The Free Market Confronts Black Poverty."

19. In the documentary *BaddDDD Sonia Sanchez* directed by Goldman and Atwater, spoken word artist Byronn Bain and The Roots lead drummer Questlove both argue that hip hop wouldn't exist as a genre or a generation if it were not for Sanchez as a critical figure in the Black Arts Movement.

CHAPTER 4: BLACK POLITICS AND THE NEOLIBERAL DILEMMA IN HENRY DUMAS'S "RIOT OR REVOLT?"

1. See Wendy Brown, *Undoing the Demos: Neoliberalism's Stealth Revolution*; Thomas Biebricher, *The Political Theory of Neoliberalism*.

2. As stated throughout this book, the National Advisory Commission on Civil Disorders chaired by Otto Kerner, governor of Illinois, released a report in 1968 (commonly known as the Kerner Report) that investigated riot-affected areas in American cities where large Black populations resided. Kerner and other committee members, including then president of the NAACP Roy Wilkins, concludes that America was moving in the direction of two societies: one Black and one white. The spark in civil unrest that the report documents between 1963–67 resulted from the grievances of American cities largely populated by Black Americans. Profoundly, the document reveals that because white America was uninformed about the United States' creation of the ghetto, its institutionalization, and its complicity in its destructive pattern that caused racial anguish in Black communities, white America was unable to connect this blight to American slavery and Jim Crow segregation. As a result, the Kerner Report attempted to push an active agenda to quell Black dissent, but in actuality it exacerbated race relations and let the police off the hook, positioning them as victims as opposed to disciplining their unchecked authority to harass and murder Black citizens.

3. See Michael Brooks et al., "Is There a Problem Officer? Exploring the Lived Experience of Black Men and Their Relationship with Law Enforcement."

4. See the Eugene B. Redmond's special "Henry Dumas" issue, *Black American Literature Forum* 22, no. 2.

5. See Elizabeth S. Anderson, *The Imperative of Integration*.

6. WSB-TV news film clip of Dr. Martin Luther King Jr. speaking about race riots in Rochester and New York City on July 27, 1964. Find the clip at the Digital Library of Georgia and Walter J. Brown Media Archives and Peabody Awards Collection, University of Georgia Libraries.

7. *Black America in the Shadow of the Sixties: Notes on the Civil Rights Movement, Neoliberalism, and Politics*.

8. *Black America in the Shadow of the Sixties: Notes on the Civil Rights Movement, Neoliberalism, and Politics*.

9. The foundation of political education during the Black Power era is reflective of radical study groups that were created during the organizing of the Black Panther

Party for Self-Defense in 1966. Anthony Bayani Rodriguez, in "Former Black Panther Marshall Eddie Conway on Revolutionary Political Education in the Twenty-First Century," addresses this point in depth. However, the direct linkage connects to the US emancipation and Reconstruction period. In "Emancipation and Reconstruction: African American Education, 1865–1919," Joy Ann Williamson-Lott, Linda Darling-Hammond, and Maria E. Hyler make the point that Black Americans after emancipation went to great lengths to educate themselves amid economic hardships and underfunding by the state. Education became a tool through which Black Americans advanced "the political, social, and economic interests of the black community" (1).

10. In "Revolutionary Women, Revolutionary Education: The Black Panther Party's Oakland Community School," former Black Panther Ericka Huggins and Angela D. LeBlanc-Ernest explain that the community schools emerged as a continuation of the liberation schools, and became a communal space where women of the movement created curriculum and instruction. This type of teaching practice educated Black students and others by encouraging their curiosity about civic engagement and global awareness.

11. See *From Head Shops to Whole Foods: The Rise and Fall of Activist Entrepreneurs.*

12. For more information about Lewis Michaux's life and the National Memorial African Bookstore, read David Emblidge, "Rallying Point: Lewis Michaux's National Memorial African Bookstore."

13. See Alex Green, "A New Generation of African-American-Owned Bookstores."

14. *The Color of the Law: Race, Violence, and Justice in the Post–World War II South.*

15. See the essay "Blacks in the Urban North: The 'Underclass Question' in Historical Perspective."

16. See the essay "Blacks and Jews: The Struggle in the Cities."

17. See Hughes, "The Harlem Riot—1964."

18. See Bell's groundbreaking essay "Brown v. Board of Education and the Interest-Convergence Dilemma," which was later presented in 1978 during a Harvard Law school symposium.

EPILOGUE

1. Toni Morrison's interview with now-disgraced journalist Charlie Rose about the 2015 Baltimore uprising on PBS. https://www.youtube.com/watch?v=SswSviVJAfc.

2. See Richard A. Oppel Jr. and Derrick Bryson Taylor, "Here's What You Need to Know about Breonna Taylor's Death," *New York Times.*

3. *Black Post-Blackness: The Black Arts Movement and Twenty-first-Century Aesthetics.*

4. See King, *Where Do We Go From Here: Community or Chaos?*

5. Trudier Harris, *Martin Luther King Jr., Heroism, and African American Literature.* Tuscaloosa: University of Alabama Press, 2014.

6. See *I Have a Dream: Dr. Martin Luther King Jr.,* published by Penguin Random House and illustrated by Kadir Nelson.

7. See *"All Labor Has Dignity": Martin Luther King, Jr.,* edited by Michael K. Honey.

8. See "(In) Justice For All Organizers Discuss Inspiration for Event," written by the *Daily Orange*, a student-run newspaper at Syracuse University. I attended the event to support my students in their mass protest and to bring voices such as Sybrina Fulton's to address state and vigilante violence. Her remarks quoted in the epilogue are from her responses to questions asked by lawyer and CNN legal correspondent Sunny Hostin, Syracuse student Nina Rodgers, and CNN news anchor Fredricka Whitfield.

9. hooks, *Killing Rage*.

10. See "(In) Justice For All Organizers Discuss Inspiration for Event," by the *Daily Orange*.

11. Collins, *Black Feminist Thought*, specifically the chapter "Mammies, Matriarchs, and Other Controlling Images."

12. See the image on Smith's website: https://www.nikkolas.com.

13. See *Selling the Race: Culture, Community, and Black Chicago, 1940–1955*.

14. See "The Historical Record and the American Imaginary: Adapting History in *Selma*."

15. John Fleming, "Who Killed Jimmy Lee Jackson?" *Sojourners* 34.4 (April 2005).

16. See Joshua Bote, "'A Riot Is the Language of the Unheard': MLK's Powerful Quote Resonates Amid George Floyd Protest," *USA Today*.

17. King, "Beyond Vietnam," King Center Civil Rights Digital Library; Jennifer J. Yanco, *Misremembering Dr. King: Revisiting the Legacy of Martin Luther King Jr.*

18. See the report at Department of Justice website: https://www.justice.gov/sites /default/files/opa/press-releases/attachments/2015/03/04/doj_report_on_shooting_of _michael_brown_1.pdf.

BIBLIOGRAPHY

"11 Major Misconceptions about the Black Lives Matter Movement." *Black Lives Matter.* blacklivesmatter.com/11-major-misconceptions-about-the-black-lives-matter -movement/. Accessed August 24, 2016.

Abu-Lughod, Janet. *Race, Space, and Riots in Chicago, New York, and Los Angeles.* Oxford University Press, 2007.

Alexander, Michelle. *The New Jim Crow: Mass Incarceration in the Age of Colorblindness.* New Press, 2010.

Alexander-Floyd, Nikol, and Evelyn M. Simien. "Revisiting 'What's in a Name?': Exploring the Contours of Africana Womanist Thought." In *Still Brave: The Evolution of Black Women's Studies*, edited by Stanlie M. James, Frances Smith Foster, and Beverly Guy-Sheftall, 92–114. Feminist Press, 2009.

Anderson, Elizabeth. *The Imperative of Integration.* Princeton University Press, 2010.

Atkins, Russell. "Henry Dumas: An Appreciation." *Black American Literature Forum* 22, no. 2 (1988): 159–60.

Atwater, Deborah F., and Sandra L. Herndon. "The Use of Public Space as Cultural Communicator: How Museums Reconstruct and Reconnect Cultural Memory." *Understanding African American Rhetoric: Classical Origins to Contemporary Innovations*, edited by Ronald L. Jackson II and Elaine B. Richardson, 69–84. Routledge, 2003.

Avilez, GerShun. *Radical Aesthetics and Modern Black Nationalism.* University of Illinois Press, 2016.

Azouz, Samy. "Amiri Baraka's Theatre of Ritual: From Staging Rituals of Unfulfillment to Performing Rituals of Political Praxis." *Journal of African American Studies* 22, no. 1 (2018): 17–30.

Bailey, Allison. *The Weight of Whiteness: A Feminist Engagement with Privilege, Race, and Ignorance.* Lexington Books, 2021.

Baker, Houston. *Blues, Ideology, and Afro-American Literature: A Vernacular Theory.* University of Chicago Press, 1984.

Baker, Houston. "Our Lady: Sonia Sanchez and the Writing of the Black Renaissance." *Black Feminist Criticism and Critical Theory*, edited by Joe Weixlmann and Houston Baker Jr., 169–202. Penkevill, 1988.

Baldwin, James. *The Fire Next Time.* 1962. Vintage, 1990.

Baldwin, James. *Notes of a Native Son.* 1955. Beacon Press, 1984.

Ball, Jared. *The Myth and Propaganda of Black Buying Power.* Palgrave Pivot, 2020.

Baradaran, Mehrsa. *The Color of Money: Black Banks and the Racial Wealth Gap.* Belknap Press of Harvard University Press, 2017.

Baraka, Amiri (LeRoi Jones). *Blues People: The Negro Experience in White America and the Music That Developed from It.* William Morrow and Company, 1963.

Baraka, Amiri (LeRoi Jones). *Arm Yourself, or Harm Yourself! A One Act Play.* Jihad Publication, 1967.

Baraka, Amiri (LeRoi Jones). "The Black Arts Movement." 1994. *SOS—Calling All Black People: A Black Arts Movement Reader,* edited by John H. Bracey Jr., Sonia Sanchez, and James Smethurst, 11–19. University of Massachusetts Press, 2014.

Baraka, Amiri (LeRoi Jones). "The Black Arts Movement: Its Meaning and Potential." *Nka: Journal of Contemporary African Art* 29 (2011): 22–31.

Baraka, Amiri (LeRoi Jones). "Black Fire: A New Introduction." 1968. *Black Fire: An Anthology of Afro-American Writing,* edited by Amiri Baraka and Larry Neal, xvii–xx. Black Classic Press, 2007.

Baraka, Amiri (LeRoi Jones). "Henry Dumas: Afro-Surreal-Expressionist." *Black American Literature Forum* 22, no. 2 (1988): 164–66.

Baraka, Amiri (LeRoi Jones). "In Search of the Revolutionary Theatre." *Negro Digest* xv, no. 6 (1966): 20–25.

Baraka, Amiri (LeRoi Jones). *The Motion of History & Other Plays.* William Morrow and Company, 1978.

Baraka, Amiri (LeRoi Jones). "November 1966: One Year Eight Months Later." *Raise, Race, Rays, Raze: Essays since 1965.* Random House, 1971.

Baraka, Amiri (LeRoi Jones). "SOS." 1969. *SOS—Calling All Black People: A Black Arts Movement Reader.* University of Massachusetts Press, 2014.

Baraka, Amiri (LeRoi Jones). "They Think You Are an Airplane and You're Really a Bird." 1967. *Conversations with Amiri Baraka,* edited by Charlie Reilly, 26–35. University Press of Mississippi, 1994.

Baraka, Amiri (LeRoi Jones). "The Works of Henry Dumas—A New Blackness." *Black American Literature Forum* 22, no. 2 (1988): 161–63.

Beckles, Colin A. "Black Bookstores, Black Power, and the F.B.I.: The Case of Drum and Spear." *Western Journal of Black Studies* 20, no. 2 (1996): 63–71.

Bell, Derrick A., Jr. "Brown v. Board of Education and the Interest Convergence Dilemma." *Critical Race Theory: The Key Writings That Formed the Movement,* edited by Kimberlé Crenshaw, Neil Gotanda, Gary Peller, and Kendall Thomas. New Press, 1996.

Benjamin, Shanna Greene. "The Uses of Anger: Wanda Coleman and the Poetry of Black Rage." *Hecate* 40, no.1 (2014): 58–79.

Bentley-Edwards, Keisha L., et al. "How Does It Feel to Be a Problem? The Missing Kerner Commission Report." *RSF: The Russell Sage Foundation Journal of Sciences* 4, no. 6 (2018): 20–40.

Bergmann, Barbara R. "The Effect on White Incomes of Discrimination in Employment." *The Journal of Political Economy,* vol. 79, no. 2, 1971): 294–313.

Berry, Mary Frances. *My Face Is Black Is True: Callie House and the Struggle for Ex-slave Reparations.* Vintage Books, 2005.

Best, Stephen, and Saidiya Hartman. "Fugitive Justice." *Representations* 92 (2005): 1–15.

Biebricher, Thomas. *The Political Theory of Neoliberalism*. Stanford University Press, 2018.

Black Arts Repertory Theatre School. United States. Federal Bureau of Investigation. 1965. Government Printing Office, 2008.

Bolden, Tony. "All the Birds Sing Bass: The Revolutionary Blues of Jayne Cortez." *African American Review* 35, no.1, 2001): 61–71.

Bote, Joshua. *Afro-Blue: Improvisations in African American Poetry and Culture*. University of Illinois Press, 2004.

Bote, Joshua. "'A Riot Is the Language of the Unheard': MLK's Powerful Quote Resonates Amid George Floyd's Protests." *USA Today*, May 29, 2020. https://www.msn.com/en -us/news/us/a-riot-is-the-language-of-the-unheard-mlks-powerful-quote-resonates -amid-george-floyd-protests/ar-BB14LQeS. Accessed July 24, 2020.

Bowman, Kenneth, and Ben Caldwell. "The Revolution Will Not Be Televised nor Staged: An Interview with Ben Caldwell." *Callaloo* 22, no. 4 (1999): 808–24.

Bracey, John H., Sonia Sanchez, and James Smethurst. "Introduction." *SOS—Calling All Black People: A Black Arts Movement Reader*. University of Massachusetts Amherst Press, 2014.

Brooks, Gwendolyn. "kitchenette building." *The Norton Anthology of African American Literature*, 3rd ed. 2 vols., 326. W.W. Norton, 2014.

Brooks, Gwendolyn. "Malcolm X." In *the Mecca*. Harper & Row, 1964, 39.

Brooks, Gwendolyn. "Mecca." In *the Mecca*. Harper & Row, 1964.

Brooks, Gwendolyn. "Medgar Evers." In *the Mecca*. Harper & Row, 1964, 38.

Brooks, Gwendolyn. *Report from Part One*. Broadside Press, 1972.

Brooks, Gwendolyn. *Riot*. Broadside Press, 1969.

Brooks, Gwendolyn. "The Wall." In *the Mecca*. Harper & Row, 1964, 42.

Brooks, Gwendolyn. "We Real Cool." *The Norton Anthology of African American Literature*. 3rd ed. 2 vols., 337. W.W. Norton, 2014.

Brooks, Michael, et al. "Is There a Problem Officer? Exploring the Lived Experience of Black Men and Their Relationship with Law Enforcement." *Journal of African American Studies* 20, no. 3–4: 346–62.

Brown, Wendy. *Undoing the Demos: Neoliberalism's Stealth Revolution*. Zone Books, 2015.

"Bury Man Killed in Subway Fracas." *Amsterdam News*, June 1, 1968, 13.

Caldwell, Ben. "Riot Sale, or Dollar Psyche Fake Out." *Drama Review* 12, no. 4 (1968): 41–42.

Camp, Jordan T. *Incarcerating the Crisis: Freedom Struggles and the Rise of the Neoliberal State*. University of California Press, 2016.

Carmichael, Stokely. "What We Want." *Let Nobody Turn Us Around: An African American Anthology*. 2nd ed. Rowman & Littlefield, 2009, 419–25.

Chan, Sewell, and Nick Cumming-Bruce. "U.N. Panel Condemns the President's Response to Racial Violence in Charlottesville." *New York Times*, August 23, 2017.

Clark, Cheryl. *After Mecca: Women Poets and the Black Arts Movement*. Rutgers University Press, 2005.

Clark, Kenneth B. *Dark Ghetto: Dilemmas of Social Power*. Harper Torchbook, 1967.

Clarke, John Henrik. "Introduction." *Harlem: A Community in Transition*. Citadel Press, 1964.

Coates, Ta-Nehisi. *Between the World and Me*. One World, 2015.

Cobb, Charles E. Jr. *This Nonviolent Stuff'll Get You Killed: How Guns Made the Civil Rights Movement Possible*. Duke University Press, 2016.

Colbert, Soyica Diggs. *The African American Theatrical Body: Reception, Performance, and the Stage*. Cambridge University Press, 2011.

Colbert, Soyica Diggs. *Black Movements: Performance and Cultural Politics*. Rutgers University Press, 2017.

Colbert, Soyica Diggs. "Black Rage: On Cultivating Black National Belonging." *Theatre Survey* 57, no. 3: 336–57.

Colbert, Soyica Diggs. "A Pedagogical Approach to Understanding Rioting as Revolutionary Action in Alice Childress's Wine in the Wilderness." *Theatre Topics* 19, no. 1 (2009): 77–85.

Collins, Lisa Gail, and Margo Natalie Crawford. *New Thoughts on the Black Arts Movement*. Rutgers University Press, 2006.

Collins, Patricia Hill. *Black Feminist Thought: Knowledge, Consciousness, and the Politics of Empowerment*. Harper Collins Academic, 1991.

Combahee River Collective. "A Black Feminist Statement." 1978. In *Still Brave: The Evolution of Black Women's Studies*, edited by Stanlie M. James, Frances Smith Foster, and Beverly Guy-Sheftall, 3–11. Feminist Press, 2009.

Cooper, Brittney C. *Beyond Respectability: The Intellectual Thought of Race Women*. University of Illinois Press, 2017.

Corrigan, Lisa M. *Black Feelings: Race and Affect in the Long Sixties*. University Press of Mississippi, 2020.

Crawford, Margo Natalie. "The 'Atmos-Feeling' of Resurrection: Feeling Black (Not Slave) in Black Arts Movement Drama." *Modern Drama* 62, no. 4 (2019): 483–501.

Crawford, Margo Natalie. *Black Post-Blackness: The Black Arts Movement and Twenty-First-Century Aesthetics*. University of Illinois Press, 2017.

Cruse, Harold. *Rebellion or Revolution?* 1968. University of Minnesota Press, 2009.

Cruz, Joelle M. "Reimagining Feminist Organizing in Global Times: Lessons from African Feminist Communication." *Women and Language* 38, no. 1 (2015): 23–41.

Curry, Tommy J. *The Man-Not: Race, Class, Genre, and the Dilemmas of Black Manhood*. Temple University Press, 2017.

Curry, Tommy J. "Michael Brown and the Need for a Genre Study of Black Male Death and Dying." *Theory and Event* 17, no. 3 (2014): 1–8.

Darity, William Jr. "The Case for Reparations." *Crisis Magazine*, September 2019. https://www.thecrisismagazine.com/single-post/2019/09/09/The-Case-For-Reparations.

Darity, William Jr. "Forty Acres and a Mule in the 21st Century." *Social Science Quarterly* 89, no. 3 (2008): 656–64.

Darity, William Jr., and A. Kirsten Mullen. *From Here to Equality: Reparations for Black Americans in the Twenty-First Century*. University of North Carolina Press, 2020.

Darity, William Jr., et al. "What We Get Wrong about Closing the Racial Wealth Gap." Samuel DuBois Cook Center on Social Equity, Duke University, 2018, 1–67.

Davila, Maria Teresa. "Discussing Racial Justice in Light of 2016: Black Lives Matter, a Trump Presidency, and the Continued Struggle for Justice." *Journal of Religious Ethics* 45, no. 4 (2017).

Davis, Angela Y. *Freedom Is a Constant Struggle: Ferguson, Palestine, and the Foundations of a Movement*. Haymarket Books, 2016.

Davis, Dana-Ain. "'The Bone Collectors' Comments for Sorrow as Artifact: Black Radical Mothering in Times of Terror." *Transforming Anthropology* 24, no. 1 (2016): 8–16.

Davis, Joshua Clark. *From Head Shops to Whole Foods: The Rise and Fall of Activist Entrepreneurs*. Columbia University Press, 2017.

Debo, Annette. "Reflecting Violence in the Warpland: Gwendolyn Brooks's *Riot*." *African American Review* 39, no. 1 (2005): 143–52.

DeFrantz, Thomas. *Dancing Revelations: Alvin Ailey's Embodiment of African American Culture*. Oxford University Press, 2004.

Department of Justice Report Regarding the Criminal Investigation into the Shooting Death of Michael Brown by Ferguson, Missouri Police Officer Darren Wilson. United States. Government Printing Office, 2015.

DiAngelo, Robin. *White Fragility: Why It's So Hard for White People to Talk about Racism*. Allen Lane, 2019.

Dove, Nah. "African Womanism: An Afrocentric Theory." *Journal of Black Studies* 28, no. 5 (1998): 515–39.

Dove, Nah. *Afrikan Mothers: Bearers of Culture, Makers of Social Change*. State University of New York Press, 1998.

Drake, St. Clair, and Horace R. Cayton. 1945. *Black Metropolis: A Study of Negro Life in a Northern City*. Harcourt, Brace & World, 1970.

Drotning, Phillip T., and Wesley W. South. *Up from the Ghetto*. Cowles, 1970.

Dudziak, Mary L. *Cold War Civil Rights: Race and the Image of American Democracy*. Princeton University Press, 2000.

Dumas, Henry. "Biography." *Black Fire: An Anthology of Afro-American Writing*, edited by Amiri Baraka and Larry Neal. 1968. Black Classic Press, 2007, 661.

Dumas, Henry. "Fon." *Echo Tree: The Collected Short Story Fiction of Henry Dumas*, edited by Eugene B. Redmond, 116–27. Coffee House Press, 2003.

Dumas, Henry. "Our King Is Dead." *Black American Literature Forum* 22, no. 2 (1988): 245–46.

Dumas, Henry. "Riot or Revolt?" *Echo Tree: The Collected Short Story Fiction of Henry Dumas*, edited by Eugene B. Redmond, 362–81. Coffee House Press, 2003.

Dunham, Roger G., and Nick Petersen. "Making Black Lives Matter: Evidence-Based Policies for Reducing Police Bias in the Use of Deadly Force." *American Society of Criminology* 16, no. 1 (2017): 341–48.

Edwards, Erica R. *Charisma and the Fictions of Black Leadership*. University of Minnesota Press, 2012.

Elam, Harry J. *Taking It to the Streets: The Social Protest Theatre of Luis Valdez and Amiri Baraka*. University of Michigan Press, 1997.

Elam, Harry J., and Michele Elam. "Blood Debt: Reparations in Langston Hughes's *Mulatto*." *Theatre Journal* 61, no. 1 (2009): 85–103.

Ellison, Ralph. *Invisible Man*. 1947. Modern Library, 1994.

Emblidge, David. "Rally Point: Lewis Michaux's National Memorial African Bookstore." *Publishing Research Quarterly* 24, no. 4 (2008): 267–76.

Fanon, Frantz. "The Fact of Blackness." 1952. *Theories of Race and Racism: A Reader*, edited by Les Back and John Solomos, 257–65. Routledge, 2000.

Farmer, Ashley D. *Remaking Black Power: How Black Women Transformed an Era*. University of North Carolina Press, 2017.

Fenderson, Jonathan. *Building the Black Arts Movement: Hoyt Fuller and the Cultural Politics of the 1960s*. University of Illinois Press, 2019.

Final Report of the President's Task Force on 21st Century Policing. President's Task Force on 21st Century Policing. United States. Washington, DC: Office of Community Oriented Policing Services, 2015.

Finley, Cheryl. *Committed to Memory: The Art of the Slave Ship Icon*. Princeton University Press, 2018.

Fisher, Maisha T. "Earning 'Dual Degrees': Black Bookstores as Alternative Knowledge Spaces." *Anthropology and Education Quarterly* 37, no. 1: 83–99.

Fitts, Mako. "Theorizing Transformative Revolutionary Action: The Contribution of bell hooks to Emancipatory Knowledge Production." *CLR James Journal* 17, no. 1 (2011): 112–31.

Fleming, John. "Who Killed Jimmy Lee Jackson?" *Sojourners* 34, no. 4 (2005). https://sojo .net/magazine/april-2005/who-killed-jimmy-lee-jackson. Accessed April 23, 2020.

Forsgren, La Donna L. *In Search of Our Warrior Mothers: Women Dramatists of the Black Arts Movement*. Northwestern University Press, 2018.

Forsgren, La Donna L. *Sistuhs in the Struggle: An Oral History of Black Arts Movement Theatre and Performance*. Northwestern University Press, 2020.

French, David. "Black Lives Matter Is Pushing Our Cities Back to the Brink." *National Review*, August 15, 2016. https://www.nationalreview.com/2016/08/milwaukee-riot -black-lives-matter-police-homicide-rate-khalif-rainey/. Accessed March 4, 2018.

Gabbin, Joanne V., ed. *Furious Flower: African-American Poetry from the Black Arts Movement to the Present*. University of Virginia Press, 2004.

Garza, Alicia. "A Herstory of the #BlackLivesMatter Movement." *Feminist Wire*, October 7, 2014. www.thefeministwire.com/2014/10/blacklivesmatter-2/. Accessed September 4, 2015.

Gerald, Carolyn. "Symposium: The Measure and the Meaning of the Sixties." 1969. *SOS— Calling All Black People: A Black Arts Movement Reader*, edited by John H. Bracey Jr., Sonia Sanchez, and James Smethurst, 46–50. University of Massachusetts Press, 2014.

Goldstein, Eric L. *The Price of Whiteness: Jews, Race, and American Identity*. Princeton University Press, 2019.

Green, Adam. *Selling the Race: Culture, Community, and Black Chicago, 1940–1955*. University of Chicago Press, 2007.

Green, Alex. "A New Generation of African-American-Owned Bookstores." *Publishers Weekly*, April 6, 2018.

Greenberg, Cheryl. *"Or Does It Explode?": Black Harlem in the Great Depression*. Oxford University Press, 1991.

Griffin, Farah Jasmine. "At Last . . . ?: Michelle Obama, Beyoncé, Race & History." *Daedalus* 140, no. 1 (2011): 131–41.

Griffin, Farah Jasmine. "That the Mothers May Soar and the Daughters May Know Their Names: A Retrospective of Black Feminist Literary Criticism." *Still Brave:*

The Evolution of Black Women's Studies, edited by Stanlie M. James, Frances Smith Foster, and Beverly Guy-Sheftall, 336–60. Feminist Press, 2009.

Hamilton, Bobb. "The Negro Image in Western Art." *Soulbook: The Quarterly Journal of Revolutionary Afro-America* 1, no. 2 (1965): 146–48.

Hamilton, Darrick, and William Darity Jr. "The Political Economy of Education, Financial Literacy, and the Racial Wealth Gap." *Federal Reserve Bank of St. Louis Review* 99, no. 1 (2017): 59–76.

Harley, Sharon. "'Working for Nothing but for a Living': Black Women in the Underground Economy." *Sister Circle: Black Women and Work*, edited by Sharon Harley and the Black Women and Work Collective. Rutgers University Press, 2002.

Harris, Trudier. *Martin Luther King Jr., Heroism, and African American Literature.* University of Alabama Press, 2014.

Henderson, Aneeka A. *Veil and Vow: Marriage Matters in Contemporary African American Culture.* University of North Carolina Press, 2020.

Henderson, Errol A. *The Revolution Will Not Be Theorized: Cultural Revolution in the Black Power Era.* State University of New York Press, 2019.

Higginbotham, Evelyn Brooks. *Righteous Discontent: The Women's Movement in the Black Baptist Church, 1880–1920.* Harvard University Press, 1993.

Hillard, David. *The Black Panther Intercommunal News Service 1967–1980.* Atria Books, 2007.

Holder, Michelle. "Revisiting Bergmann's Occupational Crowding Model." *Review of Radical Political Economics* 50, no. 4 (2018): 683–90.

Holloway, Karla F. C. "Cultural Narratives Passed On: African American Mourning Stories." *African American Literary Theory: A Reader*, edited by Winston Napier. New York University Press, 2000.

Hong, Grace Kyungwon. *Death beyond Disavowal: The Impossible Politics of Difference.* University of Minnesota Press, 2015.

hooks, bell. *Killing Rage: Ending Racism.* Holt Books, 1996.

Horne, Gerald. *The Counter-Revolution of 1776: Slave Resistance and the Origins of the United States of America.* New York University Press, 2014.

Hudson-Weems, Clenora. *Africana Womanism: Reclaiming Ourselves*, 5th ed. Routledge, 2020.

Huff, Stephanie, et al. "Gendered Occupation: Situated Understandings of Gender, Womanhood, and Occupation in Tanzania." *Journal of Occupational Science* (2020): 1–15.

Huggins, Ericka, and Angela D. LeBlanc-Ernest. "Revolutionary Women, Revolutionary Education: The Black Panther Party's Oakland Community School." *Want to Start a Revolution? Radical Women in the Black Freedom Struggle*, edited by Dayo F. Gore, Jeanne Theoharis, and Komozi Woodard, 161–84. New York University Press, 2009.

Hughes, Langston. "The Harlem Riot—1964." *Harlem: A Community in Transition*, edited by John Henrik Clarke, 214–20. Citadel Press, 1964.

Ignatiev, Noel. *How the Irish Became White.* Routledge, 1995.

Jarrett, Gene Andrew. *Representing the Race: A New Political History of African American Literature.* New York University Press, 2011.

Jefferies, Judson L., ed. *Black Power in the Belly of the Beast*. University of Illinois, 2006.

Johnson, Christine. "When You Died." *For Malcolm: Poems on the Life and the Death of Malcolm X*, edited by Dudley Randall and Margaret Burroughs, 71. Broadside Press, 1967.

Jones, Shermaine M. "Presenting Our Bodies, Laying Our Case: The Political Efficacy of Grief and Rage during the Civil Rights Movement in Alice Walker's *Meridian*." *Southern Quarterly* 52, no. 1 (2014): 179–95.

Joseph, Peniel E. *Waiting 'Til the Midnight Hour: A Narrative History of Black Power in America*. Henry Holt, 2006.

Joyce, Joyce A. "Interview with Sonia Sanchez: Poet, Playwright, Teacher, and Intellectual." *Conversations with Sonia Sanchez*, edited by Joyce A. Joyce. University Press of Mississippi, 2007.

Judy, R. A. T. "On the Question of Nigga Authenticity." *Boundary 2* 21, no. 3 (1994): 211–30.

Karenga, Maulana (Ron). "Black Cultural Nationalism." 1971. *SOS—Calling All Black People: A Black Arts Movement Reader*, edited by John H. Bracey Jr., Sonia Sanchez, and James Smethurst, 51–54. University of Massachusetts Press, 2014.

Katznelson, Ira. *When Affirmative Action Was White: An Untold History of Racial Inequality in Twentieth-Century America*. W.W. Norton, 2005.

Kaufman, Jonathan. "Blacks and Jews: The Struggle in the Cities." *Struggles in the Promised Land: Towards a History of Black-Jewish Relations in the United States*, edited by Jack Salzman and Cornel West, 107–21. Oxford University Press, 1997.

Kelley, Robin D. G. "House Negroes on the Loose: Malcolm X and the Black Bourgeoisie." *Callaloo* 21, no. 2 (1998): 419–35.

Kent, George. *A Life of Gwendolyn Brooks*. University Press of Kentucky, 1993.

Kihss, Peter. "Harlem Riots Spread Over 3 Decades." *New York Times*, July 20, 1964, 17.

Kijakazi, Kilolo, et al. *The Color of Wealth in the Nation's Capital*. A Joint Publication of the Urban Institute, Duke University, The New School, and the Insight Center for Community Economic Development, 2016.

King, Debra Walker. *African Americans and the Culture of Pain*. University of Virginia Press, 2008.

King, Martin Luther, Jr. *I Have a Dream*. 1963. Schwartz & Wade, 2012.

King, Martin Luther, Jr. "To the Mountaintop: 'Let us develop a kind of dangerous unselfishness.'" 1968. *"All Labor Has Dignity,"* edited by Michael K. Honey, 153–66. Beacon Press, 2011.

King, Martin Luther, Jr. "The Other America." 1968. *"All Labor Has Dignity,"* edited by Michael K. Honey, 153–66. Beacon Press, 2011.

King, Martin Luther, Jr. "Beyond Vietnam." Riverside Church, New York, April 4, 1967. Audio recording, Martin Luther King, Jr. Research and Education Institute, Stanford University.

King, Martin Luther, Jr. *Where Do We Go From Here: Chaos or Community*. 1967. Beacon Press, 2010.

King, Martin Luther, Jr. "WSB-TV news film clip of Dr. Martin Luther King, Jr. speaking about race riots in Rochester and New York City, New York 1964 July 27." Digital Library of Georgia and Walter J. Brown Media Archives and Peabody Awards Collection, University of Georgia Libraries, 2007. Accessed March 12, 2014.

LaBrie, Peter. "The New Breed." 1966. *Black Fire: An Anthology of Afro-American Writing*, edited by Amiri Baraka and Larry Neal, 64–77. Black Classic Press, 2007.

Lang, Clarence. *Black America in the Shadow of the Sixties: Notes on the Civil Rights Movement, Neoliberalism, and Politics*. University of Michigan Press, 2015.

Leak, Jeffrey B. *Visible Man: The Life of Henry Dumas*. University of Georgia Press, 2014.

Letort, Delphine. "The Historical Record and the American Imaginary: Adapting History in *Selma*." *Black Camera* 10, no. 2 (2019): 195–210.

Lewis, Gordon R. *Bad Faith and Antiblack Racism*. Humanity Books, 1995.

Lott-Williamson, Joy Ann, Maria E. Hyler, and Linda Darling-Hammond. "Emancipation and Reconstruction: African American Education, 1865–1919." *The Oxford Handbook of African American Citizenship 1865–Present*, edited by Lawrence D. Bobo et al., 591–611. Oxford University Press, 2012.

Malewitz, Raymond. "'My Newish Voice': Rethinking Black Power in Gwendolyn Brooks's *Whirlwind*." *Callaloo* 29, no. 2 (2005): 531–44.

Marable, Manning. 1983. *How Capitalism Underdeveloped Black America: Problems in Race, Political Economy, and Society*. Haymarket Books, 2015.

McDaniel, Caleb W. *Sweet Taste of Liberty: A True Story of Slavery and Restitution in America*. Oxford University Press, 2019.

Melamed, Jodi. *Represent and Destroy: Rationalizing Violence in the New Racial Capitalism*. University of Minnesota Press, 2011.

Melamed, Jodi. "The Spirit of Neoliberalism: From Racial Liberalism to Neoliberal Multiculturalism." *Social Text* 24, no. 4 (2006): 1–24.

Melhem, D. H. *Gwendolyn Brooks: Poetry and the Heroic Voice*. University Press of Kentucky, 1987.

Mena, Jasmine A., and Khalil P. Saucier. "'Don't Let Me Be Misunderstood': Nina Simone's Africana Womanism." *Journal of Black Studies* 45, no. 3 (2014): 247–65.

Merod, Anna. "(In) Justice For All Organizers Discuss Inspiration for Event." *Daily Orange*, October 21, 2015.

Mills, Charles W. *Black Rights/White Wrongs: The Critique of Racial Liberalism*. Oxford University Press, 2017.

Mills, Charles W. *The Racial Contract*. Cornell University Press, 1997.

Moore, Natalie Y. *Southside: A Portrait of Chicago and American Segregation*. St. Martin's Press, 2016.

Morrison, Toni. *Playing in the Dark: Whiteness and the Literary Imagination*. Harvard University Press, 1992.

Morrison, Toni. "Troubling and Cowardly." *Charlie Rose*, PBS, April 30, 2015. https://www.youtube.com/watch?v=SswSviVJAfc.

Mosby, Donald. "Threats of Violence Hit City after News." *Chicago Defender*, April 6, 1968, 1.

Moynihan, Daniel P. 1965. *The Negro Family: The Case for National Action*. Eisenhower Foundation. Government Printing Office, 2008.

Mullen, Bill V. *James Baldwin: Living in Fire*. Pluto Press, 2019.

Nash, Jennifer C. *Black Feminism Reimagined: After Intersectionality*. Duke University Press, 2019.

Nash, Shondrah T. "Through Black Eyes: African American Women's Constructions of
    Their Experiences with Intimate Male Partner Violence." *Violence against Women* 11,
    no. 11 (2005): 1420–40.
Nielsen, Inge. *Cultic Theatres and Ritual Drama: A Study in Regional Development and
    Religious Interchange between East and West in Antiquity*. Aarhus University Press,
    2002.
Neal, Larry. "The Black Arts Movement." *Drama Review* 12, no. 4 (1968): 28–39.
Neal, Larry. "Black Power in the International Context." *Visions of a Liberated Future:
    Black Arts Movement Writings*, edited by Michael Schwartz, 133–43. Thunder's Mouth
    Press, 1989.
Neal, Larry. "New Space/the Growth of Black Consciousness in the Sixties." *Visions of a
    Liberated Future: Black Arts Movement Writings*, edited by Michael Schwartz, 125–32.
    Thunder's Mouth Press, 1989.
Nnaemeka, Obioma. "Nego-Feminism: Theorizing, Practicing, and Pruning Africa's Way."
    Signs: Journal of Women in Culture and Society 29, no. 2 (2004): 357–85.
Newkirk, Vann R. "The Permanence of Black Lives Matter: A New Policy Platform from
    a Coalition of Activists Signals a New Stage in the Protest Movement." *The Atlantic*,
    August 2, 2016.
Newton, Huey P. "To the Black Movement." 1968. *To Die for the People*, edited by Toni
    Morrison, 90–93. City Lights Books, 2009.
Newton, Huey P. "The Correct Handling of a Revolution." 1967. *To Die for the People*,
    edited by Toni Morrison, 14–19. City Lights Books, 2009.
Newton, Huey P. "Fear and Doubt." 1967. *To Die for the People*, edited by Toni Morrison,
    77–79. City Lights Books, 2009.
New York City Housing Authority. *Toward the End to Be Achieved: The New York City
    Housing Authority, Its History in Outline*. New York City Housing Authority, 1937.
Nobles, Wade W. *Seeking Sakhu: Foundational Writings for an African Psychology*. 1976.
    Third World Press, 2006.
Norman, George. "To Malcolm X." *For Malcolm: Poems on the Life and the Death of Malcolm
    X*, edited by Dudley Randall and Margaret G. Burroughs, 23. Broadside Press, 1967.
Ntiri, Daphne W. "Reassessing Africana Womanism: Continuity and Change." *Western
    Journal of Black Studies* 25, no. 3: 163–67.
Obama, Barack. "Barack Obama's Speech on the Steps of the Lincoln Memorial—Full
    Transcript." *The Guardian*, August 28, 2013. www.theguardian.com/world/2013/aug/28
    /barack-obama-speech-full-transcript. Accessed August 29, 2016.
Obama, Barack. "President Obama Delivers a Statement on the Ferguson Grand Jury's
    Decision." White House Briefing Room, November 24, 2014. https://obamawhitehouse
    .archives.gov/blog/2014/11/24/president-obama-delivers-statement-ferguson-grand
    -jurys-decision. Accessed 15 June 2021.
Obama, Barack. "Remarks by President Obama in Town Hall with Young Leaders of the
    UK." Lindley Hall Royal Horticulture Halls Town Hall, London, England. April 23,
    2016.
O'Brien, Gail Williams. *The Color of the Law: Race, Violence, and Justice in the Post–World
    War II South*. University of North Carolina Press, 1999.

Oliver, Melvin L., and Thomas M. Shapiro. "A Sociology of Wealth and Racial Inequality." *Redress for Historical Injustices in the United States: On Reparations for Slavery, Jim Crow, and Their Legacies*, edited by Michael T. Martin and Marilyn Yaquinto. Duke University Press, 2007.

Oppel, Richard A. Jr., and Derrick Bryson Taylor. "Here's What You Need to Know about Breonna Taylor's Death." *New York Times* July 18, 2020. https://www.nytimes.com /article/breonna-taylor-police.html. Accessed July 24, 2020.

Osofsky, Gilbert. "Harlem: The Making of a Ghetto." *Harlem: A Community in Transition*, edited by John Henrik Clarke, 16–25. Citadel Press, 1964.

Patterson, James T. *Freedom Is Not Enough: The Moynihan Report and America's Struggle over Black Family Life*. Basic Books, 2010.

Patterson, Orlando. *Slavery and Social Death: A Comparative Study*. Harvard University Press, 1982.

Patterson, Robert J. *Exodus Politics: Civil Rights and Leadership in African American Literature and Culture*. University of Virginia Press, 2013.

Patton, Venetria K. *The Grasp That Reaches Beyond the Grave: The Ancestral Call in Black Women's Texts*. State University of New York Press, 2013.

Penrod, Josh, C. J. Sinner, and MaryJo Webster. "Buildings Damaged in Minneapolis St. Paul after Riots." *Star Tribune*, July 13, 2020. https://www.startribune.com /minneapolis-st-paul-buildings-are-damaged-looted-after-george-floyd-protests -riots/569930671/?refresh=true. Accessed July 24, 2020.

Petry, Ann. "In Darkness and Confusion." *Miss Muriel and Other Stories*, 252–95. Houghton Mifflin, 1971.

"Platform." The Movement for Black Lives. policy.m4bl.org/platform/. Accessed August 24, 2016.

Plotkin, Wendy. "'Hemmed In': The Struggle against Racial Restrictive Covenants and Deed Restrictions in Post-WWII Chicago." *Journal of the Illinois State Historical Society* 94, no. 1 (2001): 39–69.

Potter, Dave. "King's Slaying Termed Blow to Nonviolence." *Chicago Defender*, April 6, 1968, 1.

Rabig, Julia. *The Fixers: Devolution, Development, and Civil Society in Newark, 1960–1990*. University of Chicago Press, 2016.

Ragain, Nathan. "A 'Reconcepted Am': Language, Nature, and Collectivity in Sun Ra and Henry Dumas." *Criticism: A Quarterly for Literature and Arts* 54, no. 4 (2012): 539–65.

Rambsy, Howard. *The Black Arts Enterprise and the Production of African American Poetry*. University of Michigan Press, 2011.

Randall, Dudley, and Margaret G. Burroughs. "Introduction." *For Malcolm: Poems on the Life and the Death of Malcolm X*, xxiii–xxvi. Broadside Press, 1967.

Rankin, Kenrya. "The Movement for Black Lives' Policy Platform." *Colorlines*, August 1, 2016.

Ransby, Barbara. *Making All Black Lives Matter: Reimagining Freedom in the 21st Century*. University of California Press, 2018.

@realDonaldTrump. ". . . These THUGS are dishonoring the memory of George Floyd." Twitter, May 29, 2020.

Redmond, Eugene B. "Introduction: The Ancient and Recent Voices within Dumas." *Black American Literature Forum* 22, no. 2 (1988): 143–54.

Reich, David. "'As Poets, As Activists': An Interview with Sonia Sanchez." *Conversations with Sonia Sanchez*, edited by Joyce A. Joyce. University Press of Mississippi, 2007.

Report of the National Advisory Commission on Civil Disorders. 1968. Government Printing Office, 2008.

Ricks, Shawn Arango. "Normalized Chaos: Black Feminism, Womanism, and the (Re) definition of Trauma and Healing." *Meridians* 16, no. 2 (2018): 343–50.

Rodriguez, Anthony Bayani. "Former Black Panther Marshall Eddie Conway on Revolutionary Political Education in the Twenty-First Century." *Journal of African American Studies* 21, no. 1: 138–49.

Rojas, Rick, and Khorri Atkinson. "Five Days of Unrest That Shaped, and Haunted, Newark." *New York Times*, July 11, 2017.

Rose, Tricia. *Black Noise: Rap Music and Black Culture in Contemporary America*. University Press of New England, 1994.

Rustin, Bayard. "'Black Power' and Coalition Politics." *Let Nobody Turn Us Around: An African American Anthology*, 2nd ed., 430–34. Rowman & Littlefield, 2009.

Sales, William Jr. *Malcolm X and the Organization of Afro-American Unity: A Case Study in Afro-American Nationalism*. Dissertation, Columbia University, 1991.

Sanchez, Sonia. *BadDDD Sonia Sanchez*. Directed by Sabrina Schmidt Gordon, Barbara Attie, and Jane Goldwater. Performances by Sonia Sanchez, Amiri Baraka, Questlove, Ruby Dee, Talib Kweli, Haki R. Madhubuti, Ursula Rucker, Jessica Care Moore, Mos Def, and Ayana Mathis. Attie & Goldwater Productions, 2015.

Sanchez, Sonia. "blues." 1968. *Black Fire: An Anthology of Afro-American Writing*, edited by Amiri Baraka and Larry Neal, 254. Black Classic Press, 2007.

Sanchez, Sonia. "The Bronx Is Next." 1968. *SOS—Calling All Black People: A Black Arts Movement Reader*, edited by John H. Bracey Jr., Sonia Sanchez, and James Smethurst, 520–28. University of Massachusetts Press, 2014.

Sanchez, Sonia. "Poetry Run Loose: Breaking the Rules." 2004. *I'm Black When I'm Singing, I'm Blue When I Ain't and Other Plays*, edited by Jacqueline Wood, 3–14. Duke University Press, 2010.

Sanchez, Sonia. "Sister Son/ji." 1969. *I'm Black When I'm Singing, I'm Blue When I Ain't and Other Plays*, edited by Jacqueline Wood, 36–43. Duke University Press, 2010.

Satter, Beryl. "Cops, Gangs, and Revolutionaries in 1960s Chicago." *Journal of Urban History* 42, no. 6 (2016): 1110–34.

Shapiro, Herbert. *White Violence and Black Response: From Reconstruction to Montgomery*. University of Massachusetts Press, 1988.

Sharpe, Christina. *In the Wake: On Blackness and Being*. Duke University Press, 2016.

Simeon-Jones, Kersuze. *Literary and Sociopolitical Writings of the Black Diaspora in the Nineteenth and Twentieth Centuries*. Lexington Books, 2010.

Smethurst, James Edward. *The Black Arts Movement: Literary Nationalism in the 1960s and 1970s*. University of North Carolina Press, 2005.

Smith, Derik. "Quarreling in the Movement: Robert Hayden's Black Arts Era." *Callaloo* 33, no. 2 (2010): 449–66.

Spence, Lester K. *Knocking the Hustle: Against the Neoliberal Turn in Black Politics.* Punctum Books, 2015.

Spence, Lester K. "The Neoliberal Turn in Black Politics." *Souls* 14, no. 3–4 (2012): 139–59.

Sprunt, Barbara. "The History Behind 'When the Looting Starts, the Shooting Starts.'" NPR, May 29, 2020.

Steele, M. Janee. "A CBT Approach to Internalized Racism among African Americans." *International Journal for the Advancement of Counselling* 42, no. 3 (2020): 217–33.

Stewart, James T. "The Development of the Black Revolutionary Artist." 1968. *Black Fire: An Anthology of Afro-American Writing,* edited by Amiri Baraka and Larry Neal, 3–10. Black Classic Press, 2007.

Stewart, Michael Cade. "A Satyric Paradise: The Form of W. B. Yeats's News for the Delphic Oracle." *Writing Modern Ireland,* edited by Catherine E. Paul, 187–93. Liverpool University Press, 2015.

Student Nonviolent Coordinating Committee. "Position Paper on Black Power." *Let Nobody Turn Us Around: An African American Anthology,* 2nd ed., 425–29. Rowman & Littlefield, 2009.

Taylor, Clyde. "Henry Dumas: Legacy of a Long-Breath Singer." *Black American Literature Forum* 22, no. 8 (1988): 353–64.

Taylor, Keeanga-Yamahtta. *From #BlackLivesMatter to Black Liberation.* Haymarket Books, 2016.

Taylor, Keeanga-Yamahtta. "Introduction." *How We Get Free: Black Feminism and the Combahee River Collective,* edited by Keeanga-Yamahtta Taylor, 1–14. Haymarket Books, 2017.

Thornhill, Ted. "Racial Salience and the Consequences of Making White People Uncomfortable: Intra-Racial Discrimination, Racial Screening, and the Maintenance of White Supremacy." *Sociology Compass* 9, no. 8 (2015): 694–703.

Trotter, Joe William, Jr. "Blacks in the Urban North: The 'Underclass Question' in Historical Perspective." *The Underclass Debate: Views from History,* edited by Michael B. Katz, 55–81. Princeton University Press, 1993.

Tucker, Terrence T. *Comic Rage from Ralph Ellison to Chris Rock.* University Press of Florida, 2018.

Ture, Kwame, and Charles V. Hamilton. *Black Power: The Politics of Liberation in America.* Vintage Books, 1992.

Walker, Alice. "In Search of Our Mothers' Gardens." *Within the Circle: An Anthology of African American Literary Criticism from the Harlem Renaissance to the Present,* edited by Angelyn Mitchell, 401–9. Duke University Press, 1994.

Walker, Alice. "Womanist." 1983. *Still Brave: The Evolution of Black Women's Studies,* edited by Stanlie M. James, Frances Smith Foster, and Beverly Guy-Sheftall, 22. Feminist Press, 2009.

Warren, Kenneth W. *What Was African American Literature?* Harvard University Press, 2011.

Weed, Eric. *The Religion of White Supremacy in the United States.* Lexington Books, 2017.

Welsing, Frances Cress. 1991. *The Isis (Yssis) Papers: The Keys to the Colors.* C.W. Publishing, 2004.

Wheeler, Lesley. "Heralding the Clear Obscure: Gwendolyn Brooks and Apostrophe." *Callaloo* 24, no. 1 (2001): 227–35.

Williams, Chad L. "Vanguards of the New Negro: African American Veterans and Post–World War I Racial Militancy." *Journal of African American History* 92, no. 3 (2007): 347–30.

Williams, Robert F. *Negroes with Guns*. 1962. Martino Publishing, 2013.

Womack, Autumn. "Visuality, Surveillance, and the Afterlife of Slavery." *American Literary History (Review)* 29, no. 1 (2017): 191–204.

Womack, Ytasha L. *Post Black: How a New Generation Is Redefining African American Identity*. Lawrence Hill Books, 2010.

Wood, Jacqueline, and Sonia Sanchez. "'This Thing Called Playwrighting': An Interview with Sonia Sanchez on the Art of Her Drama." *African American Review* 39, no. 1/2 (2005): 119–32.

Wood, Jacqueline, and Sonia Sanchez. "'To Wash My Ego in the Needs . . . of My People': Militant Womanist Rhetoric in the Drama of Sonia Sanchez." *CLA Journal* 48, no. 1 (2004): 1–33.

Woodard, Komozi. *A Nation within a Nation: Amiri Baraka (LeRoi Jones) and Black Power Politics*. University of North Carolina Press, 1999.

Wormsby, Hollis. "Henry Dumas: Anger, Humor, Love, and Dispossession." *Black American Literature Forum* 22, no. 2 (1988): 408–11.

Wright, John S. "Introduction to Henry Dumas's *Echo Tree*." *Echo Tree: The Collected Short Story Fiction of Henry Dumas*, edited by Eugene B. Redmond, ix–xxxvii. Coffee House Press, 2003.

X, Malcolm. "At the Audubon." *Malcolm X Speaks: Selected Speeches and Statements*, edited by George Breitman, 115–136. Grove Press, 1990.

X, Malcolm. "Ballot or the Bullet." *Malcolm X Speaks: Selected Speeches and Statements*, edited by George Breitman, 18–22. Grove Press, 1990.

X, Malcolm. "The Black Revolution." *Malcolm X Speaks: Selected Speeches and Statements*, edited by George Breitman, 45–57. Grove Press, 1990.

X, Malcolm. "Communication and Reality." *Malcolm X: The Man and His Times*, edited by John Henrik Clarke, 313. Macmillan, 1969.

X, Malcolm. "A Declaration of Independence." *Malcolm X Speaks: Selected Speeches and Statements*, edited by George Breitman, 18–22. Grove Press, 1990.

X, Malcolm. "Twenty Million Black People in a Political, Economic, and Mental Prison." *Malcolm X on Afro-American History*, edited by Bruce Perry, 21–53. Pathfinder, 1989.

X, Malcolm. "Malcolm X to Organize Mass Voter Registration." *The Militant*, April 6, 1964, 1.

X, Malcolm. "Program of the Organization of Afro-American Unity." malcolm-x.org. https://www.malcolm-x.org/docs/gen_oaau.htm. Accessed February 20, 2018.

X, Malcolm. "'And This Happened in Los Angeles': Malcolm X Describes Police Brutality against Members of the Nation of Islam." Interview by Dick Elman. 1962. *History Matters: The U.S. Survey Course on the Web*. http://historymatters.gmu.edu/d/7041/. Accessed February 1, 2018.

X, Malcolm. "Who Taught You to Hate?" Educational Video Group, uploaded by Alexander Street, May 3, 2010. https://search.alexanderstreet.com/preview/work /bibliographic_entity%7Cvideo_work%7C2785586?ssotoken=anonymous.

X, Marvin, Faruk, and LeRoi Jones (Amiri Baraka). "Islam and Black Art: An Interview with LeRoi Jones." *Negro Digest* 28, no. 3 (1969): 4–11.

Yanco, Jennifer J. *Misremembering Dr. King: Revisiting the Legacy of Martin Luther King, Jr.* Indiana University Press, 2014.

Yeats, W. B. "News for the Delphic Oracle." *Yeats*, edited by Harold Bloom. Oxford University Press.

INDEX

Abu-Lughod, Janet, 6
Achebe, Chinua, 78
Africana womanism, 27, 78, 79, 89–90, 101
Afrocentricity, 80
"After the Mecca" (Brooks), 58–62, 71
Alexander, Michelle, 8
Alexander-Floyd, Nikole, 79
Anderson, Elizabeth, 114, 119
Andrews, Doug, 64
*Arm Yourself, or Harm Yourself: A Message
    of Self-Defense to Black Men!* (Baraka),
    37–39
"Aspect of Love, Alive in the Ice and Fire,
    An" (Brooks), 71, 72
Atkins, Russell, 113–14
Atwater, Deborah, 121
Azouz, Samy, 33–34, 44

BaddDDD Sonia Sanchez (Goldman and
    Atwater), 82–83, 149n19
Bailey, Alison, 99
Bain, Byronn, 149n19
Baldwin, James, 16–17, 19
Ball, Jared, 8
Baltimore (Maryland), 8
Baradaran, Mehrsa, 21, 123, 126, 140n14
Baraka, Amina, 37
Baraka, Amiri (LeRoi Jones), 12, 15, 21;
    Black rage of, 35–41; Brooks on, 62, 71;
    on Christianity, 61; on Dumas, 114; at
    Fisk University Writers' Conference,
    147n11; on restitution, 145n46; "The
    Revolutionary Theatre" by, 30, 131, 142n9;

Sanchez and, 81; *The Slave* by, 26–27,
    31–35, 41–47, 53
Beckles, Colin A., 121
Bell, Derrick, 127–28
Bentley-Edwards, Keisha, 6, 130
Bergmann, Barbara R., 86
Best, Stephen, 48–49, 145n43
"Beyond Vietnam" (King), 136
Biden, Joe, 28
Bienkowski, Peter, 111
Black aesthetic, 62, 68–69, 131
Black Arts Movement (BAM): assas-
    sination of Malcolm X inspiring, 132;
    on Black aesthetic, 68–69; in Brooks's
    poetry, 59; music in, 15; rioting in litera-
    ture of, 12, 19–22, 25, 130–31; *The Slave* as
    precursor of, 34
Black Arts Repertory Theatre and School
    (BARTS), 37
Black Bitch (fictional character), 76, 77, 79,
    85–88, 90, 99–101
Black bookstores, 120–22
Black church, 61
*Black Fire: An Anthology of Afro-American
    Writing* (Baraka and Neal), 20–21, 81
Black Lives Matter, 107, 112, 133
Black nationalism, 35; Baraka on, 37; in
    Brooks's poetry, 57–63; Caldwell
    on, 39; Malcolm X on, 115–16, 132,
    143n16, 144n25; in *The Bronx Is Next*,
    76
Black Panther Party for Self-Defense,
    120–21, 149–50nn9–10

169

ABOUT THE AUTHOR

Credit: Ross Knight

Casarae Lavada Abdul-Ghani is assistant professor of African American literature at Temple University and owns Africana Instructional Design, LLC.

CPSIA information can be obtained
at www.ICGtesting.com
Printed in the USA
BVHW050430200622
640113BV00004B/12